T0012475

Praise for Nell McShane Wulfhart's

The Great Stewardess Rebellion

"[An] astonishing exposé of [flight attendants'] long struggle for respect and equality. . . . This largely under-chronicled aspect of recent women's history is a valuable reminder of how far women have come. . . . [A] relevant and urgent read." —*The Guardian*

"Engaging. . . . *The Great Stewardess Rebellion* recount[s] journeys toward self-respect and empowerment. [It's] a trip worth taking." —NPR

"McShane Wulfhart's engaging chronicle of the labor movement launched by U.S. airline stewardesses who flew the not-so-friendly skies in the 1960s and '70s has an eye-opening anecdote on every page; even the union negotiations are entertaining and informative. . . . [*The Great Stewardess Rebellion*] demonstrates how the stewardesses' labor fight affected the state of modern American employment and helped enshrine many of the workplace rights women have today. Recommended for readers of women's history and histories of the airline industry, and anyone looking for an engaging and entertaining read."
—*Library Journal* (starred review)

"Engaging. . . . Insightful. . . . Compelling. . . . Wulfhart explains union wranglings, emerging legislation, and lengthy court battles within context, exposing the era's expectations regarding women's roles as sex objects, wives, and mothers in stark reality. This is an eye-opening chapter in the history of feminism and women's rights." —*Booklist*

"A rousing history. . . . An invigorating and inspiring story of women triumphing over discrimination." —*Publishers Weekly*

"This engaging narrative offers a fascinating look at how the intersection of the women's and labor movements helped a little-discussed, female-dominated profession achieve viability and respect. An informatively readable combination of cultural and feminist history."
—*Kirkus Reviews*

"A gripping and exciting read. . . . Wulfhart captures the urgency of the flight attendant's liberation with grace. . . . This book is a satisfying victory for anyone who has ever been put in a box and has relished proving them all wrong."
—*Bust*

"*The Great Stewardess Rebellion* has it all: '60s glam, sharp and brave heroines, and one of the most dramatic and consequential feminist battles in American history. A grippingly told and unforgettable story."
—Abbott Kahler, author of *The Ghosts of Eden Park*

"Vivid, inspiring and full of twists, *The Great Stewardess Rebellion* reveals how a pair of young women helped build a mighty union and transformed an industry forever. Wulfhart has unearthed a story of rare power, and she tells it with passion and skill."
—Jason Fagone, author of *The Woman Who Smashed Codes*

"Wulfhart's lively labor history chronicles a recent past that can feel simultaneously a million miles away and all too contemporary."
—Rebecca Traister, author of *Good and Mad*

"Nell McShane Wulfhart reconstructs the long-lost Era of the Stewardess: what she meant to the airlines, how she defined the female ideal in America, and then how she broke the mold—and helped change the world for everyone on the ground."
—Keith O'Brien, author of *Fly Girls*

"*The Great Stewardess Rebellion* should be required reading for anyone entering the modern job market—to remind them how the workplace used to be, and to honor the heroic people who stepped up and made progress possible. A fascinating, important read."
—Lisa Napoli, author of *Susan, Linda, Nina & Cokie*

Nell McShane Wulfhart

The Great Stewardess Rebellion

Nell McShane Wulfhart is a frequent contributor to the *New York Times* travel section and wrote the column Carry On from 2016 to 2019. She has written for *Travel + Leisure, Bon Appétit, Condé Nast Traveler, The Wall Street Journal Magazine*, and *T Magazine*. She is the author of the Audible Original *Off Menu*.

nellmcshanewulfhart.com

The

Great
Stewardess
Rebellion

HOW WOMEN LAUNCHED

A WORKPLACE REVOLUTION

AT 30,000 FEET

Nell McShane Wulfhart

Anchor Books
A Division of Penguin Random House LLC
New York

The Library of Congress has cataloged the Doubleday edition as follows:
Names: McShane Wulfhart, Nell, author.
Title: The great stewardess rebellion : how women launched a workplace rebellion at
30,000 feet / Nell McShane Wulfhart.
Description: First edition. | New York : Doubleday, 2022. |
Includes bibliographical references and index.
Identifiers: LCCN 2021043017 (print) | LCCN 2021043018 (ebook)
Subjects: LCSH: Flight attendants. | Sexual harassment. | Sex role in the work
environment. | Employee rights. | Women—Employment—Law and legislation.
Classification: LCC HD6073.A43 M47 2022 (print) | LCC HD6073.A43 (ebook) |
DDC 331.4/81387742—dc23
LC record available at https://lccn.loc.gov/2021043017
LC ebook record available at https://lccn.loc.gov/2021043018

Anchor Books Trade Paperback ISBN: 978-0-593-08229-4
eBook ISBN: 978-0-385-54646-1

Author photograph © Emilie Krause
Book design by Maria Carella

anchorbooks.com

Printed in the United States of America
1st Printing

Contents

Part Three: Patt and Tommie

Introduction

"THIS MORNING, SIGHT-SEEING in New York—and in about five hours, I'll meet my date for dinner in San Francisco." Thus read a 1961 newspaper ad for American Airlines that enticed would-be stewardesses with the glamour of life as a "sky girl." It was this alluring image—of a cosmopolitan career that would take you to new places, introduce you to new people, and confer upon you an aura of beauty, confidence, and desirability—that snared the imagination of young women in small towns, farms, and cities all over the United States. They wanted to escape lives that were mundane and ordinary . . . and becoming a stewardess seemed like an unmissable chance to do just that.

The opportunity to embody the stewardess ideal—slim-hipped, smiling, perfectly coiffed—and spend your time serving cocktails to Don Draper types while wearing an Emilio Pucci–designed uniform was irresistible to tens of thousands of young women. But underneath this glossy surface, the reality of the job was very different. Appearance standards mandated that the women working the cabin adhere to strict weight limits, that they be physically inspected to be sure they were wearing girdles, that they have clear complexions, perfect eyesight, even teeth, no scars, and be, as often as possible, white.

It wouldn't be much of an exaggeration to say that in the 1960s the airplane cabin was the most sexist workplace in America. Stewardesses were required to be unmarried, a demand the airlines stuck to, perversely, well after nearly every other industry had dropped this rule. Once they hit their thirty-second, thirty-third, or in some cases thirty-fifth birthday, they'd lose their jobs. And if they became pregnant, they'd be fired immediately. Virtually no one became a stewardess thinking they'd make it their life's work. And it would have continued to be that way if they hadn't taken matters into their own hands.

This is the story of how that happened.

It's about how Patt, a nineteen-year-old from Missouri whose biggest ambition was to become a stewardess supervisor, would spearhead a workers' rebellion, leading a subversive campaign to undermine one of the largest and most powerful groups in organized labor. It's about how Tommie, a rangy Texas stewardess with a sociology degree, would help run a feminist organization that made headlines time and time again, and how she'd invest heart and soul in seizing institutional power to change her industry from the inside. And it's about how the work of the stewardesses in striking down the airline industry's most sexist rules was helped along by Sonia, a single-minded Jewish refugee from Germany who would end up making legal history in more ways than one.

Their friends and colleagues aided and abetted them through court cases, face-offs with airline executives, sexual harassment, picketing, intimidation from labor bosses, and internal struggles. Through women's marches and weight checks, from hot pants to organizing campaigns, their efforts—not always unified, but with the same goals in mind—resulted in a workplace revolution.

Their actions changed their own industry forever, and along with it, the lives of women workers in the United States. They were among the first to see the potential of Title VII of the Civil Rights Act to fight sex discrimination. They launched a series of complaints with the Equal Employment Opportunity Commission, then dozens of lawsuits, in a drive to eradicate marriage, pregnancy, and age bans in the cabin. They lost more often than they won: the airline industry was highly dedicated to keeping its workforce young, thin, single, and female. But their work turned Title VII into a tool that would be wielded against discriminatory employers for decades to come, helping to cement the rules of law on disparate treatment based on sex, and establishing case law that would go on to benefit all working women.

When they had, after hard-fought battles, succeeded in turning "flight attendant" from a carefree interlude between college and marriage into a career that could span decades, it suddenly became exponentially more important that the conditions of that work—low pay, weight limits, degrading uniforms—were in every way inferior to those of their male colleagues. So they used their seductive image to their advantage, bringing public attention to the sexist standards of their workplace, and to the way their employers had created and then exploited a stewardess-as-sex-object trope to sell plane tickets. Stewardesses enjoyed a unique cultural visibility, but that had its dark side. The glamour of the job was offered up in place of tangible benefits such as retirement plans, maternity leave, a living wage, and much more.

Turning to their union for help, they found little forthcoming from the men in charge. So they decided to seize that power for themselves, looking to homegrown leaders who would take the radical step of breaking away from an extremely powerful labor organization to form their own, women-led union.

Flight attendants might seem like unlikely figureheads of the women's movement. It's hard to view them as the militant union leaders, passionate organizers, or aggressive litigators they were. It was all too easy to underestimate them, something that was quickly discovered by the very people they were fighting: the airline executives who forced them into paper dresses and go-go boots, and the unions that treated them as decorative mascots rather than workers or colleagues.

The flight attendants' achievements are, even from today's perspective, remarkable: they forced the airlines to promote them alongside men, to pay them fairly, to treat them as legitimate workers. The stewardess rebellion is a story of harnessing the energy of the women's movement to make radical change. It's a story of seizing power from the powerful. And for Patt and Tommie and many of their friends, it's a story of unexpected personal transformation. But the flight attendants' biggest victories were only achieved through tenacious collective action—and through behavior that was anything but ladylike.

Part One

Patt

CHAPTER ONE

Honeybuns
on the Charm Farm

PATT GIBBS BECAME a stewardess to get away from her mother. Gracie Gibbs was a showboat, the best-known person in Springfield, Missouri. She had six children and a thirst for fame. When she and her husband started working at Sifferman's, a local appliance store, black-and-white televisions were making their first appearance on the shelves. Gracie, who had an air of glamour and an endless belief in her own abilities, convinced the owner to let her star in his commercials, and she soon became known as the face of Sifferman's. When she and Patt's father, Bob, opened their own store—Appliances by Gracie—TV stations, still new, were in need of content. Gracie launched her own talk show, *Gracie's Good Neighbor*. Local musical talent performed (Brenda Lee, Tennessee Ernie Ford, and other eventually famous singers) between interview segments and Beautiful Baby contests. As far as Springfield went, Gracie was a star.

Patt, who was second eldest, and her five brothers and sisters all made appearances, though Gracie wouldn't let them hold a script—they were expected to remember all their lines. Patt tried her best on the show, but she never felt that she was quite what her mother had expected to get when she had a daughter. Her mother bought her ballet lessons; Patt traded them for trampoline classes. Patt asked for western gear as a Christmas gift, to wear to horse shows; instead she got modeling lessons. And while her mother's fame eased the family's money stresses, being known as "Gracie's daughter" wasn't what Patt had in mind for her life.

Patt didn't become a stewardess because she was seeking adventure. Life up to this point had been far from boring. Her parents had moved the family from town to town, state to state, her entire existence. She was born Patricia Ann Gibbs in Cincinnati during World War II, but if she had been born two weeks earlier she would have been Patricia Ann Goldberg. In 1942, "Goldberg" was too Jewish for a town like Cincinnati, which had more than its fair share of German sympathizers, so Bob decided they needed a new name. The family didn't get to choose for themselves; instead, the courts chose for them. And so Gibbs they became. They left Cincinnati, though, in part because their landlord discovered that Bob, an animal lover, was keeping a pet alligator in the bathtub. The Gibbs parents opened and then closed restaurants; they sold pots and pans door-to-door. Patt's brother Bobby ran away with a circus that passed through town one year. Later on, Patt and her siblings would all work at the circus in the summers, Patt shoveling elephant dung, performing trampoline acts, even mastering the trapeze. The family lived in Kentucky, then Indiana, then Illinois, then Ohio again, then Florida. But it was in Springfield, as they were enjoying a modicum of success thanks to Gracie, that Patt decided to make a change.

It was 1961 and Patt was nineteen when her cousin Jim came to town. Jim Thorpe, like so many people in Patt's family, had had several careers. He'd been a bass player with the Glenn Miller Orchestra, but a knife accident had destroyed his vision; he then became a recruiter for American Airlines. He was in Springfield interviewing potential stewardesses, hundreds of them, and had convinced Patt to come help him sort through the applications. "Why don't you think about becoming a stewardess?" he asked her just before he left. She couldn't, she told him, she was too fat. And what she knew about stewardesses—high heels, makeup, girdles—well, it sounded more like Gracie than her. But the idea had been planted. And several fights with Gracie later, about wanting to get away from the family and live her own life, she picked up the phone and called Jim. "Okay, I'll interview to be a stewardess," she told him. "I need to get away from home. But here's the thing: I don't want you to tell anyone at American Airlines that we're related. I don't want my mother's input, I don't want your connections. I just want to do it myself."

Patt's impression of the glamour girl type that made the ideal stewardess wasn't far off the mark. Looks were by far the most important factor in the interview process. The 1963 American Airlines supervisor handbook would emphasize that when it came to hiring, "the first fundamental is appearance. A stewardess must be attractive. We can sometimes pretend a person is attractive, if we admire them for some other reason. This should be avoided." The beauty of stewardesses was so well known that an American Airlines Barbie debuted in 1961. She had bright red lips, high heels, a flight bag with the AA insignia, and a neat blue hat perched atop her voluminous hair. (Captain Ken wouldn't show up until 1964.)

At five foot three and 121 pounds, Patt wasn't Barbie-slim. And slim was a requirement. Weight limits were uncompromising at every airline. At the same time Patt was considering her new career, an article titled "A Tale of the Scale" appeared in *The Delta Digest*, the airline's employee magazine. It told the story of stewardess Hildy Hoffman, who was five foot three and had weighed 170 pounds in high school. She lost fifty pounds in one summer, plus an extra five as requested by the airline, and was rewarded with a job. "I love it," Hildy was quoted as saying. "It's every bit as interesting and exciting as I thought it would be, even if hard work too. And I don't miss a single one of those pounds I gave it up for."

If Patt was going to make it to training school, she'd have to drop a few pounds like Hildy. She put herself on a strict diet. And it worked. Filling out the application for American Airlines, she happily entered "110 pounds" in the blank space for "weight." The form also required her bust, waist, and hip measurements, her marital status, disclosure of debts or a criminal record, and whether she rented or lived with her parents. She filled it out, sent it off, and went back to the set to learn her lines.

Different airlines preferred different kinds of stewardesses. These women were the most visible of the airlines' employees, after all; they were walking, talking brand representatives. Pan Am, with its international routes, looked for elegance, sophistication, and a cosmopolitan air. United, wanting to appeal to the middle-class American, looked for a girl-next-door type. TWA, like Pan Am, wanted its "air hostesses" to project exclusivity and worldliness. Pacific Southwest was known to hire the blonde and pert, with an hourglass figure strongly preferred. Delta, based in the South and priding itself on its conservative nature, hired for "high moral character"; its recruiters were known to prefer a demure, wholesome smiler to a bombshell.

Delta's ads boasted about its stewardesses' "superior background," and claimed that "we can't give her that gracious air, that friendly spirit. They come of home and heritage." Delta's evocation of old southern traditions was code for white and Christian; the homes and heritage it was scrutinizing in its search for candidates were pretty uniform.

American Airlines steered a course between worldly, respectable, and sexy, landing on its perfect stewardess: the "all American" girl. I could do that, Patt thought. She knew she wasn't a bombshell, but she figured she could pull off sweet and cute.

The reason Patt had known she was too fat for the job was because the recruitment material made no bones about what the airlines were looking for. A *New York Times* classified ad for Eastern Airlines requested "a high school graduate, single (widows and divorcees with no children considered), 20 years of age (girls 19½ may apply for future consideration). 5'2" but no more than 5'9", weight 105 to 135 in proportion to height and have at least 20/40 vision without glasses." Patt never wore makeup or spent much time on her hair, but she had clear skin and was newly thin; she figured it was worth a shot. Besides, she couldn't spend the rest of her life as a recurring character on *Gracie's Good Neighbor.*

She was offered an interview in March 1962. Patt's father drove her to Love Field, the Dallas airport. She dressed modestly, with her short hair curled in a bang over her forehead. An interviewer named Fred Hazard began by looking her up and down. He asked her to walk over to the wall, turn around, and walk back. He brought his face near to hers to examine her complexion, looked closely at her hair. He had her show him her hands so he could check for scars and signs of nail biting. Patt suddenly felt a discomfiting resemblance to a prize steer at auction. At the end of the interview, he sat her down and said, "Well, I'd like to give you an opportunity to become a stewardess, but you've got a space between your two front teeth, about an eighth of an inch. If you can do something with those teeth, send me a picture and then we'll see."

Energized, Patt went back to Springfield and made an appointment with a dentist. "How soon can you pull these teeth together?" she asked him. He fitted her for braces and had her come back once a week for tightening. Her mouth was always in pain, but she com-

Patt with the gap in her teeth.

forted herself with the fact that the pain meant she ate less. Fred Hazard had given her a May deadline to send the photo, so she had the dentist take the braces off after a couple of months, smiled wide for the camera, and sent the snapshot off to Hazard. Within a week, her acceptance letter had arrived. She was to report to training school in June.

Patt was under twenty-one, so she was sent a contract for her parents to sign. It stated, "I will abide by the policy of the Company that my employment as a Stewardess will not be continued beyond the end of the month during which my 32nd birthday falls." The contract also specified that "among the qualifications and regulations of a Stewardess position are those of an attractive appearance, a pleasant personality, an even temperament, neatness, unmarried status, and the ability and desire to meet and serve passengers, and the failure to maintain such qualifications or to meet other standards required of Company employees will also be cause for the termination of my employment."

It had been less than a decade before, in 1953, that American had implemented the age restriction, the first airline to do so. According to American, automatic termination upon turning thirty-two was necessary because "basic among the qualifications is an attractive appearance. Such an appearance ordinarily is found to a higher degree in young women. Therefore, the establishment of an age limit will best effectuate and preserve the concept of Stewardess service as it is understood in this Company."

The stewardesses' union had made efforts to protest this stricture but succeeded only in limiting its application to new hires: stewardesses hired before December 1, 1953, would be "grandmothered" in and allowed to work past the age of thirty-two. Other airlines soon added their own age limits. In 1956 Northwest imposed an age ceiling of thirty-two, and the next year TWA started retiring female stewardesses at thirty-five—though male flight attendants could fly into their sixties. By the middle of the 1960s, more than 60 percent of stewardesses worked for airlines that demanded they resign when they reached either their thirty-second, thirty-third, or thirty-fifth birthday.

"I'm nineteen," Patt thought. "I'm never going to get old." Both turning thirty-two and getting married seemed so far away as to be unimaginable. Her parents signed, she signed, and by June, Patt was back in Dallas, unpacking her bag in the dormitory of the American Airlines Stewardess College.

When Patt stepped onto the campus, she felt like she'd entered a whole new world, one of affluence and sophistication. American had opened its million-dollar training school just five years earlier. The school was spread over twenty-two acres near Love Field, and had its own swimming pool, as well as shuffleboard and tennis courts. It looked like a college campus, with enticing green lawns and sofa-strewn lounges filled with students taking notes, or just relaxing and chatting. The only difference was that they were all women and they were dressed in identical navy blue skirt suits, pumps, and hats. And this campus was surrounded by a chain-link fence that, for the first few years, was electrified—whether to keep the women in or men out was hotly debated. On one of the lush lawns sat the famous statue of a kiwi bird. The kiwi gave its name to the Kiwi Club, a group of former American Airlines flight attendants. Once the students were no longer working, it was explained, they would be eligible to become Kiwis. But they'd no longer have their wings. Since they were mostly former only because they'd been grounded upon marriage, pregnancy, or turning thirty-two, the symbolism of

Patt just before heading off to stewardess college.

a flightless bird was a little on the nose. (Other airline clubs had equally dispiriting names: Eastern Airlines had the Silverliners, United the Clipped Wings, and Continental the Golden Penguins.)

American's inspiration for building a school dedicated solely to the training of stewardesses was twofold: the growth of air travel, and the increasing realization that its young women were its best and most eye-catching asset. Other airlines soon followed American's lead. Braniff International Airways opened an International Hostess Training College (bars were affixed to the balconies of the dorm rooms, and an alarm system alerted dorm supervisors if a window or door was opened against regulations). United launched a stewardess school, called "Cloud College," in Chicago. In addition to safety training, the curriculum offered lessons on how to put your coat on properly, posture instruction, and rules for carrying gloves and a purse ("carry everything on one side if possible"). Continental sent its trainees directly to the John Robert Powers Modeling School, tacking on a half day of training in emergency procedures. The American Airlines Stewardess College, which started churning out impeccably styled stewardesses at assembly line speed, quickly became known as "the charm farm." Its students were given a nickname of their own. C. R. Smith was the founder and president of American Airlines, and he had a courtly yet dominating personality that made him immediately identifiable as the man in charge. The inhabitants of the charm farm, with their clear skin and white teeth, were always called—by the students, the instructors, and C.R. himself—"C.R.'s honeybuns."

The United States was entering a period of rapid cultural change, but you wouldn't have guessed it from observing life on the charm farm. Government approval of the birth control pill, the opening of the first Playboy Club, and the Greensboro lunch counter sit-ins all launched the 1960s with a bang. But inside the chain-link fence, the students' world was reduced to practicing walking in high heels and scheduling visits to the on-site beauty salon where former models, who had been hired as instructors, would test out makeup and hairstyles. It was regimented but bewitching, and Patt thrilled to the newness of it all. She was away from home, out from under the eye of her mother; she loved flying and dreamed of someday becoming a supervisor like the impossibly elegant women who instructed her.

Life at college was strictly regulated. Supervisors kept a close eye on what the women ate, and scales were everywhere. An entire class was dedicated to nail care: how to file nails correctly, the approved colors of polish, cuticle management. Haircuts in the style the airline had decided on for that year were mandatory. As the weeks went by, the women started looking more and more alike. They *were* alike—all white, mostly Protestant, within a small range of height and weight. When Patt started working, American Airlines had no Black stewardesses; it wouldn't hire Joan Dorsey, its first, until 1963. Before that, airlines argued that they couldn't hire Black women. Such women would diminish the glamour of the job, they claimed, and white women would no longer want to work as flight attendants. By 1965, once the Civil Rights Act had made discrimination illegal, airlines had started hiring a few Black women, though there were still only around fifty Black stewardesses out of a total of about fifteen thousand.

Stewardesses might have entered training school with individual hairstyles, makeup, clothes, and habits; they came out almost identical. There was a saying among stewardesses that a pilot gained his identity when he put his uniform on, and a stewardess lost hers. Patt didn't mind. "Stewardess" was an identity she craved. She'd been loved at home, she knew, but she'd always felt slightly out of place. But here the rules for how to fit in couldn't have been more clear.

Break one of those rules and she'd be sent home with alacrity (coming back from a day of classes to find a roommate's bed empty and her things gone was not an uncommon occurrence). Patt and her fellow trainees, around 120 on the campus at a time, were housed in dorms, five or six per room. They each had a small closet, a locker, and a narrow twin bed. The bathroom was shared, as was a desk that ran down the center of the room. The girls' boarding school ambience was complete when Patt put in her retainer every night; she had to use it in case her teeth moved back, but wearing it around the instructors would have resulted in quick dismissal. If she gained back the weight she'd lost, or had an attitude the instructors didn't like, she'd get the boot. She stayed on the alert—she wasn't about to get sent back to Springfield to live under Gracie's thumb again.

"You walk like a gorilla." This shot was fired by Kelly Flint, a former John Robert Powers model, who had been hired by American as an instructor. "What are you doing with your arms out like that?" she asked Patt. "You need to learn to walk like a lady." With these words, Patt was condemned to hours of what she thought of as "remedial walking." Up and down the stairs, in heels, with a book balanced on her head and her elbows glued to her waist, she practiced every day for an hour before class. She had barely worn heels in her life.

Patt spent the rest of her time learning how to apply makeup, style her hair in the new cut she'd been given, and paint her nails in regulation color. She nodded along as instructors talked about the importance of a girdle. In the beauty salon, she'd sit in front of a mirror, draped in a hairdresser's smock, applying mascara as Kelly Flint teased a fellow student's hair with a comb, a can of Aqua Net within easy reach. She was slightly disappointed to learn how much the training was focused on appearance. She'd never been "girly" in that way, but she gave it her best.

The service classes weren't inspiring either—they didn't practice with passengers on a real plane; instead they handed out cardboard food to pretend passengers seated in old surplus airplane seats that had been lined up in rows. But Patt threw herself into the process, even volunteering to make the phony food and trays, creating steaks out of cardboard and patiently cutting out fake milk cartons. Her goal, she'd decided, was to get into management, and she was sure that this show of willingness would help. She'd gotten used to her family being in charge—they'd moved into the management class with the opening of the appliance store—and she thought of herself as a future airline instructor, maybe even a supervisor.

She did manage to get on a real airplane when they practiced emergency evacuations. The trainees walked across the street from the charm farm to Love Field, where they boarded a plane that had been grounded for maintenance checks. They'd rehearse rushing to get the canvas slide out of its compartment, nicknamed "the dog-

Patt (on the right) in grooming class; grooming instructor Kelly Flint on the left.

house," then running it back to the exit to hook it up and practice sending their "passengers" jumping into it. But they only practiced this part once. If they needed to evacuate passengers on a real-life flight, the instructors told them, "you get six strong men and tell them to hold the slide out like this."

On the charm farm, everyone ate together: the instructors, the supervisors, and the trainees. Eating wasn't a pleasurable experience; with the threat of dismissal hanging over their heads if they gained a couple of pounds, few of the women could unthinkingly enjoy a meal. Patt knew not to put anything on her plate that looked like it had too many calories because she would be pulled into a supervisor's office and weighed if they spotted so much as a slice of bread on her tray. The food in the serving dishes was mostly the diet food of the '60s: salads, cottage cheese, skinless boiled chicken, iceberg lettuce, each with a sign denoting the number of calories. There were no soft drinks.

Patt had never worn makeup before; her skin was sensitive and the powder provided made her face break out. The school ordered hypoallergenic Almay powder for her (she was dismayed when she learned she had to pay for this herself), and when it arrived Kelly Flint ordered her up to her dorm to put it on. Patt, in what was perhaps a tiny reaction to the "gorilla" comment, had a moment of rebellion. She went upstairs, smoked a few Marlboros, and came back down. Her teacher enthused about how much better she looked with the new makeup. Patt laughed about it later with the other students, but soon found herself in trouble. A classmate had ratted her out. Hearing your name called over the PA system ("Patt Gibbs, please report to Miss Alford's office") was usually a sign that you were being sent home. You'd be ordered to your dorm to clear your locker and pack up your clothes, and you'd be gone before your classmates had finished the day's lessons. So when Patt heard her name, she got a sinking feeling in her stomach. What a stupid way to have lost her chance! But luck was on her side, in the form of an instructor named Peggy Sullivan. She argued in Patt's favor, telling Miss Alford, "She's going to make a really great stewardess." Patt was duly chastised, told she'd better straighten up her act or she wouldn't graduate. And she did, vowing not to put a toe out of line again.

Six and a half weeks later, Patt had made it. July 18, 1962, was graduation day and she was twenty years old; she'd celebrated her birthday at the charm farm. She was grinning with pride and excitement, although there was a tiny nagging feeling that she'd gotten away with something she shouldn't have. She'd worked hard, sure. She hadn't wanted to fail, to hear her name called on the PA and be sent home in disgrace. A fellow classmate had been dismissed and sent packing the very day before graduation. But even with the high heels, she was still short and stocky, and her classmates were taller, thinner, more feminine—more like the American Airlines Barbie than Patt would ever be. She knew her background—the circus, the name change, the alligator, the constant picking up and moving to a new town—wasn't the same as most of her fellow students'. She felt supremely lucky to be chosen. She had been, as the airline's ads boasted, one of thousands of applicants.

A print ad from 1960 featured a photo of graduating stewardesses lined up neatly on the staircase at the training college, their lipstick all the same color, their light blue uniforms neat and trim. The ad copy declared, "We choose just 1 in 23 from over 15,000 annual applicants for an intensive 77-subject course at our Stewardess College, the only one of its kind. The young ladies graduate with honors in the gracious art of making people happy." Patt believed it, too. They were the cream of the crop. At least her fellow students were. But she'd made it through.

There was one final test. She was carefully writing out the name cards for the pre-ceremony luncheon, another job she'd happily volunteered for, when she heard it: "Patt Gibbs, please report to Miss Alford's office." She was sure this was it: she'd been found out somehow. She walked into the office.

"Do you know Jim Thorpe?" Miss Alford asked her.

"Yes, I do," said Patt.

"I'm glad you didn't lie," Miss Alford told her, adding, "I know he's your cousin. If you'd said you didn't know him, I would have sent you home. But you told the truth, so now you can make a name card for him because he'll be coming to the graduation luncheon."

Weak with relief, Patt went back to her calligraphy.

Graduation day meant the execution of a number of traditions. The graduates lined up on the training school's staircase, where every class had their photo taken. It was here, neatly uniformed, with their caps perched over their matching hairdos, that the resemblance among the newly minted stewardesses was most obvious. All white, all slender, with matching smiles—they were so alike that when she looked for herself in the photo later on, Patt would have to remind herself, "Well, I was in the front row, I know that . . ." It would always take a moment or two to find her own face.

After the picture, each took her turn having her silver stewardess wings pinned to her uniform. Jim pinned on Patt's with a grin. The women sang the graduation song they'd prepared in advance, changing the words of a popular tune to describe how thrilled they were to start their careers as stewardesses. They marched down to the kiwi bird statue for the final ritual. Every stewardess in every graduating class would place a penny in the slot under the bird and make a wish, like children at a birthday party.

Then, hugging each other goodbye, Patt and her classmates packed their things and headed off to their assigned bases. After the month and a half of training school, they'd start their careers on a six-month probation period, officially working as flight attendants. In the parlance of the airline industry, Patt was going "on the line." And she couldn't wait.

CHAPTER TWO

Gloves to Grievances

FIRST, PATT HAD to buy her uniforms. These were tailor-made: two light blue summer uniforms with fitted jackets that buttoned down the front, two navy blue wool winter uniforms, and six blouses with removable buttons for easier ironing. A winter coat, a trench coat, and a serving garment called a topper. Flat shoes, and heels. A purse, a suitcase. Hat, gloves. Though she was just beginning her employment, she had to pay $650 ($5,648 in 2021 dollars) for these things, money that would be automatically deducted from her paycheck month after month. In later years, Patt would negotiate with the company for paid uniforms, but in 1962 she was so thrilled to have made it as a stewardess that it never occurred to her to question it. The clothes came with a long list of rules. Hats and white gloves had to be worn at all times in public if you were in your uniform. The uniforms couldn't be stained or appear worn in any way. Girdles and bras were required, as were high heels when on the plane. Stewardesses who left off the girdle, removed their gloves, or were unlucky enough to spill something on their uniform (or have a passenger spill something on it) would be disciplined. No problem, thought Patt. If she knew the rules, she could follow them.

Just before she started work, Patt got a haircut. The charm farm hairdo, the one they had given to all of her classmates, featured wings of hair that puffed out on either side of their hats. The window for changing your hair was a short one—you weren't allowed to change it at college, and once you got to the base the supervisors wouldn't like it if you cut your hair because you'd be demonstrating the wrong attitude, showing that you didn't want to look like every-

Patt in her first uniform, on one of her first flights.

one else. Afros were specifically forbidden (in 1969, United would fire one woman, Deborah Renwick, for hers), and some airlines would require the few Black women they employed to straighten their hair. Patt had her hair cut short so she could comb it back, making sure it would fit under her uniform hat, which had to be positioned exactly two finger-widths above her right eyebrow. With her wide grin and chubby cheeks, she looked fresh and eager to get to work.

She was assigned to the Fort Worth base. Her first flights were on a DC-6, a piston plane that didn't have the fuel range to do long nonstop trips. She rapidly learned that since you were only paid for the time on board and not for layovers, the most coveted flights were the longest ones. Each stewardess would fill out her "bid sheet" monthly, carefully listing the flights that would suit her schedule the best and hoping she'd get them, though at some airlines Black stewardesses were discouraged from bidding on flights that included southern states, because they'd be more likely to encounter racist and hostile passengers. The crew schedulers then handed out assignments on the basis of seniority: the women who had been on the job the longest were the most likely to get the flights they wanted.

Because she was so low on the seniority list, Patt was only eligible for the worst flights, such as the eight-hour journey that flew from Love Field to Fort Worth to El Paso, made three stops in Arizona, went on to San Diego, and ended in Los Angeles. The DC-6 didn't have space for cooking food, so Patt handed out box lunches: fried chicken—always fried chicken—an apple, a brownie, and a napkin. Beverages were served after takeoff, the only hot things on the plane, and passengers could choose from coffee, tea, or milk. Up, drinks, box lunch, down, then up again and off to the next destination.

One of her first trips to Los Angeles was an all-nighter. She'd stopped by a coffee shop in the airport to get something to eat before they flew out and spotted a senior stewardess from American sitting at the counter sipping her coffee, hat resting on the stool beside her. Patt did some asking around, found out her name, and, when she got back to Dallas, reported her to management. Ratting out a fellow worker to a supervisor was a sisterly violation of the highest order, and word traveled fast along the galley grapevine. Patt wasn't required to report uniform infractions, but she hadn't thought twice: the rules said they had to wear full uniform in public, hat included, and this woman was breaking that rule. Her future union comrades would never let her live it down. At the time, though, Patt wasn't even aware that the stewardesses had a union.

Money was tight, and it was common for four or five stewardesses to share an apartment because their salaries were so low. New employees earned around $350 a month ($3,000 in 2020 dollars), out of which they had to pay their uniform deduction, their dry cleaning, their transportation, and all their living expenses. Patt had learned at the charm farm that she didn't want to live with so many people; she needed some time and space to be alone. She figured that she could live on her own if she found a really cheap spot, but when she started looking she discovered she couldn't afford even a studio on her salary. Then inspiration struck. She went over to the Tower Motel and Trailer Park and rented a twenty-four-foot travel trailer. It was tiny and didn't have air-conditioning, but she had it all to herself.

✈

Patt got a shock when she was handed her first disciplinary rebuke. It was one of Dallas's sweltering July days, and she had been heading to the airport on the employee bus. No passengers were aboard, just crew and supervisors, and Patt was sweating in the heat so she removed her white gloves. A supervisor reported her. Patt was suspended. And devastated—why had she let down her guard for even one moment? Any discipline, documented in a C-314 form, went into your permanent file. She worried about her chances for promotion. She became even more careful when she checked her uniform in the mirror before going to work each day, applying her mascara with extra care and making sure to pin on her hat at exactly the right angle. Still, it wasn't long before she incurred another disciplinary action. Trying to save money, she'd sold her Austin-Healey Sprite and bought a motorcycle. She'd learned how to ride while performing with her brothers in the circus. She started driving herself to the employee parking lot on her bike, in full uniform, but was quickly suspended for three days for conduct unbecoming to an American Airlines stewardess. The motorcycle, while efficient, apparently did not fit the image American wanted its female employees to project. She was only three months into her probationary period and she was already somehow breaking the rules. What was wrong with her?

She tried to dismiss these thoughts and focus on her goals. She continued to volunteer her time at the stewardess college, creating training aids and constructing cardboard meals for the students. She wanted to do more, wanted to show them she could become a supervisor. She could fit in, she knew it. She kept trying.

Patt was never sure what made her go to the union meeting. It was held at the Transport Workers Union hall at Love Field, more often home to meetings of airplane mechanics. She'd grown up thinking unions were full of militant people, something she wanted no part of. Still, she was curious and had the night off. She assumed the hall would be full of angry women wanting to tear the place down. And she was right, although there were only five women there. There were 250 stewardesses on the base, but just twenty-five were members of the union. The hall was dingy, with limp flags leaning in their stands, and the women were sitting around a table cluttered with beer and cigarettes. They wore slacks and sweatshirts, were smoking like chimneys, and sipped from warm cans of Lone Star beer. Patt, who was dressed in jeans and a leather motorcycle jacket, helmet under her arm, looked like she'd walked right out of *West Side Story.* She didn't look like the kind of woman who'd be shocked by beer drinking and cursing, but she was still a small-town purist at heart. She never drank alcohol and was taken aback by the swearing and complaining. Someone said "Fuck them!" about management; another called their supervisor "that damn fucking Bob Ferris"; they all talked nonstop about how they were being screwed. Patt reeled. Her first thought was that this was all so disloyal to the company. Her second: "I don't want to be part of this group!"

Patt didn't say a word in the meeting. She just sat there smoking and listening to the others complaining, wondering why she had come. Everyone was so angry at the company; it was mystifying. She stayed less than an hour, then left, thinking, "Well, I'm never going to go to one of *those* things again." A week later, a letter arrived in the mail congratulating her on becoming a union member. A mistake, she thought. She certainly hadn't paid any dues or filled out any paperwork. She threw the letter in the trash. A couple of weeks later, a second letter arrived. This one congratulated her on her election to the position of union vice chairperson of the Fort Worth base. She threw that one away, too.

She soon found out that just by turning up at that meeting she'd demonstrated enough interest to have the others sign her up for membership and pay her $10 union dues. Then they'd voted her in as base vice chair, ignoring the fact that she knew nothing about union work and had no interest in even attending a second meeting. This was in September. By November, the chair, Kip Rose, had gone on medical leave, and Patt Gibbs, somehow, was now the acting union chairperson for the entire base.

Then the phone rang. It was Nancy Collins, the union's master executive chairperson, calling to give Patt a quick primer on the group she was now a part of. Nancy was a slim, good-looking woman with light brown hair, blue eyes, and a clear complexion; unlike nearly everyone else, she didn't smoke. In her calm voice, she explained to Patt that her union, the Air Line Stewards and Stewardesses Association (ALSSA), represented the stewardesses and the (many fewer) stewards at several airlines. Its function was to help the stewardesses when they'd been disciplined, bargain with management for better working conditions, and try in various ways to help them keep their jobs and make those jobs better. Management and the company were powerful, and the union was the women's only source of help. If a stewardess had been treated unfairly by her supervisor, Nancy said (Patt's mind went immediately to the white gloves incident), the union would help her file a grievance, and she might be able to avoid getting fired or suspended. ALSSA, Nancy went on, had just joined the Transport Workers Union. Even Patt had heard of the TWU. It was a massive union of subway workers, bus drivers, and airline workers, including ground workers, maintenance workers, and baggage handlers. The TWU structure was pyramid-shaped: at the top were the TWU leaders, a handful of men who had risen from jobs on subways and buses to become hugely powerful directors of this giant labor organization. Under their leadership were different divisions. ALSSA, with its stewards and stewardesses from American, TWA, Eastern, and other airlines, was part of the TWU's air transport division.

That meant that stewardesses like Patt had to pay dues to the TWU, but could get help from them in exchange. The TWU membership was enormous, Nancy pointed out, the union was an essential part of the country's economy, and power came from numbers. An individual stewardess couldn't do much on her own if she was badly treated by her employer, but with a giant union behind her, she'd have a fighting chance.

Patt still didn't want anything to do with a union, but she couldn't help being charmed by Nancy. She was, Patt thought, the perfect leader. She was a union woman through and through, she had lots of experience, she could talk to anyone, and she was an expert at defusing tension with a few well-chosen words. And she was persuasive. But Patt wasn't convinced.

The one thing she had known about unions is that they were always fighting management, and a management job at American was where she'd set her sights. And it was obvious the union wasn't popular. The Dallas base had been so hard up for members that they had paid Patt's membership fees for her! With automatic termination upon marriage, the average stewardess stayed on the job for just a couple of years. So the union was constantly losing members. Most women considered the job an interlude between high school or college and marriage, so they gave little thought to improving working conditions, pensions, or other benefits. Patt certainly wasn't thinking of these things. She was focused on making it through her probationary period without further discipline.

The phone rang; Nancy again. She had news: a fellow flight attendant had been suspended, and was "grieving" the suspension, which meant a meeting between the stewardess and management. "Patt," said Nancy, "I need you to go to the grievance and represent this woman." Patt, bemused, protested that she didn't know anything about grievances. "I'll walk you through everything," Nancy reassured her. She was so positive that Patt believed her. How hard could it be? She hadn't even been to a second union meeting, but she was accustomed to obeying authority. She agreed.

The issue was this: Pat Suchecki, a fellow stewardess a year senior to Patt, had spilled coffee on her light blue uniform while on a flight. She was suspended for three days because she had had to wear the stained uniform on her next flight—she hadn't brought a second uniform with her, and it had been impossible to get the uniform to a dry cleaner on her layover (she'd arrived in Chicago late on a Saturday night and her flight out was at 8 a.m. the next day). She felt that the suspension was unfair. Patt was twenty years old, but her job was to represent Pat in a meeting with the manager of the Dallas base, Bob Ferris, and to try to get the suspension lifted.

Patt didn't like Bob. He was, she thought, a pig; he was consistently condescending and he treated the women like dirt. He'd take advantage of his right to conduct girdle checks to run his hands over the stewardesses' bodies anytime he pleased, getting what they referred to as a "free feel." Bob wasn't the only one at liberty to do a girdle check; all the supervisors and even the pilots could exercise this right. But Bob exercised it, in the minds of Patt and her fellow stewardesses, much more than was necessary.

Patt and Pat met at the airport and walked into Operations. Lined with cubbyholes, this busy area was where the stewardesses would pick up their mail and memos. There was a scale for weight checks. And in the corner was Bob Ferris's office, with two chairs outside the door. They sat down and conferred quickly. Pat gave her reasons: there had been turbulence that made her spill the coffee, the flight the next morning was an early one, and no dry cleaners had been open. "You should have had an extra uniform with you," Patt admonished her. Stewardesses were encouraged to travel with spare uniforms for exactly this kind of situation, but carrying a garment bag everywhere on the off chance that you'd need it was a hassle. Even Patt didn't usually do it. And she did think that a three-day suspension was overkill. Nancy had made sure Patt had received a copy of the union rulebook, but Patt hadn't read it. If Nancy was sending *her*, none of this could be that big a deal.

Bob Ferris came out of his office and greeted them with, "Oh, you must be Patt Gibbs."

"Yes, Mr. Ferris," she said. "I'm Patt Gibbs, and this is Miss Suchecki."

He said, "Well, Patt, go ahead and take your seat out here." He took Pat into the meeting, leaving Patt sitting outside.

The meeting didn't last long, but it went on long enough for Patt to leaf through her book and discover that she was supposed to be *in* the meeting, not sitting in a chair outside the room. And the book stated clearly that if someone in management called you by your first name, you called them by theirs. This was news to Patt. The airline industry was rigidly hierarchical. A stewardess never addressed a captain by his first name—they'd always be called "Captain LastName"—but the pilots never called the stewardesses by anything other than their first name, unless it was "sweetheart" or "darling." A few minutes later, Bob walked out of the room and said, "Well, Patt, the hearing is over and she lost the grievance."

Wait a second, she thought. She realized how naive she'd been. She stood up. "Bob," she said, pointing her finger at him, "she lost this time, because I didn't know I was supposed to be in there. But she's going to win this grievance. You wait and see." She took Pat by the arm and left.

Although she'd claimed that they would have won the grievance if she'd been in the room, Patt was fully aware that she wouldn't have known what to do if she had been. But she did know she hated feeling so stupid. She called Nancy and told her Pat had lost. Nancy pointed out that Patt should have been in the meeting. Patt responded that she hadn't known, and acknowledged that she'd looked foolish. "But," she said, "in my defense, I did call him Bob."

After this incident, Nancy came out to Dallas to start training Patt as a union rep. Nancy taught her how to file an appeal, and Patt was determined to do better this time around. She prepared for hours. At the appeal, she pushed her way into the room, determined to avoid being shut out again, and made her presentation defending Pat's uniform infraction. And she won. The suspension was lifted. Patt was hugely relieved and a little proud; she had, she thought, redeemed herself. She'd had a taste of being treated badly, and she'd pushed back. Pat's suspension had been unfair, but it wasn't the main motivating factor. Patt had somehow come up against a line she wasn't willing to cross. There were, she realized, limits to what she'd put up with. It was an epiphany that would shape the course of her life. She'd seen how the airline management, in the form of Bob Ferris, would treat stewardesses like they didn't matter. She could either accept that, she thought, or she could fight back.

Being made a fool of by Bob Ferris was also the beginning of the end of Patt's ambitions to get a management job. Managers were, in their essence, rule followers, and she'd followed the rules every way she knew how. She had volunteered her time at the learning center, had even ratted out a fellow stewardess. She had been hoping those things would get her through the door. She now knew that that wasn't how you got through the door. You had to get picked, and she didn't have what they were looking for. She looked at the system and saw one that wanted homogeneity, people whom they could, she thought, brainwash. They'd been told from the beginning how special they were, and how lucky they were to be there. She'd believed it. But Pat Sucheki's disciplinary action destroyed any illusions she'd had.

CHAPTER THREE

The Air Strip

THE FIRST TIME Patt met Jimmy Hoffa, she shouted at him. She was in Chicago for the 1964 ALSSA convention. Her inadvertent election to base chairperson meant that she could attend as a representative, and as she entered the ballroom of the Palmer House Hotel on the first day, her jaw dropped. There were women there from all over the country, stewardesses from Western, Eastern, Northwest, TWA. For the first time Patt could see what Nancy had meant by power in numbers. She was a convert now, her belief in the union as strong as her trust in the benevolence of American's management had once been. This, *this*, was how the stewardesses would get things done.

The other American attendees with her were far more experienced. Nancy was there, of course, as well as Kathy Russo, an old hand who was the chair of the Boston base. Patt had stars in her eyes, thrilled by the sight of hundreds of women union leaders, but Nancy and Kathy tamped down her enthusiasm fast. The TWU leadership was almost entirely male, they pointed out, and it made its priorities clear: men—such as airline mechanics and maintenance workers—had families to support, and they needed the most money and benefits. Stewardesses, in the TWU's view, were temp workers. Though they believed in the power of the union, Nancy and Kathy told Patt that the TWU thought of them as mascots, not workers in the way a mechanic was a worker. They'd spent years watching the TWU fight for wages, pensions, and benefits for other groups while doing little to support the stewardesses, who wouldn't be around long enough for it to really matter anyway.

After the day's meetings were over, Nancy turned to Patt. "Come on," she said. "We're going to another meeting here in the hotel." Patt thought they were heading to an internal caucus, but they took the elevator to the penthouse. Stepping through the doorway behind Nancy, Patt recognized the man in the center of the room right away. It was Jimmy Hoffa.

Jimmy Hoffa, the president of the Teamsters, had been making overtures to stewardesses since the late 1950s. He wanted to add airline workers to his 1.7 million transportation workers (many of them truckers) and had offered stewardesses their own special division with the Teamsters back in 1961. The Teamsters were a formidable union, and though the government had attempted to reduce their power through accusations of corruption and links to organized crime, they were aggressively effective. Kathy, who had been to school with one of Hoffa's lieutenants, had set up this clandestine meeting.

The rest of the women were visibly thrilled to be meeting Hoffa: he was the king of the Teamsters, the bold, swaggering, hard-nosed leader of the American labor movement, the man who could shut down the country with a single call for a strike. He came over to say hello. Patt was stunned. And confused. "What the hell is going on?" she asked. "Why are we here with the Teamsters?" What she knew about the Teamsters was what she had read in the papers—they were chain-wielding, crowbar-carrying mobsters who blew up trucks. When Hoffa turned to Patt and introduced himself with a casual, "Hi, I'm Jimmy," she lost her cool. "I know who you are," she exploded. "I don't know what's going on, but I'm out of here. I'm not staying in this room. I'm not a Teamster. I will never be a Teamster!"

The rest of the women ran over to her, panicking, and started frantically shushing her. "Patt, this is *Jimmy Hoffa*! Don't insult *Jimmy Hoffa*!" Hoffa said only, "We're not that bad." Patt turned on her heel and left. She couldn't believe what had just happened. It was the height of disloyalty to meet with the Teamsters when they were there on the TWU's dime. And what would a group of female stewardesses do in a truck drivers' union, anyway? She ran back into the elevator, jabbing at the buttons, then stormed her way through the lobby until she spotted Colleen Boland, the president of ALSSA.

The American union reps, she told Colleen breathlessly, were meeting Hoffa to discuss breaking away from the TWU and going with the Teamsters.

The meeting with Hoffa didn't go anywhere, and the women who had attended were called in to individual meetings with the TWU leadership and had the fear of God put in them. Patt, who had ratted her colleagues out, became an outcast for a while.

Patt had made it past probation, was well into her working life, and she hadn't been fired. The shine had worn off, though. The freedom-filled, sophisticated lifestyle she'd been expecting hadn't materialized. Work did have its pleasures, its excitements, even its dangers. Once, going into St. Louis on a DC-6, she'd had to prepare for a gear-up landing, a situation where the plane's landing gear didn't extend, with the possibility of the aircraft landing on its belly. She'd been scared; had had to run back to pull the slides out of their compartment and haul them to the exit doors. Everything had worked fine in the end, but she had gotten her first real-life example of how necessary stewardesses were in case of emergency. She wouldn't forget it.

Still, much more of her life than she'd expected was taken up with girdle checks and petty grievances, patronizing supervisors and small paychecks. She started dating a man named Johnny, whose mother worked in airport catering. He lived nearby, and was a nice guy, fun to be around. But Patt knew she would never sleep with him. It wasn't that she disliked him, exactly, but something, she felt, was missing from their relationship. When she made it clear she was neither going to marry him nor go to bed with him, Johnny took it badly. He volunteered for the army and went off to fight in Vietnam. Patt was hugely relieved when he came back alive.

Nancy continued to encourage and mentor Patt in the ways of the union, and she started to become friendly with other union members. Nancy sent her reading material about the importance of unity, of building the membership. This was stock union messaging, but for Patt it was new and eye-opening. She decided to start recruiting. Most of the stewardesses who worked at the Fort Worth airport lived in small groups in apartment complexes known as "stew zoos." Patt had driven eighteen-wheelers when she worked for the circus, so she hatched a plan. She went to a General Motors dealership and convinced them to lend her a motor home. "People will see lots of women stepping in and out of it," she told them confidently. "It's free advertising!" They agreed.

She would niftily pull her motor home into the parking lot at a stew zoo, then she'd go around and knock on doors. They wouldn't come to union meetings, so Patt was bringing the meetings to them, luring people in with offers of food (she'd learned fast that free cake was a building block of power). Her energy was compelling, and she signed up new members at a rapid pace, pointing out all of the things that the stewardesses were putting up with.

At the upper levels of the union, things were getting tense. The people in the TWU assigned to keep an eye on the stewardess division reported back to the leadership that the stewardess union leaders were inept, that union meetings were sparsely attended, and that there was a general lack of interest in the union. Well, of course, Patt thought to herself: what with firing women when they got married, or turned thirty-two, the airlines had made the job tenure so short that it was hard to motivate flight attendants to get active in the union. Why bother, when they'd soon be out of a job anyway? Frederic Simpson, the TWU's chief staff organizer and the man in charge of overseeing the stewardesses, came to a different conclusion on why women weren't interested in the union: women were too obsessed, he decided, with thoughts of men and dating.

Not Patt. And by the time the next election came around, she had her own ideas of how a union should be run. She ran against the base chair, Kip Rose, and won, elected by many of her own new recruits for an eighteen-month term. She'd be the Dallas chair for the next six years.

On April 17, 1963, eight stewardesses held a press conference in New York's Commodore Hotel. Boasting toothy smiles, glowing skin, and impeccably pressed uniforms that displayed plenty of leg, they lined up in front of the gathered reporters and defied them to guess which of the stewardesses was over the age of thirty-two. Barbara Roads, aged thirty-five and known to everyone as "Dusty," issued a challenge: "Do I look like an old bag?" she asked, with an audacious grin. The stewardesses, all slim and smiling, were between twenty-three and thirty-six years old, and this stunt made headlines around the country. The answer to Dusty's question was a loudly expressed *no*, both from reporters and the readers who saw the photo in their daily paper and took their own guess as to which of the stewardesses was over the limit. The *Daily News* described Roads as "poured elegantly into a form-fitting uniform (measurements, 36-24-36) . . . Dusty stands a long-legged five ft. eight and weighs one-hundred-twenty-five pounds and has natural blonde hair, if you get the picture, fellows."

Dusty, a charming, strong-willed stewardess, was an ALSSA leader, and she and her close friend Nancy Collins had organized the event to call attention to the age issue as the union and the airlines battled over the automatic-termination-at-thirty-two rule. Dusty, who had been hired in 1950 before the rule was implemented, wasn't even affected by it—according to the arrangement made between American Airlines and ALSSA, she'd been one of the group "grand-mothered" in, and could continue flying even past her expiration date.

The age issue went all the way to Congress. Dusty had been petitioning members of Congress, schmoozing them, even dating them, in an attempt to get a law passed that would permit stewardesses to stay on the job past thirty-two, but to no avail. Then, in 1965, federal hearings were held on employment issues faced by older workers. Could they get rid of the age rule this way? The stewardesses decided to try.

A group of seventeen stewardesses, including ALSSA president Colleen Boland (age thirty-six) and Northwest stewardess Mary Patricia Laffey (age twenty-seven), headed to Capitol Hill to testify about the airlines' retirement policy. The House of Representatives Select Subcommittee on Labor was considering the issue of age discrimination in employment, debating whether to create a law against it and, if so, which ages should be protected. They included the stewardesses in their debates over age discrimination and related problems, and hopes were high that Congress could force a change on the airlines. The women appeared before a three-man panel that seemed to view their presence as more of a joke than anything else. Representative James H. Scheuer even asked Colleen, "Would you be good enough to have the members of your group stand so we can visualize the dimensions of the problem?"

Colleen delivered a strong statement, hammering home the point that age had nothing to do with a stewardess's ability to do her job. But the congressmen were more interested in the view than in what she had to say. Representative Scheuer asked, "Would the airlines tell us that these pretty young ladies are ready for the slag heap?" He followed this with the generous statement, "I for one would oppose to my dying breath the principle that a woman is less attractive, less alluring, and less charming after age 29 or 32 or 35. I think my colleagues on this committee will agree." Representative James G. O'Hara responded, "Especially if we want to be reelected." Cue general laughter. When Colleen finished her testimony, O'Hara expressed his appreciation to her and her fellow workers "for adding some beauty and grace" to the hearings.

The proceedings came to an end without any progress on age discrimination; the government had nothing to offer stewardesses who crossed the invisible age line. The women were bitterly disappointed. They had, though, made the news: the papers avidly covered the hearings, with titillating headlines such as "Airline Stewardess over the Hill at 32? Congressional Girl-Watchers Say 'No!'" (the *Atlanta Constitution*) and "Stewardesses Pushing 32 Stack Up Well in Age Plea" (the *Baltimore Sun*). But it was paltry compensation.

Firing stewardesses at the age of thirty-two didn't always mean that the women disappeared at that age. Some were reassigned to ground jobs, though these were usually lower status, paid less, and might involve moving to another base in a completely different part of the country. Many stewardesses who aged out found employment at the Admirals Club (the airport lounge for valued customers), and the few who had been grandmothered in still worked the line. They became known as "gold wingers" because after five years of service, the silver wings that had been pinned on them at graduation were exchanged for gold ones.

Patt became friends with a gold winger, Ann Davis, and they often flew together. Passengers boarding the plane would see Ann's gray hair and crack jokes ("Oh, look at this, a mother-daughter team!"). Ann would laugh and smile, saying nothing; Patt followed her example. One day they had to prep the plane for an emergency evacuation, and Patt noticed that suddenly none of these wisecracking passengers wanted to talk to her anymore. They directed all their questions to Ann, seeking reassurance from the woman who clearly had more experience. All at once the human toll of the age discrimination issue was made real to Patt, who'd signed her contract without a second thought. Pilots had gray hair, she realized, and no one cared. It wasn't long afterward that Patt and Ann were in Operations waiting for a flight. Bob Ferris, the base manager, was walking out the door when he caught sight of them. "Hey, Ann!" he shouted. "Why don't you wear silver wings instead of your gold wings so they match your hair?" He guffawed at his own joke as he left the room, but Patt didn't laugh. And for Ann it wasn't anything new; it was just one more dig, one more unsubtle encouragement to leave the line.

The airline eventually convinced Ann to resign by promising her a job as an instructor at the charm farm. She had finally tired of the jokes, the spoken and unspoken pressure to get out of the cabin and make way for the younger women. The disappointed faces of male passengers who'd clearly been expecting a fresh-faced twenty-year-old started to undermine her confidence. So she took the instructor job. When she arrived, though, she found herself put in charge of supplies instead.

Keeping track of inventory felt like a token job to Ann. It wasn't instructing, it wasn't working the cabin, it wasn't important. She couldn't stop thinking about how she was too old to be on the airplane, too old, according to American Airlines, to even appear in front of the public. She became depressed. After a few months, she suffered a nervous breakdown, and she checked herself into a psychiatric hospital for treatment. But it didn't help. She hadn't been there long before she committed suicide, suffocating herself with a plastic bag she'd found in a garbage can. She had left behind, Patt would learn, a note. It said that she felt old and useless.

Ann Davis wasn't the only stewardess over thirty-two who committed suicide. She was one of six individuals who had been forced off the line for being too old and had been unable to come to terms with being discarded after years of service. Appearance was everything at the airlines when it came to stewardesses, and passengers had been trained to expect young, smiling women welcoming them into the cabin, not women with gray hair and lines etched on their faces from all that smiling.

As the stewardesses were fruitlessly looking for help from Congress, the airlines decided to double down on marketing their sexual appeal. The industry started launching advertisements and uniform changes that would get more and more extreme, veering at times into the truly bizarre. In 1965, Patt and her fellow stewardesses watched in disbelief as Braniff International Airways took the lead, hiring designer Emilio Pucci to revamp its uniforms. The new look included futuristic clear plastic bubble helmets to keep off the rain, skirt suits, shift dresses in primary colors for serving dinner, and knee-length "harem pants" with tight-fitting mock turtlenecks for dispensing digestifs. Braniff then debuted the "Air Strip." During the flight, its stewardesses would, bit by bit, shed pieces of their elaborate new uniforms. The print ads, bright with color and seductive smiles, portrayed the whole event as a striptease—who knew where it might end? The television commercial, set to bawdy flute music, featured a woman unzipping a coat, then slipping off a shoe, then unwrapping a skirt, as a man's voice intoned, "When a Braniff International hostess meets you on the airplane,

she'll be dressed like this . . . When she brings you your dinner, she'll be dressed this way . . . After dinner, on those long flights, she'll slip into something a little more comfortable . . . The Air Strip is brought to you by Braniff International, who believes that even an airline hostess should look like a girl." There was also a Braniff Barbie, who came with four stewardess outfits. Ken, in his pilot uniform, was sold separately.

The fitted nature of the eye-catching new clothes meant that stewardesses even had to remove their girdles. Unashamedly performative, the new job description for a stewardess was less about safety than it had ever been before. This campaign, along with "the end of the plain plane" (Braniff painted their planes in seven new colors, including blue, yellow, orange, and turquoise), was the brainchild of Mary Wells, advertising's best-known female executive. Gloria Steinem would later say that "Mary Wells Uncle Tommed it to the top." Wells issued a blunt rebuttal: "I worked as a man worked. I didn't preach it, I did it."

A year later, Braniff reported a nearly 50 percent increase in revenue. The "Air Strip" pointed the way: stewardesses were now a financial driver.

CHAPTER FOUR

Sonia in Fantasyland

ON MARCH 26, 1963, a thirty-four-year-old lawyer named Sonia Pressman testified before the House Committee on Education and Labor. She was working for the National Labor Relations Board but she had ended up in front of the House in the roundabout fashion typical of Washington, D.C.: she'd noticed paperwork on a colleague's desk and, curious, asked what it was. He told her he volunteered at the American Civil Liberties Union. She contacted the director of the Washington office, Larry Speiser, who briskly enlisted her into his volunteer corps. His first ask was that she write a speech for him to deliver in Congress in favor of the Equal Pay Act, currently up for debate. She wrote it and handed it over. He read it, then looked up and suggested she deliver it herself. So she did.

The Equal Pay Act was pushed through Congress by the Kennedy administration, and signed into law on June 10, 1963. It was now officially illegal to pay workers different wages based solely on their sex. Equal pay for equal work was the law of the land, or would be when the act became effective in 1964.

At five foot three, Sonia was dwarfed by most of her colleagues. But she had a bulldog-like tenacity to hold on to an idea, and an incorruptible sense of right and wrong. She'd arrived in the United States at the age of five, fleeing with her parents from Nazi Germany, and progressing through a childhood in the Catskills, college at Cornell, a series of desultory jobs, and eventually law school, before arriving in D.C. to work for the government. With her face pale underneath the thick dark hair cut to her ears and puffed up above her head, set off by earrings or a pearl necklace, she wasn't a physically intimidating presence. But she was a fighter, one who would spend her career campaigning for women's rights, and she was there at some of the women's movement's most pivotal moments. Especially those that involved the second piece of legislation that would change the stewardesses' lives forever: the Civil Rights Act of 1964.

Signed into law on July 2, the Civil Rights Act outlawed discrimination based on race, color, religion, sex, or national origin. Title VII of the act, which specifically prohibited employment discrimination on the same grounds, was the provision that the stewardesses would seize upon, changing their futures and setting precedents for all women workers. It banned discrimination when it came to salaries, advertising for open positions, hiring and firing, benefits, and much more. The act needed to be enforced, so it also established the Equal Employment Opportunity Commission, which would be the official agency in charge of making sure every business in the United States fell in line with Title VII.

This piece of legislation hit the airline industry like an explosion. Making discrimination in employment illegal cut directly to the heart of its business model. And the stewardesses took notice. Title VII, they realized, could be used as a lever to challenge almost every one of the airlines' sexist hiring practices. Still, there was one loophole in Title VII that gave the airlines a chance to reject every attempt the stewardesses might make for a more equitable workplace: the BFOQ. In certain situations, the law allowed, employers would be permitted to discriminate on the basis of sex if they could prove that sex was a bona fide occupational qualification and "reasonably necessary to the normal operation of that particular business or enterprise."

The staff were still taking typewriters out of the boxes and setting up their desks when Dusty Roads and her fellow American Airlines stewardess Jean Montague turned up at the newly formed Equal Employment Opportunity Commission. Mostly Black, the employees weren't sure what to make of these two blondes in stewardess uniforms. One woman approached them and asked bluntly, "What are you doing here?"

"Well," Dusty replied, "we have a problem."

She said, "You're white, you're free, and you're twenty-one. What is it?"

"Honey, sit down," Dusty said. "I got a long story to tell you."

She and Jean helped the staff unpack the typewriters, then sat down and told them about the airline industry: the weigh-ins, the marriage and pregnancy bans, the way stewardesses were fired in their thirties. "They don't fire the pursers," said Dusty. "They don't fire the flight engineers. And they don't fire men in cabin service." She pointed out that Pan Am and TWA both employed men as cabin attendants, usually as pursers. Purser was a better-paid job than stewardess, and involved slightly more responsibility because the duties included dealing with foreign currency and customs forms on international flights, but it was not by any measure significantly different. But those men didn't lose their jobs when they turned thirty-two. The EEOC staff, shocked by their stories but still not quite sure if these women belonged in their office, typed up their complaint, and Dusty and Jean went on their way, sure that they had a winning case.

The EEOC had a clear mandate: enforce Title VII's antidiscrimination provisions. Although the EEOC had no power to take anyone to court (and wouldn't until 1972), its rulings were meant to be taken seriously and EEOC decisions empowered plaintiffs to file lawsuits. The EEOC was a big deal; it would be tackling workplace discrimination head-on, with implications for nearly every worker and business in the country. But despite the fact that "sex" had been one of the conditions listed in the act, virtually no one expected sex discrimination to be an issue that the EEOC would take up. The newspapers were full of the fight for racial equality, which was inflaming public opinion. A few months before the EEOC was scheduled to open, Malcolm X had been assassinated. The march from Selma to Montgomery, to demand voting rights for Black people, had taken place and had been met with police violence. In the eyes of the president, the EEOC commissioners, the staff, and the public, the commission's remit was race. But then Dusty Roads had walked in.

She was the first, but she wasn't the only one. By October, there were 143 charges of sex discrimination on the EEOC's books. By the end of the first year, almost 2,500. Around 27 percent of the total complaints filed were sex discrimination. And stewardesses were coming to the EEOC in droves: within a year and a half of its opening, stewardesses alone had filed more than 100 complaints. For a commission expecting to deal almost entirely with racism, this was deeply unsettling. Most of the commissioners and staff refused to take the sex discrimination charges seriously. But for one person, those charges deserved attention.

Sonia Pressman was still working for the National Labor Relations Board. She was thirty-seven years old, restless, and looking around for something new. She'd enjoyed volunteering for the ACLU, but needed more stimulation. She complained to a friend, Jackie Williams, that she'd been having pointless lunch after pointless lunch with people she hoped could help her find an exciting new job, but nothing had emerged. Jackie knew about a brand-new agency that had just opened; one of her teachers at Howard University had started working there. She suggested that Sonia talk to him. Sonia, never one to let the grass grow under her feet, immediately made an appointment. Charlie Duncan, his desk covered in application forms, hired her with barely an interview (Sonia suspected Jackie had put in a good word).

There was one hitch. Charlie required a reference from a congressperson before he could bring her on board. Sonia was stumped; she wasn't a Washington insider and didn't know anyone in power. But then something occurred to her. She'd once heard Senator Edmund Muskie, who would later become governor of Maine, deliver a speech sympathetic to immigrants and refugees. Back then, in need of a job, Sonia had written him a letter, leaning hard on the fact that she'd been a refugee herself. An assistant to Muskie, George Mitchell, had responded and she'd met with him, though no job had materialized. Now, she reached out again. Mitchell quickly got back to her. He'd be in D.C. on business soon, he said; could she meet him for a drink at the Mayflower Hotel? She could. They drank. They danced. He told her about his wife, who had just had a baby. She reminded him that she needed a reference from Muskie. Then she readied herself to leave. She had almost reached the elevator when he asked her to go with him to his room.

Mitchell would later go on to play a major role in American and global politics, serving as Senate majority leader and helping to craft the Good Friday Agreement in Northern Ireland. In 2019, he'd also be publicly named as one of the alleged participants in Jeffrey Epstein's underage sex abuse ring. But in 1965, he was propositioning Sonia, though without success. She hopped into a cab. But she berated herself all the way home. In the books she read, women were going to bed with men all the time, and moving up in their careers. What was wrong with her? She finally decided she just wasn't the type to go around sleeping with lots of people, but she did feel sure that she'd lost her chance at the new job. But then the reference arrived on Charlie's desk. Sonia was hired. She was the Equal Employment Opportunity Commission's first woman lawyer.

Though she was, almost unwittingly, a pioneer, it wasn't the growing women's movement that made Sonia a feminist. It was logic. The EEOC had been in business for three months before she arrived (always neatly turned out in houndstooth or checked dresses and skirt suits, never trousers), and the sex discrimination complaints, starting with the one Dusty had filed, were piling up. But no one ever took them on. She watched as the women's cases were pushed to the bottom of the heap. Indignant, she raised the issue with her bosses, but she was ignored. Was she going crazy? The EEOC was there to enforce an act, there was a provision about women in the act, but no one was enforcing it. Surely that was wrong? But no one else seemed to care.

She kept up an ongoing debate with herself. She felt scammed, somehow. Or was the fault hers? Had she been stupid to believe that the agency would actually tackle sex discrimination? She knew the EEOC had limited funds, and that sex discrimination raised legal questions to which no one yet knew the answers. And she didn't think of herself as a feminist. But it still seemed to her that she was pointing out the elephant in the room to no avail.

The EEOC had five commissioners. Franklin Delano Roosevelt Jr. was one, and also the EEOC's first chairperson, but he left after a few months, though not before Sonia overheard him describe his office as smelling like a "French whorehouse." The other commissioners were Aileen Hernandez, Richard Graham, the Reverend Luther Holcomb, and Samuel C. Jackson. A *New York Times* article announcing the appointment of these five ended with the memorable sentence "Mr. Jackson and Mrs. Hernandez are Negroes." The other three, it didn't need to specify, were white. Holcomb, a Texas minister, had been a friend of Lyndon Johnson, who appointed him as a spy who would keep him abreast of what was happening

Sonia in her EEOC years.

at the EEOC. He knew, Sonia quickly realized, nothing about civil rights and was unabashedly opposed to women's rights. Then Herman Edelsberg was appointed executive director. He, too, had little respect for women's rights, and Sonia felt even more disappointed in him; she had expected more from a fellow Jew. At his first EEOC press conference, Edelsberg spoke to reporters about his personal belief that he, and every other man, was entitled to a female secretary if he wanted one: "There are people on this Commission who think that no man should be required to have a male secretary— and I am one of them."

When Dick Berg was appointed as the EEOC's acting general counsel in 1967, Sonia became even more despondent. Berg, like Edelsberg, discounted the sex provision of Title VII completely. He was even in favor of the so-called protective laws that many states had in place; these often excluded women from jobs that were hazardous, physically demanding, or even just required night work or overtime, all in the name of "protecting" women. Berg argued against the EEOC becoming involved in a case that dealt with a California protective law that barred women from working overtime in certain industries. It would, he said, take "efforts and attention from other projects ... deserving of higher priority." (The Reverend Dr.

Pauli Murray, the activist and attorney, was then a consultant at the EEOC, and she refuted his claim in a memo, pointing out that "Congress indicated no intention that any one class protected by Title VII was to receive higher priority than another.") Berg, Sonia soon saw, believed that a woman's place was in the home.

There were a few bright spots. Dick Graham, she felt, was sympathetic to women. Aileen Hernandez believed in women's equality. And Sonia was happy with her boss, Charlie Duncan, who, though Sonia privately considered him a womanizer, was happy to take lessons from her on women's rights. Like so many of the EEOC staff, he'd come on board thinking only about race. But when Sonia drove it home that the mandate included sex, and pointed to the rapidly growing stack of complaints submitted by women, he quickly agreed with her. He did, however, nickname her "the sex maniac," because at every meeting she'd interrupt the discussion of race-based discrimination to ask what they were going to do about women, and when.

The stewardess cases in particular stuck in Sonia's mind. She read all the complaints about their treatment by the airlines, and was alternately shocked, disgusted, and outraged by what was going on. The airlines were in clear violation of Title VII, she thought as she paged through case after case. It was apparent in every line about mandatory termination upon marriage or pregnancy, every detail about the age limit. The insistence on young women as the only ones who could do the job was absurd . . . and, she knew, it was now illegal.

Angered, Sonia attempted to speak to Edelsberg again about the EEOC's lack of progress on women's rights. "We can't act," he replied, "because we don't know what the women want." With the women's movement gathering steam apace, Sonia felt that this was a poor excuse. After each conversation with Edelsberg that went nowhere, she'd cry tears of frustration on her way home. No one had appointed or elected her to fight for women's rights, she knew. She had no power. She was facing off against the executive director, the deputy general counsel, a majority of the commissioners—men who made all the decisions. "How," she asked herself, "did I get into this?" She felt completely alone.

Title VII was still new, and employers were unfamiliar with how it would affect their businesses. So Sonia was deputized by the EEOC to travel around the country and give speeches, telling employers about the new law and how it would change their hiring and employment practices. Her first talk was given to the Women's Department of the United Auto Workers, and it was memorable mostly because she had packed her speech in her suitcase, and then picked up someone else's luggage at the airport. Future talks would be memorable for a different reason. She'd speak about the new law and inform her audience they had to comply with it or the EEOC would come after them. When she referred to women's rights, the reaction of the executives wasn't much different than that of Luther Holcomb and Herman Edelsberg. The idea was so absurd that her audience would laugh. She couldn't decide whether to be angry or mortified; she settled on both.

One talk was canceled before it took place. When she called to confirm the details of her upcoming speech at D.C.'s Army and Navy Club, she was told that she'd have to enter the building through the back entrance. The club was only for men, and women couldn't come in the front door.

"Why not?" she asked.

"There might be club members walking around who aren't completely dressed," they told her. "So we can't have you coming in that way."

"I've seen men in underwear before," Sonia replied calmly, hiding her anger.

But they insisted. Sonia snapped. "You're asking me to speak on women's rights and I can't come in the front door?" she asked. "Goodbye and good luck." She didn't go.

Although Sonia felt isolated in her fight for women's rights at the EEOC, she did have one prominent ally. Congresswoman Martha Griffiths, a Michigan Democrat, was using her powerful voice to shine a spotlight on the fact that the EEOC staff spent more time on the ludicrous and hypothetical aspects of potential gender-bending than fighting the real issue of sex discrimination. She took to the floor of the House to decry this: "At the White House Conference on Equal Opportunity in August 1965 [the EEOC] focused their attention on such silly issues as whether the law now requires 'Playboy' clubs to hire male 'bunnies.'" (The specter of the male bunny would be raised again and again in the press.)

Sonia with President Lyndon Johnson, April 11, 1968. Johnson was signing
the Civil Rights Act of 1968, and Sonia was invited to the White House.
Lady Bird Johnson is on the right. Photographer: Frank Wolfe.

Griffiths was a friend of Dusty Roads, and she went on to single
out the airlines, which had been vehemently protesting the idea that
a man, or an older woman, or a married woman, could do the job of
stewardess. The industry had latched on to the law's loophole, the
bona fide occupational qualification, proclaiming that hiring only
young, single women was essential to their business model. Griffiths
pointed out that the airlines "would not be making such a ridiculous
argument if the EEOC had not been shilly-shallying and wringing
its hands about the sex provision. Since both men and women are
employed by the airlines as flight attendants, how in the name of
commonsense can it be argued that the employment of either sex
alone is 'reasonably necessary to the normal operation' of the airlines? . . . If any EEOC official believes this kind of foolishness, then
the headquarters of EEOC, at 1800 G Street NW, should be called
'Fantasyland.' "

Her speech was shortly to have a powerful effect on women's rights. Not quite in the way she'd hoped, but in the formation of the country's most prominent women's rights organization.

The Feminine Mystique, published in 1963, was an explosive exploration of the frustration, anguish, and anger American women were experiencing in their roles as housewives and mothers who weren't part of the 38.3 percent of women who worked outside the home. The author, journalist Betty Friedan, became instantly famous, and by 1966 her book had sold almost three million copies. Betty decided to follow up this book by writing about the progress women had made since its publication; this included investigating the EEOC and its mandate to enforce the sex discrimination provision of Title VII. Conducting interviews in the D.C. office, she spotted Sonia, the agency's only female attorney, and came to her office to chat. Sitting in the chair opposite, Betty asked, "What are the problems here? What's going wrong?" Sonia wanted to confide in her, but worried that she would lose her job. She told Betty everything was fine.

Two weeks later, Betty returned. Sonia had just left a meeting with Herman Edelsberg, and was so vexed at his intransigence on taking on women's cases that when she spotted Betty, she pulled her into her office. The words spilled from Sonia's mouth in a torrent of frustration. The EEOC wasn't enforcing the law for women, she told Betty. Nothing was happening. "This country needs an organization to fight for women," she said, tears in her eyes, "like the NAACP does for Negroes."

By such small incidents are seismic changes launched. The second catalyst was the Conference of Commissions on the Status of Women, held in June 1966 in Washington, D.C. Attendees at the conference, inspired by Martha Griffiths's recent speech, decided to pass a resolution that pertained to the EEOC. Their goal was Sonia's idée fixe: the enforcement of Title VII as it applied to women. They were quickly told that they didn't have the authority to pass resolutions, which was true. The conference was being held under the aegis of the Department of Labor. One federal agency can't dictate to another federal agency; the commission had no power to pass resolutions prescribing work for the EEOC.

The attendees were furious, possibly because they understood this prohibition to mean they were being told that their commissions, which had been set up to keep track of progress on women's issues, were powerless. At lunch, Betty and a group of fellow activists channeled their rage into action: they decided to start an organization that would, as Sonia had suggested, be for women, by women, and push for women's equal rights. The other women in the group, twenty-eight in total, each contributed $5 as seed money, and the group that would become the National Organization for Women (NOW) had had its first meeting. Betty jotted down the acronym on a napkin.

The second meeting was held on a Saturday morning on Halloween weekend 1966. The location was the basement of the *Washington Post* building. Sonia walked in to find nineteen women and two men, all sitting on folding chairs, briefcases and handbags tucked down by their feet. The purpose of the meeting was to adopt bylaws and establish NOW's mission statement. Sonia had plenty of suggestions and spoke up, improvising the legalese of that document on the fly, and insisting on careful wording that would later on save NOW from lawsuits. She didn't know most of the other people at the meeting. They worked in government, for the press, some in labor unions, but the thing they had in common was vexation at the inferior status of women, fury at what they saw as sabotage of Title VII, and a compulsion to do something to fix it. Betty wrote the group's statement of purpose: "To take action to bring women into full participation in the mainstream of American society now, exercising all the privileges and responsibilities thereof in truly equal partnership with men." That meeting also established NOW's next steps: inaugurating task forces, committing to work for the enforcement of Title VII, and creating a Legal Committee to take action on behalf of the flight attendants, those whose initial complaints to the EEOC had received so little attention.

Sonia was a little in awe of her fellow founding members. Betty Friedan was famous, of course. And Sonia already knew Pauli Murray, who had done work at the EEOC and was the woman who had pushed back on Dick Berg's assertion that fighting sex discrimina-

NOW's second meeting, basement of the Washington Post *building, Halloween weekend 1966. Sonia is in the front row, third from the right; Betty Friedan is on the right. Photographer: Vincent J. Graas.*

tion should take a back seat to fighting race discrimination. Murray, one of the very few nonwhite people involved in NOW's inception, was a Black woman, and a lawyer, civil rights activist, labor organizer, and Episcopal priest whose work would be found behind the scenes of nearly every important activism project of several decades, from sit-ins to gender discrimination arguments made before the Supreme Court by Ruth Bader Ginsburg. Colleen Boland, president of ALSSA, the stewardesses' union, was also a founding member. Other pioneers of the second-wave feminist movement were there. Mary Eastwood, a Justice Department attorney, would author, with Pauli Murray, the groundbreaking article "Jane Crow and the Law: Sex Discrimination and Title VII," on legal discrimination against women. Catherine East had a place, from 1962 to 1977, on every presidential advisory committee on the status of women. Caruthers Berger was a government attorney who would work on nearly all the Title VII test cases. Dick Graham, one of the EEOC's commissioners, joined, and was even elected vice president in October 1966.

Phineas Indritz was another of the few male founding members. A lawyer, feminist, and civil rights activist who, Sonia knew, also wrote most of Martha Griffiths's speeches, Indritz would go on to write the Pregnancy Discrimination Act of 1978, a major victory for NOW. Sonia was, she felt, in illustrious company. For the first time in a long time she felt hopeful. She'd been spinning her wheels, but now, finally, perhaps she could do something.

Indritz, Eastwood, and Berger helmed the organization's Legal Committee. Stewardesses were first on their agenda. This was a win for both groups: NOW had a picture-perfect group of women to capture media attention, and the stewardesses suddenly had the backing of a resourceful organization that was already aware of—and angry about—the EEOC's reluctance to investigate sex discrimination. The stewardesses made the perfect face of NOW's dynamic campaign to ensure that Title VII was enforced in a real, tangible way.

Sonia, though not officially on the Legal Committee, formed an unusual partnership with its members. Her frustration at the EEOC's obduracy had finally found an outlet: she offered to pass, in complete secrecy, information on the EEOC's activities (or lack thereof) to NOW. She was a mole, spending her days at the office attending meetings where issues relating to sex discrimination would come up. Time after time, she'd watch her bosses dismiss them. Then once a week, in the evening, she'd take the bus to southwest D.C. to the apartment of Mary Eastwood. There, Sonia would meet Eastwood, Indritz, and Berger and tell them what had happened at the EEOC that week: the sex discrimination cases they'd neglected to take up, the growing heap of stewardess complaints they'd ignored. These meetings were all business—Eastwood didn't even offer coffee—but Sonia reveled in them; she was no longer alone. The group used her information as the basis for its campaigns. On the back of Sonia's intel, NOW members picketed the EEOC offices to ask why it wasn't doing anything for women's rights. They sent letters full of probing questions about why the agency hadn't found sex discrimination in a particular case, or demanding action on complaints lodged. NOW initiated lawsuits against the EEOC for disregarding the sex discrimination complaints that thousands of women had submitted. It petitioned the EEOC to hold public hearings. At work, Charlie

Duncan would assign Sonia to write up the agency's decisions; at night, she'd take them directly to her cadre of lawyers. Nobody ever thought to ask how NOW had access to the EEOC's decision-making process.

In the times when she wasn't at work or at Eastwood's apartment, Sonia fought a battle with herself over what she was doing. She felt that divulging this information to NOW was wrong, maybe even unethical. But she couldn't shake the knowledge that the EEOC was failing women. It certainly wasn't, she'd reassure herself, following the law. For her, most things in life had always been black and white. But this was something that made her wrestle with her conscience. She continued with her secret work, conflicted, until she finally hit upon a reason that would justify her treachery: things at the EEOC, she thought, had to be beyond the pale, be really, truly terrible, to compel her to break this rule. Then she felt better.

The pressure NOW exerted, and the result—a growing public awareness of the agency's negligence of its directive to tackle sex discrimination—started to make an impact. NOW members picketed the EEOC in protest of a decision it had issued on help wanted ads: that it was legal for newspapers to advertise jobs in two separate columns, one "for men" and one "for women." (One picket sign read, "Title Seven has no teeth, EEOC has no guts.") Sonia had long found this egregious. The jobs listed for women were nearly always less skilled and lower paid than those listed for men. And she knew that, convention aside, a man could be a secretary and a woman a company director. She'd hated this segregation of help wanted ads so much that at a NOW meeting she'd even proposed bombing the presses at the *Washington Post*. The *Post* wasn't the only paper advertising jobs for men and women in different columns, but it was the nearest. Her bombing plan wasn't taken up, but the picket, which had been organized at Mary Eastwood's apartment, worked: the agency changed its mind, deciding that employers would no longer be able to advertise open positions in columns separated by sex. Jobs, at least most jobs, had to be open to men and women, and people would have to be treated equally once employed.

Sonia wasn't the only one working in secret. Other feminists employed by the government were also doing their part. Mary Eastwood, Catherine East, and Caruthers Berger were actually using government equipment to write the first sex discrimination briefs. They'd stay late in their government offices, typing out documents for NOW's first legal cases on their government typewriters, Xeroxing them on government machines. NOW never went so far as to thank the federal government for its contribution to the feminist movement, but it did play a small, albeit unknowing role.

Sonia's intel, and NOW's resulting publicity campaign, meant that the EEOC could no longer squirm out of its responsibilities. It was finally forced to take action on behalf of its most persistent complainants: the stewardesses. The agency started issuing decisions on the stewardesses' cases. And it decided to hold hearings to determine whether or not being female was a job requirement for a flight attendant. Sonia was thrilled.

There was a neat synergy in the cycle of women helping women. Flight attendant grievances had fueled Martha Griffiths's speech about the lack of action at the EEOC. Griffiths's speech helped inspire the formation of NOW, later that month. NOW went after the EEOC (with Sonia's help). And, finally, the EEOC started helping flight attendants, which would, through the establishment of case law around sex discrimination, help other women win rights in the workplace.

The male EEOC leadership's refusal to take women's rights seriously had ended up radicalizing women like Sonia. It was an unexpected turn of events. But it was one that would be repeated, in similar circumstances, a few years later when the battle between the stewardesses and their union would change the entire airline industry.

CHAPTER FIVE

What the BFOQ?

SUDDENLY, PATT WAS fired. The reason was so petty, she couldn't help but think it was tied to her increasing union activity. She'd inadvertently written a bad check to a hotel. It wasn't a huge amount, just $25, but she'd asked a friend to deposit her paycheck and the friend had forgotten, so the check was returned. The next day Patt was called into her supervisor's office and terminated for bringing bad publicity to American Airlines. She was in shock.

When she woke up the next day, she stayed in bed for hours, staring up at the ceiling. She had no backup plan, no other options. Being a stewardess was what she did, and it was what she was good at. She felt unmoored; her very essence had been judged by the company and found wanting. Then she looked down at her body. I still have all of the fingers on my hands, she thought. I have all my toes, my eyes. I haven't died. Nothing that bad has happened. Suddenly something occurred to her: "I just need to unplug this umbilical cord that I apparently plugged into the airline." She'd been so convinced this was the world's greatest job, that she was so fortunate to have been chosen for it, she realized, that she'd almost believed that losing her job was like losing part of herself. Instead of being crushed, she suddenly felt wide awake.

She turned to the union for help. To pay the bills she got a temporary job driving across the country to repossess cars, but she wasn't taking her termination lying down. She filed a grievance, went to the hearing, lost, filed an appeal, lost again, appealed again, and won, sort of. She was reinstated, but without back pay for the forty-five days she'd been out of work. Patt went back on the line.

She realized she'd been trying to prove herself to be a good person by becoming a good stewardess. Maybe, she thought, it was because she knew, though still barely acknowledged, that she wasn't quite like other women. She had on occasion found herself attracted to women. She'd rigorously quashed those feelings every time they came up; homosexuality was classified as a mental disorder, and she'd been raised to believe the Bible said people like that would burn in hell. She certainly didn't know any lesbians; at least, no lesbians who were open about it. Since the day she'd sent in her application to American Airlines, she'd felt a strong compulsion to justify herself, to demonstrate that she was doing all the right things. She'd been a model stewardess and employee. But, she realized now, what she'd been doing so far wasn't working. Patt had never felt like she belonged, and now she knew it.

Unplugging the umbilical cord, as Patt thought of it, was a Sisyphean task. If the airlines were to continue to attract the young women they wanted but not to pay them well, they had to compensate in other ways. Promoting the job as glamorous and highly exclusive did the trick, with the added bonus of letting the airlines sell tickets on the strength of their flight attendants' good looks. In 1967, Eastern Airlines even launched a marketing campaign focused on how many applicants they turned away. A print ad featured the bold header "Presenting the Losers" over a photo of nineteen slim, white, glum-faced women. The copy read:

> Pretty good, aren't they? We admit it. And they're probably good enough to get a job practically anywhere they want. But not as an Eastern Airlines stewardess.
>
> We pass up around 19 girls, before we get one that qualifies. If looks were everything, it wouldn't be so tough. Sure, we want her to be pretty . . . don't you? That's why we look at her face, her make-up, her complexion, her figure, her weight, her legs, her grooming, her nails and her hair.
>
> But we don't stop there. We talk. And we listen. We listen to her voice, her speech. We judge her personality, her maturity, her intelligence, her intentions, her enthusiasm, her resiliency and her stamina.
>
> We don't want a stewardess to be impatient with a

question you may have, or careless in serving your dinner, or unconcerned about your needs. We try to eliminate these problems by taking a lot more time and passing up a lot more girls.

It may make our job a lot harder. But it makes your flying a lot easier.

The accompanying television ad was simply a parade of young women passing by the camera, while a male voice pronounced what was wrong with each one: "She bites her nails," "Not very friendly," "She wears glasses," "She's married." And the job was truly exclusive. In 1965, around one million women interviewed to be stewardesses, though there were only about ten thousand open positions. New ones were opening up all the time, though—that same year, American reported the resignation of 80 percent of its stewardesses due to marriage. And in 1967, fewer than 3 percent of aspiring stewardesses made it through TWA's application process.

Before getting back on the plane, Patt had to do one more thing. Every year, the company doctor conducted a medical exam of each stewardess. He would take measurements, do blood work, and, of course, weigh them. Patt always suspected the doctor checked the blood work for signs that they were taking drugs or, worse, were pregnant. Since she'd been fired, she'd have to undergo an extra medical exam before she was permitted to go back to work. For this particular exam, the inspection was even more in-depth. The doctor asked questions about how she felt toward the company now, after being fired. Was she angry or resentful? "I feel fine," she said. He asked more questions, then gave her the all-clear to go back on the line, but not before she'd noticed something on his desk. A personnel file, labeled "Patt Gibbs."

What would the doctor want with her personnel file? Those files were employee records—they detailed disciplinary infractions, supervisors' reports, discussions with management. They weren't relevant to a medical exam. The only reason that file would be on the doctor's desk was if the Employee Relations department had sent it over. It was suddenly obvious: the file was there to encourage the doctor to find a reason not to bring her back. Now they knew she was a troublemaker.

Meanwhile, Patt was paying close attention to something happening over at Braniff Airways. In November 1964, a supervisor at Braniff discovered that stewardess Betty Green Bateman had been secretly married for a year and a half. Bateman, perhaps not coincidentally a union leader, was immediately fired. Her union filed a grievance. Braniff resisted, hard, repeatedly denying her requests for arbitration until the union had to get a court order to have the matter adjudicated by a referee. Finally, Bateman was reinstated. She'd succeeded in keeping both her husband and her job.

Patt was astounded. It had never occurred to her that this was something that could be changed. The mandatory retirement age, she knew, had only been established the previous decade—that was a rule she could envision getting rid of, someday. But marriage? It was barely on her radar. She was new to the airlines, still, and figured that the company had these rules in place for a reason. Nancy and Dusty, who had long lost their faith in the company's goodwill toward its women workers, were also following the case avidly. They were in the midst of negotiating a new contract for the stewardesses.

Contracts were momentous; each one covered a period of several years during which the contract terms could not be changed. Each detail of the stewardess job, from small to large—salaries, uniform allowance, seniority allocation, whether or not gloves had to be worn, benefits, vacation days, meals on planes, hours between flights—was included in the contract. Though many different airlines belonged to ALSSA, contract negotiations were conducted separately for each airline. This was when the stewardesses would tell their union what changes they most wanted to see, and the union would then go into bargaining: arguing and bartering and making deals with the company until a list of demands had been agreed upon. This was a months- and sometimes years-long process that involved meeting after meeting, with the company on one side of the table and the stewardesses (and their union reps) on the other. The reps, sent from the TWU, would bargain on behalf of the stewardesses, asking for increases in pay, or fewer hours, or that the company pay for the uniforms. American Airlines management would counter with its own demands. Eventually, the two sides would come to an agreement, the stewardesses would vote to approve it, and the contract would be signed for the next three years, locking in wages, working conditions, and employment regulations. The contracts were even printed and bound into small books and handed out to each stewardess so she knew the rules and her rights.

Nancy and Dusty, like Patt, immediately realized the importance of Bateman's win. Braniff stewardesses could get married and keep their jobs! Maybe they could use this as leverage at the bargaining table, putting pressure on American to get rid of its own marriage ban.

What was it like for a man to get on a plane knowing that every stewardess was single and, theoretically at least, available? Not that they were always truly single: some estimates recorded that up to 30 percent of stewardesses were secretly married, and certainly most of them, contrary to public opinion, were there to work, not to find a husband. But the illusion was a powerful one.

The cost and stress of maintaining a secret marriage was high. Some women would pay for two phone lines, one with a number that she gave only to the crew scheduler and that her husband could never answer. Maiden names, not married names, went on their mailboxes, and wedding rings stayed in the jewelry box. Some supervisors would scan hometown newspapers for marriage announcements, trying to catch stewardesses who wanted to keep working. Continental Airlines removed its no-marriage rule earlier than most, in the spring of 1966, and even allowed stewardesses to use their married names . . . but still insisted that they be introduced as "Miss," not "Mrs." For women to keep up the perpetual pretense of singledom, the job must have been worth it to them.

In the early 1960s, when Patt joined American, 70 percent of women in the United States married before the age of twenty-four. And the airlines usually hired women who were nineteen or twenty, so high turnover was inevitable. The average length of service for a stewardess was only thirty months. One American Airlines ad jokingly complained that "people keep stealing our stewardesses," and boasted that most of them didn't even last two years in the job before getting married. This was, the copy asserted, because "a girl who can smile for 5½ hours is hard to find. Not to mention a wife who can remember what 124 people want for dinner."

At United, women stayed for an average of 32.4 months before marrying, and Charles M. Mason, United's senior vice president for personnel, considered this the upper limit. "If that figure ever got up to 35 months," he was quoted as saying in the *New York Times,* "I'd know we're getting the wrong kind of girl. She's not getting married."

People keep stealing our stewardesses.

Within two years, most of our stewardesses will leave us for other men. This isn't surprising. A girl who can smile for 5½ hours is hard to find. Not to mention a wife who can remember what 124 people want for dinner.

(And tell you all about meteorology and jets, if that's what you're looking for in a woman.)

But these are not the things that brought on our problem. It's the kind of girl we hire. Being beautiful just isn't enough.

(We don't mean it isn't important. We just mean it isn't enough.) So if there's one thing we look for, it's girls who like people. And you can't do that and then tell them not to like people too much.

All you can do is put a new wing on your stewardess college to keep up with the demand.

American Airlines

Firing women upon marriage had had a chilling effect on Patt's ability to convince people to join the union. Why bother going to all that trouble if they'd be heading down the aisle soon and out of a job? Knowing this, Nancy and Dusty had convinced their TWU reps to fight to get rid of the marriage ban as they hammered out the 1965 contract with the company. Finally, the union and the company came to an agreement, changing the wording in the contract ("Stewardesses may be released any time following the expiration of six months after her marriage") to indicate that after a stewardess got married, the airline had six months in which to review her job performance. Patt celebrated with Nancy and Dusty: this change in the wording must mean that they could get married and stay on the line; they knew full well that marriage had no impact on how anyone did the job. The contract had some bad news for stewardesses, too. Pregnancy still meant immediate termination. And there was no letting up on the push to get older women out of the cabin: stewardesses who had been grandmothered in got a strong incentive to leave, a hefty payment of $4,500 if they resigned voluntarily. Patt thought of Ann Davis, browbeaten into leaving the line. Any means necessary, she concluded glumly.

Still, it was a huge accomplishment. According to the stipulations of the contract, stewardesses were still required to notify American when they married. They obediently did so. Six months later, the company fired them all. Nancy and Dusty were furious. But not just with American. They were furious with the union. How had they let this happen? The marriage issue was forcing women out of work every day, and the TWU leadership didn't seem to care.

Dusty had expected Title VII to solve the stewardesses' problems, with the EEOC leading the charge. But she was disappointed. The EEOC's first decisions, while ideologically helpful, were toothless in terms of practical assistance. In September 1965, the commission weighed in on whether airlines could fire women who married. It seemed to side with stewardesses, issuing employment guidelines that said that employers who placed restrictions on the employment of married women but not married men were violating Title VII. Stewardesses understood this to mean that the airlines' termination-upon-marriage rules were now illegal. Not so fast. Just twelve days later, Charlie Duncan, Sonia's boss, qualified this decision after being queried by panicking executives. He said, "It would be my opinion that the rule announced by Chairman Roosevelt would not apply to airline stewardesses . . . If an airline may give preference to females only as stewardesses, i.e., if sex is a bona fide occupational qualification for the job of airline stewardesses, it would follow that an airline company could impose further qualifications with respect to such jobs and require that the employee be single and under a certain age."

The airlines got the hint: if they could prove that sex was a bona fide occupational qualification for the job of stewardess, they could make whatever rules they wanted regarding their employment.

Northwest Airlines decided to submit a formal request that the EEOC declare whether or not sex was a BFOQ for working as a stewardess. Northwest was joined by the Air Transport Association, an industry group that represented many airlines, setting the stage for a showdown. If the EEOC ruled that sex was a BFOQ, airlines could continue to get away with their regulations on pregnancy, age, marriage, appearance—or at least they'd be sheltered from accusations of sex discrimination. They wouldn't be discriminating against women in favor of men; they'd be simply creating rules that *anyone* in the job had to follow. They wouldn't have to follow the rules of employment under Title VII. Or, as Sonia put it to herself as the date for the hearing approached, "they could hang those women up by their fingernails."

It was a risky move for the airlines. If the EEOC decided that sex was *not* a BFOQ, then the rules the airlines were using against women would be considered sex discrimination. And that, thanks to Title VII, was illegal. If the airlines lost, they'd have to open up the ranks to married women, older women, women who wore glasses. Or—worst of all—*men*. If being a woman was no longer an essential qualification for the job, airline executives thought, the floodgates would open.

But the airlines were confident they could win. So confident that they had suggested the hearing themselves. The stewardesses knew that whatever decision came down was going to make or break their rights as workers, and their chance to turn a temporary job into a career.

On May 10, 1966, Mary Pat Laffey walked into a room where the hearing would be held, flanked by a group of her fellow stewardesses. She was twenty-eight years old, and nervous; she was wearing her uniform in defiance of airline rules that said you weren't to do so in anything that involved publicity (unless, of course, the airline had asked you to). It was her first foray into the public debate on stewardesses, although a few months later she'd attend the congressional hearings on age discrimination. But she and her fellow stewardesses from Eastern, TWA, and Southern were optimistic. The inclusion of "sex" in Title VII made it clear, they thought, that what the airlines were doing was illegal, and having the EEOC declare it so would give them a leg to stand on when it came to negotiating the age and marriage rules out of their contracts. The stewardesses there were all union members; ALSSA president Colleen Boland had convinced them to attend as a kind of visual argument. The lawyers did most of the talking, but the ranged stewardesses, each in her uniform, each trying to hold on to her job though many were married or over thirty-two, made a powerful impression.

The airlines presented their arguments for hiring only women; the unions presented theirs for why that was wrong. It was like a contract negotiation, each side facing off against the other, only writ large. The airlines had hired Jesse Freidin, an attorney from the prestigious New York firm Poletti, Freidin, Prashker, Feldman & Gartner, to represent their alliance. (The firm would continue to represent the airlines in every post–Civil Rights Act discrimination case.) Freidin was a specialist in labor disputes, accustomed to representing management from major industries. His arguments for the airlines hinged on the unique womanly traits that he termed "essential" to the airlines' business model. One of the major questions up for debate was whether or not men could perform the "nonmechanical" tasks that the flight attendant job required. The airlines didn't try to argue that men couldn't serve dinners and open emergency exits. What men couldn't do, they insisted, was "convey the charm, the tact, the grace, the liveliness that young girls can—particularly to men, who comprise the vast majority of airline passengers."

According to the airlines, men simply couldn't handle the emotional labor the job required. They could pour drinks and hang up jackets, sure, but they couldn't create the atmosphere of welcome, comfort, and enjoyment that women could. There was a reason why many of the airlines used the word "hostess" instead of stewardess. And, Freidin argued, men just didn't look good enough: "Girls who are young and pretty have been employed as stewardesses because they are girls, and being girls, had a particular kind of attribute for the particular kind of job that the airlines thought ought to be performed by girls who are rendering in-flight service to passengers." Girls. Girls. Girls. With the repetition of this one word, Freidin was astutely hammering home the point that these were not regular workers who deserved a chance at a career. They were temporary workers, young and only in it for a couple of years—an impression that the airlines were working as hard as possible to make a reality.

United Airlines, powerfully motivated to keep its workforce young and female, prepared a document nearly eighty pages long, each page suffused with reasons why "attractive young women" were uniquely qualified to be stewardesses. Section headings included "This Is a Female Job" and "Stewardesses Have Effectively Produced the Desired Results and Have Done So Because of Their Inherently Female Make-up." They provided testimonials from psychologists, who argued, "[Men] cannot create for the passenger the psychological impression of a memorable occasion . . . add to the pleasure of the trip, the loveliness of the environment or the ego of the male passenger."

Marriage, added the airlines, was incompatible with the stewardess lifestyle. The schedules were too irregular for wives, whom they argued would value their domestic lives above their jobs: "The contemporary habits of our society make a girl's first interest after marriage her husband and her home, rather than her job." Freidin declared that keeping the job restricted to young, single women would even benefit society at large: "As an acceptable and useful job for young girls, as a training ground for future wives and mothers, as a stepping stone from school to a lifetime career, as a happy assistance to innumerable passengers, the stewardess corps serves an important social purpose and is universally recognized throughout the nation as being a very good thing."

The idea that being a stewardess was the perfect training for a future wife wasn't new. The airlines frequently used it as a selling point for their services. One United ad featuring a photo of a hard-working stewardess came with the reminder, "She's going to make someone a great wife," tucked just under the "fly the friendly skies of United" slogan.

Another ad was predicated entirely on the eligibility of the airlines' stewardesses. A close-up of a smiling, big-eyed woman was titled, in bold, "Old Maid." The copy read:

That's what the other United Air Lines stewardesses call her. Because she's been flying for almost three years now. (The average tenure of a United stewardess is only 21 months before she gets married.) But she's not worried. How many girls do you know who can serve cocktails and

dinner for 35 without losing their composure? And who
smile the whole time like they mean it? (They do.) Not too
many, right? That's part of the reason why only one of every
30 girls who apply for stewardess school becomes a United
stewardess. But still, since United invented the stewardess
back in 1930, we've trained over 15,000 smiling reasons
to fly the friendly skies. Maybe that's why more people
fly United than any other airline. Everyone gets warmth,
friendliness and extra care. And someone may get a wife.

Work in the cabin, in other words, was the perfect wifely training, even serving, as Freidin claimed, an important social purpose.

As the hearing progressed, the stewardesses fought back. Colleen
Boland, as president of the stewardess union, presented arguments
on behalf of the women. Sex was obviously *not* a BFOQ, she declared;
in fact, a few airlines already hired men as flight attendants. And
that some airlines had no marriage and age restrictions made it clear
that such rules were not essential to doing business. Marriage had
no effect on a stewardess's ability to do her job, and, she pointed out,
in 1963 American Airlines—one of the airlines that was clinging to
the marriage ban like a life raft—had actually employed married
flight instructors as flight attendants during an employment short-
age. They hadn't been allowed to wear wedding bands or use their
married names, but they'd performed just fine.

The fact that so many stewardesses had married and continued
to fly, hiding that fact successfully from their employers, was a point
in her favor. Colleen, in a gesture that echoed Dusty Roads's "old
bag" gimmick, even challenged the EEOC commissioners to pick
out, on appearance alone, which of the stewardesses in attendance,
sitting to one side, were married.

The hearing took just five hours. Mary Pat left feeling confident
that they had won. She'd watched the commissioners hear the arguments, and they hadn't, she thought, seemed inclined to agree with
the airlines. She was thrilled with the idea that they might have
beaten the company on these issues; it had the potential to change
everything.

The EEOC had six months to make a decision. Patt, Nancy, and
Dusty spent those six months with a veneer of anxiety, interspersed

The glamorous life of a stewardess

This is a non-public appearance of a United Air Lines stewardess. United "invented" the airline stewardess back in 1930 to make air travel a little easier for our first customers.

In those days the specifications were: Registered nurse, not over 25 years of age, weighing 115 lbs. or less, not over five feet four inches tall.

This made sense because these petite first ladies of the air had to squeeze their way through narrow aisles serving up thermos jugs of hot coffee and reassuring smiles to a nervous new flying public.

Today you don't have to be a registered nurse, or under 115 lbs., or five feet four inches tall.

But, you do have to know how to put "extra care" in action: soothe a first-time flyer, relax a tired business-

man, quiet a baby, or laugh with a child.

Our stewardesses go through tough competition for their wings. Only one applicant in 30 makes it.

We have the finest flock of stewardesses in the airline business. And the largest: 2,754 smiling reasons why it's a friendly sky when you fly United.

fly the friendly skies of United.

with short bursts of optimism, layered over their working lives. They knew the outcome would dramatically change their jobs: it would either be the leverage they needed to get rid of a dozen sexist restrictions in one fell swoop, or it would be another door slammed in their faces. But then something happened. The EEOC commissioners voted on November 9 and it became known that they had decided in favor of the stewardesses. But before the commissioners could announce the official decision, the airlines suddenly threw a wrench in the works: they sued to prevent the release of the very ruling they had requested.

Their reasoning: Commissioner Aileen Hernandez, one of the four to vote on the ruling, had joined NOW, and had even been elected, though in absentia, executive vice president. She'd officially resigned from the EEOC and was finishing out her notice period when she'd voted against the airlines. The airlines argued that she couldn't possibly, as a feminist and an elected NOW officer, have been objective about sex discrimination. The judge agreed, and issued an injunction against the use of the decision. An entire new set of hearings would have to take place.

The stewardesses were thwarted again when Delta Airlines had its own no-marriage rule upheld in court. Eulalie Cooper, a Delta stewardess, had been fired upon discovery of her marriage. Delta's workers weren't unionized, so Cooper was on her own. She had brought an EEOC complaint against Delta, and the EEOC had authorized her to bring suit, something that was required for filing a lawsuit alleging discrimination. She took Delta to court on the grounds that she had been discriminated against on the basis of sex. But the judge agreed with Delta that being a single young woman was an essential qualification for the job of stewardess. Stewardesses needed to be single, Delta had argued, because they were less likely to get pregnant, were more accommodating of flight schedule changes, and because passengers preferred them to married women. These arguments would become depressingly familiar to the stewardesses as they continued to push back against the no-marriage rule.

Upon hearing the outcome of the *Cooper* decision, Martha Griffiths took the issue to the House floor. She made speeches about the judge's disregard of Title VII, as well as blasting the judge directly in a letter that spanned five pages. Griffiths's letters were becoming famous; she had already written angry screeds to United's Charles M. Mason, the senior VP who had said that if stewardesses stayed on the job for more than thirty-five months without getting married, they were "the wrong kind of girl." Her letter to Mason of October 10, 1966, asked him the unforgettable question, "What are you running, Mr. Mason, an airline or a whorehouse?" She would continue for years to support the stewardesses in their fight for workers' rights; a future flight attendants' union would eventually name its most prestigious award after her.

Though her case set a disheartening legal precedent, Eulalie Cooper got her job back eventually, when Delta got rid of its no-marriage rule in 1971. The tide was turning, although not fast enough to save the jobs of many women employed in the last years of the 1960s. The unions that represented the stewardesses—which had, in previous contracts, given in to the airlines on the termination-on-marriage rule—started making noises about how it was unreasonable. Too little, too late, thought Patt. When at the bargaining table, the union had clearly considered other issues more important than the marriage ban. Elimination of the marriage rule was treated as a bargaining chip, not a priority, even though it was the number one cause of stewardesses leaving their jobs.

CHAPTER SIX

Black Mollies

PATT'S REALIZATION THAT rules could be changed, whether they were about marriage, or age, or wearing white gloves, had somehow flipped a switch. She threw herself into union work, running for master executive chairperson in 1966, and quickly moving up the union leadership ladder, always backed by Nancy and Dusty. They'd been behind her since the beginning: Dusty out there, publicly voicing her support, Nancy preferring to remain behind the scenes.

The name Patt Gibbs was becoming very familiar to her supervisors, but it wasn't just management who frowned on what she was doing. Even now that union membership had skyrocketed—in the middle of the decade, a union security clause had been negotiated, which meant that every stewardess was now automatically a dues-paying union member—union leaders were still flagged as troublemakers by other stewardesses. Not only were they challenging the company and being annoying by pestering workers to come to meetings, but they projected an image that was the polar opposite of the smiling, docile ideal. They were loud and belligerent. They rarely, in fact, shut up. It wasn't an image that appealed to the average stewardess.

Then Patt got fired for the second time. She was convinced it was related to her union activities; she was being made an example of now that she was rising in the ranks. The incident itself was negligible: while making a passenger announcement on a turbulent flight, she'd cracked a joke about handing out Alka-Seltzer instead of dinner. This comment was, she was told when her supervisor fired her, degrading to the company. By this point, she knew what to do. She filed a grievance immediately.

Patt had toughened up by now. The first time she'd been fired, she had lain in bed, staring at her hands, and reassuring herself, "I'm still alive. I'll survive this. I'm still worthwhile." This time, the second time around, she didn't need that reassurance. Upon her firing her supervisor was supposed to cut up her employee ID, like a credit card that had been declined. "Don't bother," Patt told her. "I'll be back."

She was confident that the TWU would be there to back her up. She had seen it supporting ground workers and taxi drivers. Now it was her turn. The issue was going to arbitration. This was the next step after filing a grievance, and was more serious. It was like a court case in miniature, with a panel of arbitrators, who were supposed to be neutral, deciding whether the company had been right to fire her, or whether it had been unfair and Patt should get her job back. Patt, nervous, wanted a lawyer to represent her in the arbitration. The TWU said no.

Patt was astonished. Then she got mad. She called ALSSA union officers higher up the ladder and complained. Then they called the TWU and complained in turn. "You'll happily take our dues as long as we don't ask for anything" was the gist of the argument. But the TWU leadership continued to resist; this level of grievance didn't merit, they said, a lawyer's fees. Finally, Patt said, "If I have to, I'll get the flight attendants to strike if I'm not put back to work." This was a real last-ditch effort; a strike would have been illegal and American would have been livid. And the threat was an empty one: if Patt had gone to her fellow stewardesses and asked them to support her by walking out, they probably wouldn't have done it. But it sounded good. The TWU caved and hired Gil Feldman, a staunch labor advocate. When Patt met him, she dismissed him as a slob; he had neither neat clothes nor combed hair. But he was, she quickly learned, an excellent lawyer. Still, she pushed back when he insisted that she not act defiant in front of management; instead, she should try to appear as pious as possible. She'd gotten a reputation, he pointed out, so she had to appear sweet—think nun, or choirgirl—so that the arbitrators would think she couldn't possibly be as bad as the supervisors said she was. She thought about it. A case of this level wouldn't normally have gone all the way to arbitration, she realized, or take two days instead of one, or be held in a big conference room. The company must want to make an example of her. She followed his instructions and played along. The Alka-Seltzer joke was repeated, the arbitrators agreed it didn't merit a firing, and the hearing ended on St. Patrick's Day. Patt and Gil celebrated her win with a green beer in a New York bar.

It was around this time that her colleagues made Patt an unusual gift: a toy gun. Someone snapped a photo of her, seated in a bar, glass of beer in front of her, ski cap on her head, and sunglasses covering her eyes. She was jokingly aiming the gun at someone. It was clear from the gift that the way people saw Patt had changed. No longer meek, but militant.

American Airlines liked to lean on the group of retired stewardesses who made up the Kiwi Club to demonstrate the alternative to becoming someone tough and noisy, like Patt. The Kiwis would be asked to come in and talk to new hires, telling them that when their flying careers were over, they'd have the privilege of joining the club. It wasn't explicitly stated, but it was understood that if you were a union leader, marching around, sporting a union pin, you wouldn't be welcome at the Kiwi meetings. By this time Patt was picketing like a pro. She was the anti-Kiwi: she held rallies, orga-

Patt and her toy gun, mid-1960s.

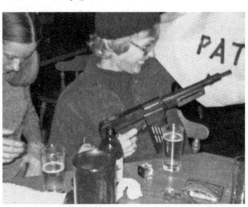

nized meetings, brainstormed how to get more people to participate in the union. She had some success, although mostly during contract bargaining time, when stewardesses knew their working conditions could change for the better (or worse). But even in those periods, Patt found it almost impossible to get her fellow stewardesses to picket, or even to distribute leaflets. They worried that the company would discipline them—they'd seen Patt get fired, and she was the leader! If the company could terminate her, they could terminate anyone. Patt would tell them, yes—but they didn't get away with the firing. That was the point. It was a message that only got through some of the time.

Appearance remained the most important function of the job. The "stewardess as sex object," dressed to impress in eye-catching uniforms, wasn't just on the plane handing out magazines—she was in the magazines. By the late 1960s, the biggest carriers, including American and United, were spending more than $20 million a year on advertising. No holds were barred as the last years of the decade saw a rash of ads that winked provocatively at potential customers, emphasizing both the nubile allure of the stewardesses and their heartfelt dedication to passenger comfort.

A 1967 ad gave credit to the stewardess college for turning the "friendly, intelligent, attractive" "Miss Butterfingers" into a great stewardess. Another boasted about the increased size of United's new planes ("And you'll need all that room. Because you'll be swiveling around a lot looking at the stewardesses.") American took another tack, boasting that it was "against the living doll school of airline stewardesses," because "the world doesn't need any more beautiful girls that just stand there," although Patt, working the galley and running up and down the aisles carrying trays, would have been grateful for an opportunity to just stand there for a minute or two. The "beautiful" part, though, was nonnegotiable. Especially when it came to weight.

For Patt, the battle with her weight was never far from her thoughts. She was always too close for comfort to her permitted maximum, and she, like every stewardess, could be weighed by any

The former Miss Butterfingers.

Two months ago Sheri Woodruff couldn't even balance a cup of coffee.

But she was friendly, intelligent, and attractive. And wanted more than anything else to be a great stewardess.

So we put her to the test. (We take only one out of thirty applicants.) Five and a half weeks at United's Stewardess School.

We taught Sheri how to serve a gourmet dinner, how to soothe a first-flyer, how to apply everything from make-up to first-aid. Along with courses like aviation principles and geography.

Today she can warm a baby's formula with one hand and pour four cups of coffee with the other.

But more than that.

She's still the same Sheri Woodruff. Friendly, intelligent, attractive. And wants more than anything else to be a great stewardess.

She is.

fly the friendly skies of United.

"This is what I call a balanced meal."

We've improved everything on our Chicago nonstop except the stewardesses.
(We know when to leave well enough alone.)

You won't recognize our nonstop flight to Chicago anymore.

Now it leaves an hour and a half earlier. At 5:30 PM. This means you can make a fast getaway from the office. And get to Chicago almost before you know it.

The plane itself has been changed, too. Now it's a 737 jet. (We now have total jet service to Chicago.) Our 737 is the newest thing in short-hop jets. It's not only fast—it's comfortable. Inside, you get as much head, shoulder, and knee room as the biggest jet we fly.

And you'll need all that room. Because you'll be swiveling around a lot looking at the stewardesses.

One final thought: if our 5:30 PM flight isn't convenient for you, we have 3 other Chicago jets leaving morning, noon, and night. (Who could improve on that schedule?)

For reservations call your Travel Agent, or United at 746-0301.

fly the friendly skies of United.

The world doesn't need any more beautiful girls who just stand there.

We are against the living doll school of airline stewardesses.

The passenger who wants his dinner, or a pillow, or an answer about flight connections, or for that matter a dry martini or a dry diaper, wants to see somebody do something.

So our Stewardess College takes almost 2 months (longer than anybody else in the business) just to teach a girl everything that you might expect of her on one flight across the country.

We run American with the frequent traveller in mind. Any Travel Agent can tell you what it takes to get fliers like this.

We can't afford the sweet young thing who just stands there, and we bring up our girls on just that basis.

Slink or swim.

American Airlines
The airline built for professional travellers. (You'll love it.)

supervisor at any time. The scale sat in the middle of the bustling Operations room, surrounded by offices; pilots, crew schedulers, managers, and other stewardesses were walking by all the time, and the humiliating lack of privacy was an additional incentive for the stewardesses to keep their weight down. The scale was weaponized—if you had pissed off management in any way, or been spotted picketing, or stepped out of line, they'd put you on frequent weight checks. Stewardesses often skipped meals for a few days before a scheduled weigh-in. Patt flew with one woman who was so stressed about getting her weight under the limit that she had breast reduction surgery to try to beat the scale. There was one loophole: you could get away with being three pounds above the maximum weight for your height if you told the supervisor you were menstruating. But you couldn't use that excuse every time.

The weight limits were derived from charts that had first been developed for the Metropolitan Life Insurance Company in the 1920s. The charts, different for men and women, allocated "healthy" weights for people based on their height and whether they had a "small," "medium," or "large" frame. They were flawed from the beginning, based on an unscientific contemporary trend of thinness that meant a majority of the population was suddenly "overweight." Age, and the change in physiology that came with it, was not taken into consideration. By using these charts as a guideline for their own women workers, airlines were enforcing standards of thinness that for many were nearly impossible to maintain over time. The charts overwhelmingly mandated that women keep their body weight low, adhering to the "small" or "medium" frame specifications; at Pan Am, which hired male stewards, men were expected only to stay under the maximum number laid out for the "large" frame. At American Airlines, a woman standing five foot five had to weigh 129 pounds or less.

When Patt was hired she'd weighed 110 pounds, and it was almost impossible for her to stay that way; before deciding on a stewardess career, she'd hovered around 121, a comfortable weight for her frame. When her weight started creeping up, her supervisor sent her to Medical. The company doctor looked her over, put her on the scale, and then wrote her a prescription. "Diet pills," he told her. "They'll help you keep your weight down." She was hopeful; maybe this was the solution to constant worry, calorie-counting, avoiding catching her supervisor's eye as she hurried through Operations. She filled the prescription.

The pills worked. She drank black coffee, smoked cigarettes, and had no appetite. And when she flew all-nighters—signing in late in the afternoon for an overnight flight, getting back around seven in the morning—she no longer had problems staying awake. She never fell asleep at work, or even got tired. She took the pills for several years, until she started experiencing paranoia. She couldn't sleep at night; she became afraid someone was trying to kill her. She'd imagine people trying to break into her bedroom. What she'd been taking, it turned out, was speed, although the stewardesses always called them "black mollies." Still, she was reluctant to give them up. Finally, the paranoia made her realize she had to stop.

But she still had to lose weight. She went to the drugstore and bought a bottle of Geritol. She'd seen ads for it, aimed at the elderly, and thought, "If it's good enough for these old people, maybe it'll work for me." Geritol was an alcohol-based liquid dietary supplement, advertised as being intended for those with "iron-poor tired blood." Dieting made her feel weak and tired; Geritol might help. Maybe vitamins would keep her weight down without the assistance of black mollies. She embarked on a new exercise regimen, too. She had a banana seat bicycle that she would ride whenever possible. One long weekend she wasn't scheduled to fly, but she was full of anxiety, as worried as a boxer or jockey that she might not "make weight." She decided to head out on a three-day bike ride through East Texas, certain she'd come back thinner. She put a pup tent into her backpack, along with a few cans of tuna and her Geritol. She also packed a .22 pistol for protection while she camped. She'd had the pistol since her Missouri days, when she'd used it for target practice. Backpack strapped to the front of the bike, she was pedaling and puffing her way across a bridge, shorts and T-shirt soaked with sweat, when she noticed a car drive by her, one, two, three times. When she reached the other side, she found the car parked, front door open, and the driver sitting there masturbating. She reached into her backpack, pulled out the .22, and aimed it at his crotch. He peeled out and disappeared, car door flapping.

Pleased with herself, Patt continued cycling until she reached Jim Hogg State Park, in the East Texas Pineywoods. She put up her tent and settled in for the night. It wasn't long before the town sheriff came by and asked what she was doing there. "Trying to sleep," she pointed out drily. He told her there was a criminal on the loose, that he'd escaped from the local psychiatric hospital, and that she was a sitting duck. Patt gave up. The sheriff took her to a gas station with a pay phone, where she called a friend and asked for a ride. When she got home, she weighed herself. She had gained two pounds.

There was another thing the scale could give away: pregnancy. Around the time that Patt was riding her banana seat bicycle around East Texas, her roommate became pregnant. Patt had moved from her trailer into an apartment in Irving, Texas, and was sharing it with another stewardess, Joan. It was summertime, but Joan wore her uniform raincoat to work to hide her changing body as best she could. Eventually, a supervisor caught on and dragged her to the scale. The secret was out, and she was fired. She moved out, and Patt heard later that she'd had the baby adopted. This wasn't uncommon among stewardesses, who were by definition unmarried. If they got pregnant, they'd try to take leave long enough to deliver the baby. On occasion, Patt knew, stewardesses would try to get injured so they could get the necessary time off work to either have an illegal abortion or deliver the baby and put it up for adoption. There was an adoption agency in Dallas to which Patt would refer women who didn't want to have a clandestine abortion. The shame of pregnancy was bad, but the stigma attached to abortion was worse. Stewardesses would often end up quitting their jobs, going back to their families, and admitting they were pregnant rather than have an abortion and continue to fly. The birth control pill had been approved in 1960, but laws restricted its sale in many states, and access would remain limited until the early 1970s. In most states in the 1960s, it was illegal to prescribe birth control to anyone under the age of twenty-one.

As a union leader, Patt's duty, as she saw it, was simple: to help women keep their jobs. Pregnancy was one of the biggest threats to employment. Abortion was illegal, and dangerous, but for many of the stewardesses it was either that or be fired. Patt went with one stewardess to get hers. Peggy had become pregnant by a married pilot at the age of twenty-two; she'd only been flying for a year. She was devastated, and came to Patt for help. Patt considered, then told Peggy she'd try to get a doctor she knew in Dallas to do the procedure. The pilot handed over $600, and Patt took Peggy to have her abortion. There was no nurse there, just the doctor, but it was over quickly. Six hundred dollars was a lot in 1966, but it was cheaper than child support. And it was cheaper than a divorce.

At TWA, it was the same story. If you had the baby and didn't put it up for adoption, you'd be gone forever. If you miscarried, or the baby was stillborn, you could come back to work. Women hid their pregnancies as long as possible. Other stewardesses might know, but they'd never tell. Kathleen Heenan, a stewardess at TWA, always kept other people's pregnancies secret; the idea of squealing to management was anathema. It was "us" in here, and "them" out there, and it was the rare stewardess who would cross that line. Abortions were clandestinely available; the airline didn't frown on them, and Kathleen had an idea that TWA might even help you put a baby up for adoption. Women did on occasion manage to successfully hide children from the airline. They'd work until they began to show, then take sick leave, if possible getting a doctor to write a note saying they had a protracted illness like mononucleosis. They'd have the child, then breeze back into work, suddenly cured! They could never mention their children at work, though, or show a snapshot to a supervisor. Kathleen had heard a story about a particularly audacious woman who had cobbled together sick leave and educational leave and had two children in secret. She then made up an elaborate back story to explain their existence: her best friend had been killed in a car accident, she told everyone, and now she and her husband were responsible for her children. She'd even hand around photographs of the kids, talking about how she'd adopted them after the crash. That was an outlier, though. Usually, once a stewardess became pregnant, she'd quit and not come back.

Kathleen started at TWA in 1965 after graduating from the University of Minnesota, but she had thought about becoming a stewardess long before that. When she was seven years old she'd been at the airport with her parents and seen a beautiful redheaded stewardess step off a Northwest Stratocruiser, a brand-new plane that seemed to epitomize the thrill of the "golden age" of travel. The allure of that life stuck with her. Like Patt, Kathleen was presented with a contract agreeing to resign at a certain age (at TWA, it was thirty-five). She knew she would be married with children by the age of thirty-five; why would she want to continue flying after that? The friends she'd gone to college with were becoming teachers, or nurses, or getting married. Kathleen wasn't doing those things. But then, she thought to herself, she didn't want to. She signed her contract and packed her bags.

When she completed stewardess training, she was sent to New York. She was thrilled; she had always wanted to live there. She moved into a one-bedroom basement apartment in Queens, piling in with three of her classmates. The apartment owner, Mrs. Goluck, was like a sitcom version of a landlady, always grumbling but making a fortune collecting security deposits from her transient stewardess tenants. Life as a junior stewardess in New York came as a shock. The salary was low for big-city life, around $5,000 a year (around $44,000 in 2021 dollars). And Kathleen was starting out on the bottom of the seniority list, always on reserve, and without the years of service necessary to "hold" good flights. Her life was completely dictated by TWA's crew schedulers. Still, because the airlines were growing rapidly and stewardesses were leaving to get married every day, she moved up the ladder fast and managed to hold a flight fairly quickly. That meant she had a regular schedule throughout the month, and didn't have to sit around waiting for the phone to ring, then grab her suitcase and leg it to the airport. She passed language tests, Spanish and German, and started flying overseas. This was when the impression she'd always had of stewardess life— cosmopolitan, glamorous, and full of exciting destinations—finally became a reality. It was a thrilling time. She flew around the world, her horizons widening with every new country and every unfamiliar meal. And it was fun! Flying into a destination city, stepping into the crew bus with the rest of the stewardesses and the cockpit crew, being transported to a good hotel in Milan, Paris, London. This wasn't the age of shuttle buses and airport Marriotts; they stayed at high-end hotels and traveled in style. The work was hard, but Kathleen was happy she wasn't stuck in a nine-to-five job. If she'd been working as a secretary in Manhattan, she'd be eating a grilled cheese at a diner on her lunch break. Now when she was hungry she'd help herself to some of the passengers' pâté and caviar (TWA spent a lot of money on service). The exchange rate favored the dollar, and she was free to explore new cities, walking, shopping, stopping to sample a gelato, or a cone of frites, or a glass of wine at a sidewalk bistro. Even when she'd flown all night, she'd force herself to get out of bed after three or four hours' sleep, spending the afternoon sightseeing before returning to the airport. And though New York was expensive, her rent was cheap, especially split four ways. If she went on a date, the man would always pay.

Patt was brandishing her gun and getting herself a reputation as a troublemaker, but Kathleen was making the most of her job at TWA. In later years, as the job got harder, the planes bigger, and the working conditions far less comfortable, she'd look back on these as the salad days. She finally moved out of the packed basement apartment in Queens, bidding an unregretful goodbye to Mrs. Goluck, and into a two-bedroom in Manhattan, this time with only two other flight attendants. She and her friends occasionally dated passengers they met on the plane, but mostly they met men in the city, sometimes pilots they'd run into at parties. She met her husband. Life was good. Still, she couldn't shake a growing sense that something wasn't quite right. She'd gone to a Catholic girls' school, and sometimes felt that she'd never left. The strictness of the rules about appearance and behavior chafed. Constantly feeling that her looks and the way she acted were being scrutinized wasn't easy. And her salary was still frustratingly low.

Then Kathleen found herself wearing a uniform made of paper. In 1968, TWA decided to entice passengers with an exotic new idea: "Foreign Accent" flights. These flights were domestic, but they each had a theme (French, English, Italian, and, incongruously, Manhattan) that the airplane played up with music, food, magazines, and newspapers from that location. The airline issued stewardesses paper uniforms that corresponded to each flight's theme. Olde English was a ruffled white blouse and short skirt, French was a gold minidress, Italian was a belted white "toga style" robe, and Manhattan Penthouse was a slinky pajama outfit. The print ads featured four women, each in one of the costumes, looking coyly at the camera and posed next to the dishes they'd serve on the flight. The copy read:

> Fly "Foreign Accent" with us and forget about counting
> the hours. We make a new thing of it every time, first-class
> and coach, beginning with our special "Foreign Accent"
> hostesses. Their ruffles, bows and minis, and sheer delight
> in being girls, as well as expert hostesses, makes something
> wonderful happen inside the plane. Atmosphere!

Kathleen, along with her fellow stewardesses, hated the paper uniforms. They tore and stained almost immediately, and the pushback soon got rid of them. The ads, Kathleen noted wryly in an article she'd go on to write for the *Civil Liberties Review*, "pictured us wearing our flimsy outfits while we served exotic food and drink to our passengers. Actually, we spent most of our time taping, stapling, patching, and otherwise repairing our ripped dresses."

The provocative photos in the ads were hard for Kathleen to swallow. Passengers, she was realizing, didn't really understand

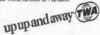
why the flight attendants were necessary on the plane. She'd been on a flight leaving London when an engine caught fire; the plane had to turn around and fly back, everyone fearful that the leaking gasoline would cause the wheels to catch on fire. She'd kept her cool, reassuring panicking passengers, moving calmly through the cabin. When they pulled into their spot at Heathrow, she'd shuffled the

passengers off as fast as possible, helping them run off the plane onto the bridge and into the airport, leaving all their bags behind. On another flight a man had a heart attack; they'd had to take care of him until landing. A friend had a passenger die on her flight. They'd stored him in one of the bathrooms; there was nowhere else for him to go. There was a spate of hijackings in the early 1970s. Kathleen hadn't been trained on how to deal with hijackers, but she'd be in charge of passenger safety if anyone tried to take over the plane. *She* knew she was there in case something went wrong. *They* thought of her as a flying waitress—a glamorous one, to be sure, who stayed in fancy hotels in a different city every night, who lived out of a suitcase, who had a man in every (air)port—but still, someone whose primary function was to serve. She resented the way the pilots and supervisors talked down to her, but she couldn't speak up for fear of being reprimanded or taken off duty for a few days. Kathleen hated it when pilots, pursers, or passengers referred to the stewardesses as "the girls," but that, she reflected, was what they were. They weren't, at least in the minds of others, fully formed adults who thought for themselves. She wanted people to know she had a brain in her head. She decided to become a union representative. In part because she wanted to be more involved, to really get to know what was going on instead of just being told what to do all the time. And in part because as a union rep she'd be taken more seriously. A union rep has credibility, she thought. And maybe I'll get some more respect.

CHAPTER SEVEN

Think of Her
as Your Mother

THE STEWARDESSES WERE reaching their breaking point. Despite Title VII, mandatory retirement at thirty-two hadn't gone away at most airlines, and their position was becoming more and more ludicrous. Patt could see women climbing career ladders all around her. She watched as women won seats in Congress, succeeded as lawyers, thrived in business. But in her industry, thirty-two was a glass ceiling they couldn't seem to break. While the age rules had been put in place back in the 1950s, stewardesses were hired so young that it had taken a decade for the rules to start to affect them in significant numbers. But now it was becoming intolerable.

Throwing fuel on the fire was United Airlines, which *added* an age limit of thirty-two right in the middle of the protests in 1966, just as a few airlines had finally begun getting rid of their age restrictions and flight attendants were taking the issue to court. TWA had, unusually, eliminated its no-marriage rule back in 1957, but in the same year it installed a replacement rule, which forced stewardesses to leave the line at age thirty-five. Pan Am was an exception; stewardesses had been able to get married since 1949, and the airline had never had an age limit. But broadly speaking, in a time when the economy was thriving and women were moving into the workforce more rapidly than ever before, the airlines went the other way, adding rules and restrictions just as other businesses were loosening them. It was an entire industry alarmingly out of sync with cultural and political change.

And that industry was booming: in 1967, there were over twenty thousand working stewardesses, more than twice as many as at the start of the decade. But for them, the sense of powerlessness—you could hide a marriage, but you couldn't hide your age, and there was no recourse—was stifling.

Another attempt was made to get help from the government. Having resolved nothing in its 1965 hearings on age discrimination in employment, Congress was holding new ones in 1967. And Patt's hopes were high. Could Congress pass legislation that would ban this kind of age discrimination?

It could, it turned out, but it wouldn't be of any use to flight attendants. The testimony given was varied in the extreme. Representatives from both airline management and the airline unions arrived to try to influence the listening senators. In their testimony, American Airlines executives broadly hinted at menopause as an argument for firing women at age thirty-two, submitting a statement that read, "Senior stewardesses may experience emotional problems resulting from the absence of a permanent home and family relationship." This was far from the first or the last time that this argument—that middle-aged women went a little crazy—would be used as a way to keep age restrictions in place. They could be, it seemed, a danger to themselves and others.

Colleen Boland, the union president, was there, testifying about how the age restrictions had impacted flight attendants. She skillfully walked the line between getting her point across and presenting a pleasingly feminine mien. She urged Congress to eliminate the minimum age for discrimination, so that the stewardesses could be included. She pointed out that Pan Am had no age limit. She talked about how TWA's male stewards could continue working until they were sixty. She smiled.

Senator Claiborne Pell suggested that a woman of sixty would have more problems meeting the strict airline appearance standards than a woman of thirty. Patiently, Colleen replied, "Perhaps she has more problems in that regard but if she is capable of meeting that challenge, then should she not have the right to do it?"

By the end of her testimony, Colleen was becoming increasingly exasperated by the senators' stonewalling. She decided to drop a bombshell. Standing up before the committee, she declared, "To us a few more months of pleading, talking, or of pouring thousands of dollars into various courts may make a strike far more feasible and practical." Striking was always, for a union, a very last resort. Colleen's threat demonstrated just how desperate the stewardesses were becoming.

In these hearings, as in many others, the stewardesses had freely used their looks to push back on sexist regulations. They never argued, either in front of Congress or at the EEOC, that being attractive wasn't an essential requirement for a stewardess. Instead, they promoted the idea that attractiveness was not restricted to the young. You think women are only good-looking until they turn thirty-two? they were asking. Fine. Say it out loud. It was a successful tactic, though there was little thought given to the idea that if they had been Black or brown women, this strategy might not have worked. As well, they knew that rowdiness, belligerence, or shouting would destroy in an instant the idealized stewardess image. So they played along: unthreatening, conventionally pretty, feminine, soft-spoken, white. They knew not to alienate their fellow workers or the flying public with visible anger or raised voices. The popular idea of how a stewardess should look and act stayed intact. And although this approach—not that hiring on looks was bad but that good looks didn't disappear at thirty-two—would change in the next decade as the feminist movement took hold, for the moment the stewardesses played the game and played it well.

The result of the hearings was the passage of the Age Discrimination in Employment Act of 1967. But the bill's protection was, dismayingly, restricted to workers between the ages of forty and sixty-five. Had the age minimum been thirty rather than forty, that single change would have altered the career trajectory of thousands of stewardesses. As it was, with age discrimination only considered applicable to those over forty, it was worse than useless. The stewardesses would have to find another way.

Having watched the attempt in Congress fail, Dusty Roads decided to try another tack. She was on a mission to get American Airlines to abolish the age rule, and decided to take it to the public. Patt, still full of fury at Ann Davis's suicide, was inspired by her passion. Dusty was an organizer's organizer: able to talk to anyone, outspoken, attractive, liked by all. She took Patt and a group of fellow stewardesses to New York to petition the state's Commission for Human Rights on the issue. They lined up for a photo on the steps outside the statehouse, each wearing her miniskirt uniform, with her hairpiece pinned on top of her real hair (these were common; when they got home, or to a hotel room after a flight, they would lift off their wigs and plop them on the desk, where they'd sit until the morning). In their similarity, there was an uncanny echo of the stewardess college graduation photo.

Their age protest took its rallying cry from American Airlines itself. In 1968, American had launched an ill-conceived national print ad campaign. The ad was dominated by a slim white woman in the current uniform, a white dress that ended mid-thigh. She was sitting on a chair, legs tucked underneath her, chin in her hand, gazing directly into the camera. The copy read:

She only wants what's best for you.

A cool drink. A good dinner. A soft pillow and a warm blanket.

This is not just maternal instinct. It's the result of the longest Stewardess training in the industry.

Training in service, not just a beauty course.

Service, after all, is what makes professional travellers prefer American.

And makes new travellers want to keep on flying with us.

So we see that every passenger gets the same professional treatment.

That's the American Way.

The headline, black and bold, read, "Think of her as your mother."

Patt cut the ad out of a magazine and plastered a few words above it: "Would you fire your mother at 32?" That became their picket sign.

The group held more protests, focusing on the airports with the most stewardesses who strongly supported the union. This included Los Angeles, where Dusty and Nancy Collins were based. Each city had a leader who was in charge of the pickets. In New York, it was Claire Corbett, who picketed AA headquarters in Manhattan. Patt was in charge of Dallas's Love Field. She shepherded her protesters, with their signs, to the grassy area each car had to pass as it entered the airport. That way the maximum number of people would see them: perfectly coiffed young women in impeccable makeup and spick-and-span uniforms (they always wore their uniforms), asking for the privilege of keeping their jobs past the age of thirty-two.

Patt found it hard to gather more than a handful of people to protest, though. Usually she couldn't corral more than five at a time. They were afraid of the repercussions. Plus, a flight attendant's job was to make people feel comfortable, safe, and happy, not to piss them off. The women had been trained to be agreeable, and Patt was asking them to make waves, to voice their opinions, even just to get angry. It was like pulling teeth. Patt eventually realized that they wouldn't do anything, even something as mild as attend a union meeting, until she could show them that an airline policy was having a quantifiable effect on their lives. Even finding the "Think of her as your mother" ad offensive was not universal. The agitators— Patt, Dusty, Nancy—were horrified, but the majority of the stewardesses weren't in the habit of finding such things repugnant. And protests, picketing, marching, holding up signs—these were not in any way ladylike behaviors. The process of changing young stewardesses into militant union members was a long one.

The law had failed them, and while picketing had garnered some public sympathy, there was still no indication from American Airlines that the age rule would be rescinded. So the stewardesses turned to their penultimate option: contract negotiations.

Nineteen sixty-seven was the first year that Patt would be involved in negotiating contract terms. This was a weighty responsibility: as ever, the results of this bargaining—stewardesses on one side, management on the other—would determine working conditions, wages, and the strictures the stewardesses would have to follow for the next three years. Leading their bargaining team was Colleen Boland. She had been a stewardess at TWA, but she no longer worked the line; she was now president of ALSSA, the division in the Transport Workers Union to which American Airlines stewardesses belonged. This meant that Colleen had close relationships with the higher-ups at the TWU, the men whose job it was to oversee the stewardess division. She was experienced, and the TWU had invested a lot of training in her.

Charlie Pasciuto arrived just in time for bargaining on the 1968 contract (bargaining always began months in advance). An Italian American, like so many of the executives at American Airlines, he had come from TWA to work in Employee Relations, later known as Human Resources. Pasciuto quickly moved up the ladder to become the vice president of personnel and labor relations. Dark-haired and baggy-eyed, he was usually seen with a Lucky Strike in his mouth, the pack on the table in front of him. He had a master's degree in labor relations from Cornell and would from the date of his arrival at American be the company's designated representative in every conflict with the stewardesses. He was a stickler for the rules: you got what you negotiated for, and no more. Used to dealing with men—pilots, mechanics—or with the upper echelon, like Colleen Boland, with whom he had been friendly since their TWA days, he had a knack for making Patt feel worthless. His attitude, she came to feel, was less "Let's bargain as equals" and more "I'm going to tell you girls what to do." The stage was set for a bargaining session that was likely to be, at a minimum, very lively.

The due date for agreeing on the 1968 contract was August, but as always, bargaining and discussions between the union and management started much earlier. Patt was eager to sink her teeth into it. She knew what she wanted to fight for, and she was ready. Charlie Pasciuto would be negotiating on the other side; it was also his first contract at American. They were all meeting in New York (where the TWU and American Airlines were both headquartered) at the Dryden East Hotel. Patt sat at the table, quietly thrilled to be there, along with Marge Norris and Kathy Russo, dressed in sleeveless shift dresses with carefully chosen jewelry. Marge had experience; she'd been grandmothered in and hadn't had to quit at thirty-two. She'd worked on other contracts. Kathy was also a longtime union leader; she'd been the one to organize the illicit meeting with Jimmy Hoffa four years earlier.

Age and marriage were the subjects of most of the initial discussions. There was a heated argument about the last contract—the one where the company had started firing stewardesses six months after marriage, though management had let union negotiators believe that the marriage ban was finished. The company gave it up for good this time around, though, agreeing quickly that the termination-upon-marriage rule would disappear. But American wouldn't budge on pregnancy as a cause for instant dismissal, and the negotiators knew it. And it was still holding out on the age issue, too, refusing to allow stewardesses to age past thirty-two. This, they were going to fight.

Another major issue up for debate was wages. Stewardesses were being paid less than $5,000 a year (less than $44,000 in 2021 dollars). Patt would tell her members "if you can't afford to eat, go apply for food stamps." And then she leaked it to the papers: stewardesses were so underpaid, they had to use food stamps! It made American look bad. And the TWU wasn't helping. Fred Simpson, the TWU's representative in charge of the stewardesses, lectured them, telling them not to expect too much, and then insisting that they were to follow the pattern bargaining model, using what other airlines were paying their stewardesses as a standard. He explained the "nickel more" theory: you made incremental progress, adding "a nickel more" to each contract based on what the other units were getting. Patt could smell sexism here. The TWU had gone all out for the mechanics and the cleaning services workers, all of whom were better paid than the stewardesses. The stewardesses were getting lowballed because they were women, and their union wasn't doing its job.

Patt resented Fred's proposal hugely: Why should it matter what Pan Am was paying their stewardesses? *Her* members were on food stamps. She felt that the TWU was dismissing the stewardesses' concerns. Colleen Boland was the official negotiating team spokesperson, but Marge was sure she couldn't be trusted. Colleen wasn't now and never had been an American Airlines stewardess. Patt respected Marge's opinion; she had been dealing with these people for years. And Nancy Collins, whom Patt had called for advice, had instructed her, "Do what Marge tells you to do." Colleen was a TWU loyalist, but Patt, Marge, and Kathy were starting to lose faith in the TWU's strategies. Adding to their distrust was something they'd seen one evening: Colleen, Fred Simpson, and Charlie Pasciuto drinking together in the Dryden East bar. Drinking with management was a very bad look. In Patt's book, anyone who was friendly with management couldn't truly be on the side of the members.

Patt, Kathy, and Marge started putting together their proposals, writing down the list of things they wanted changed in this new contract, although Colleen, as the spokesperson, would be the one to put them forward. Very early on, they saw that they wouldn't be involved in the discussions—it would be Colleen talking to the company. Patt, Marge, and Kathy had surveyed their members and knew what they wanted. A survey was more than just information gathering: it was a way of showing management that the workers stood behind the negotiating team. But Patt quickly realized that the TWU would be making the decisions, not the union reps who were still working stewardesses like her. She was being shut out. And seeing Pasciuto on the opposite side of the table, while Colleen was on theirs, didn't help. They're buddies from TWA, she thought.

That's not good for us. As talks progressed, Patt and the others tried raising their concerns with Colleen and Fred Simpson, to no avail. They tried to speak up in the bargaining sessions, and were put off: "No, not now, we'll talk about that later."

It was the first time Patt had bargained against Charlie Pasciuto. Charlie, she thought, really curated his image as a New York tough guy. He enjoyed playing up the kind of behavior most people would associate with the Mafia. For one, he was always flanked by two men. They were nominally part of his staff, but they were physically intimidating and almost never spoke. Charlie had lost a lot of people their jobs over the years and it was clear he brought the men along for protection. He was infuriatingly dismissive with Patt, probably because he knew how much it angered her. He got a kick out of reminding her she was "just a stewardess." And he addressed her as "Gibbs," a habit that would continue for decades. She, the lesson of her first arbitration firmly etched in her memory, always called him "Charlie."

Frustrated, Patt, Kathy, and Marge huddled together in a hotel room and triaged. They decided that, whatever happened, they weren't going to let the TWU come away from the bargaining table with just "a nickel more" for their members. Patt held a quick internal debate with herself, then took a deep breath. "Kathy," she said, "I think it's time for you to call your Teamster friend again."

Patt was no longer tempted to shout at Hoffa about his reputation. She had become so angry that she didn't care how they got the pay increases. If it required a tire chain, or a crowbar, or they had to blow up a few planes, fine—she was all for it. Her members were not being paid fairly, and she was determined to do something. Maybe another union would serve the stewardesses better. The TWU had always worried that they would leave and go with the Teamsters. They would, Patt decided, use this as leverage. Kathy made the call.

First, the Teamsters took them for a fancy dinner at Toots Shor's, a popular hangout spot for celebrities and the New York mob. They showed them their proposals, and the Teamsters gave advice. As bargaining went on, Kathy, Marge, and Patt continued to have meetings with the Teamsters representatives, always at Toots Shor's. They were getting more and more disillusioned with the bargaining process. Sometimes they'd be so frustrated with the lack of results that during breaks in bargaining they'd go into the women's bathroom at the Dryden East and pitch pennies against the wall, cussing out the TWU at the same time. As they blew off steam, they'd discuss: Should we call the Teamsters again? Should we leave the TWU? They had almost convinced themselves when the Teamsters, realizing they were serious, sent them to D.C. on Frank Sinatra's private jet for a meeting with Hoffa. (Patt knew where Sinatra came into it: he was based in Vegas, where the casinos had been funded by the Teamsters' pension funds.)

The Teamsters' D.C. headquarters were huge, and Hoffa's office was on the very top floor. He recognized Patt right away. Patt stammered out an apology for losing her cool four years before. She pled youth and ignorance. They wanted to be part of the Teamsters, she said; she knew now it was the only way they'd really get a seat at the table. Hoffa had a small sign on his desk in Latin, and Patt, desperate to establish camaraderie, asked what it meant. "Don't let the bastards get you down," Hoffa told her. He picked up the sign and handed it to her as a gift. She would find out later that he had dozens of these signs and gave them away all the time, but her apology had clearly been accepted. The Teamsters produced authorization-to-act cards: these, if signed by enough workers, would authorize the Teamsters to represent the stewardesses, replacing the TWU. Half tremulous, half thrilled, Patt, Marge, and Kathy went back to their hotel, cards carefully tucked inside Patt's handbag.

Later that evening, two strange men started banging on the door of Marge's room. They were from the TWU, and they were looking for the cards. Marge quickly called Patt in her room and told her TWU thugs were on their way up and that they were going to search her room for the authorization-to-act cards; Patt had to get rid of them. Patt gathered them up and ran into the bathroom. She flushed the cards down the toilet.

Patt, shaken, figured the TWU had bugged their rooms. Or maybe they'd had them followed to the meetings with the Teamsters. How else would they have known about the cards? But the TWU did know, that much was clear. Patt, Marge, and Kathy tried to keep their panic in check when they returned to New York for the next round of bargaining. Patt wasn't sure what would happen next. What did was a surprise.

Now that the threat had been identified, the company backed down. Patt, Marge, and Kathy had made no bones about the fact that they had issues with the TWU; now the TWU knew just how far they'd go. Backdoor talks proceeded. Fred Simpson and Colleen Boland went to the company and said there was no point in raising wages; no matter what American offered the stewardesses, all they wanted was to join the Teamsters. (Both Fred and Colleen had, in previous years, signed contracts that agreed that stewardesses had to resign at age thirty-two.) But American executives hated the Teamsters; they didn't want them on the property, and they certainly didn't want them representing their stewardesses. Charlie Pasciuto conferred with his colleagues. They decided to accept the wage proposal Patt, Kathy, and Marge had made: raises of 25 to 40 percent, depending on length of service. The three women were in shock. Later on, they'd guess that the TWU had done such a good job of convincing management that the stewardesses would never accept any offer that American had figured they might as well risk it. But that the company had decided to fork over huge raises rather than risk them leaving to join a more militant union . . . well, that was useful information.

Patt, Marge, and Kathy were over the moon, but they didn't show it. "We'll have to think about it," they said. They left the room, and celebrated, quietly, covering their mouths to keep their squeals of excitement hushed. Then they went back and accepted the offer.

CHAPTER EIGHT

Do Women Age Faster
on Airplanes?

AFTER A DELAY of many months, the EEOC was preparing for another try at deciding the stewardess question: Was sex a bona fide occupational qualification? The cancellation of the first decision meant that fourteen months had gone by, during which women had continued to be forced out of their jobs via the marriage, pregnancy, and age rules. The BFOQ question *had* to be decided. The decision would either confine stewardesses to whatever rules the airlines wanted to make, validating their claims that only young, thin, single women could do the job, or it would change everything.

Few things had excited as much sympathy in Sonia as this question. The airlines, she thought, were treating the stewardesses disgracefully. It was clear to *her* that the termination upon age or marriage or pregnancy was both illegal and morally wrong. When Jesse Freidin, the lawyer for the airlines, came to the EEOC offices for the hearings, they'd have heated discussions about the issue. She was slightly awed by him—he was representing the biggest airlines in the United States, he practiced at a top private firm in New York, and she was not that long out of law school, still relatively new to the law, and almost twenty years younger than him. But she didn't let him intimidate her; when she ran into him on his visits to the EEOC offices, they had lively debates about the stewardess issue. He was, Sonia knew, a good lawyer, but he was on the wrong side. The idea that only women could do this job was as ridiculous as anything she'd heard. She knew the EEOC commissioners had been on the brink of making the right decision the last time, before the airlines had used Aileen Hernandez's NOW affiliation to wangle a second hearing. She was hopeful they would do so again.

The second hearing took place on September 12, 1967. This time, the airlines hired psychologists to discuss the personality differences between men and women. The psychologists submitted statements agreeing that yes, more women than men had the specific character- istics required by the job. Women, they argued, possessed many qual- ities men did not. They produced a list of these, including mothering, comforting, ministering, femininity, warmth, compassion, gracious- ness, charm, sensitivity to passenger needs, and a natural interest in food, service, and decor. They claimed that women could more satis- factorily perform duties such as smiling at and greeting passengers, assisting mothers traveling with young kids, helping anyone who got airsick, and caring for old, sick, or infirm passengers.

United Airlines argued that the very lack of possibility for advancement was what made the job more appealing to women than to men, because most flight attendants only used the job as an interlude between "girlhood" and marriage. The stewardess was the face of the industry, American protested, and the job needed to be performed with enthusiasm, something that senior stewardesses would inevitably lose as they grew older; women between the ages of thirty-eight and fifty, it claimed, underwent physical, emotional, and personality changes that would negatively impact their job per- formance. And because, the airlines added, society placed the burden of raising children and making a home on women, married women who had to fly several days a week would naturally cause a disrup- tion in family harmony. The airline executives worried aloud that they would have to deal with angry phone calls from stewardesses' husbands regarding their absence from the home.

The union leaders at American sent stewardesses to testify against the BFOQ, but they chose carefully. They sent women who were thirty-two but looked younger. And they sent married women. The point was to prove that these women could do the job and that the rules were arbitrary: who could tell which stewardess was too old or too married to work?

The union reps, arguing on behalf of the stewardesses, were quick to declare that being over thirty-two or thirty-five didn't pre- clude a woman from being either attractive or competent at her job.

They pointed to the fact that a couple of domestic airlines did allow women to continue working past those ages, and many foreign ones did as well. One union rep, Margie Cooper, submitted a document listing the age policies of non-American airlines. Swissair and Belgium's Sabena had compulsory retirement ages of forty, she pointed out. At Germany's Lufthansa and Britain's BOAC (the precursor to British Airways), stewardesses could work until they turned fifty-five. Air France had no mandatory retirement age at all. And these airlines continued to stay in business.

The need for attractiveness, now as in years before, wasn't questioned by the stewardesses or their spokespeople. But they did query, hard, the idea that women were better than men at all the duties of a stewardess, but only until they got married, or hit their midthirties. It took extraordinary twists of logic to argue that marriage restrictions were necessary when some airlines didn't have them and their planes didn't fall out of the sky. Still, the airlines tried their best.

The slate of people testifying on the stewardesses' behalf was impressive: Betty Friedan (she was then the president of NOW), Jean Marcous (on behalf of the National Woman's Party), Esther Peterson (on behalf of the Interdepartmental Committee on the Status of Women), Senator Maurine Neuberger (on behalf of the Citizens' Advisory Council on the Status of Women), Aileen Hernandez (the former EEOC commissioner whose NOW membership and elevation to office had been the reason for the year-and-a-half postponement), and more.

After listening to argument after argument, the EEOC finally decided no: being a woman was not an essential qualification for working as a flight attendant. They released this decision on February 24, 1968; it was the same conclusion they'd come to in 1966, and almost three full years had passed since the stewardesses had first started filing their complaints at the brand-new EEOC. The decision was not unanimous—Luther Holcomb, Sonia's nemesis, was the dissenting vote—but it was final. The stewardesses had won. Now women could become pursers, men could become flight attendants, and no matter if passengers preferred young women—that didn't mean the airline could exclude all other candidates. Although the EEOC had no ability to compel the airlines to obey these new rules, it was setting up a robust legal foundation for challenging any airline that refused to do so. Three individual decisions on the age and marriage rules followed a few months later, setting precedents for EEOC cases in progress and cases to be filed in the future. (All the plaintiffs in these cases were stewardesses and the defendants airlines.) These cases would serve as a basis for case law on sex discrimination.

In *Dodd v. American Airlines*, June Dodd had challenged the grounding of stewardesses at a certain age, in her case on her thirty-third birthday. The airline had attempted to argue that senior stewardesses would experience emotional problems, that enthusiasm was necessary to successful performance of the job, and that such enthusiasm was lost with age. Here, the EEOC declared that the age rule was a violation of Title VII: "Various airlines currently have male flight attendants in their employ or employed them in the past; no policy reassignment or termination for reaching their mid-thirties was or is applied to them. Obviously, therefore, the requirement of being under the mid-thirties in age is not related to satisfactory performance as a flight attendant but to the sexual identity of the incumbent."

The second case, *Colvin v. Piedmont Aviation*, dealt with marriage. Virginia Lane Colvin had been fired upon her marriage, but Piedmont, a smaller airline (today it operates as a subsidiary of American Airlines), was one of the few that also employed men as stewards, though they were not fired upon marriage. Another violation of Title VII, said the EEOC.

Neal v. American Airlines took the marriage problem further. American, still firing stewardesses six months after they married, claimed to have added the six-month "probation" period to keep pregnant stewardesses from flying. Then the airline argued that because it only hired women as flight attendants, sex discrimination couldn't apply. The EEOC rejected the airline's argument that it wasn't discriminating on the basis of sex and decided that any employment rule, like this one, that applied to a class of employees because of their sex was indeed sex discrimination. There didn't have to be differences in the way men and women were treated in the same job to qualify.

That summer, the EEOC also took a public stand on the stewardess cases, releasing a statement that made crystal clear the EEOC's position that terminating stewardesses on marriage, and terminating or grounding them on reaching the age of thirty-two or thirty-five, was unlawful. And Sonia was the one who wrote it, becoming forever a part of the stewardesses' story.

But she almost didn't. Charlie Duncan had assigned the writing of this statement to Sonia, the "sex maniac." When Holcomb found out, he told Charlie to take her off the assignment. She was prejudiced, he explained. When Charlie asked exactly how Sonia was prejudiced, Holcomb replied, "She supports women's rights," the very same argument the airline had used to claim that Aileen Hernandez couldn't be objective. Charlie, to his everlasting credit, refused the order. Sonia wrote the statement.

She was more emotionally involved with the stewardess cases than any that had come up in her three years at the EEOC. Helping stewardesses was, she would think later, the most important work she'd done in her career as an attorney. When the commissioners decided that the airlines were breaking the law, she was ecstatic. Her first thought was that justice had been served for the stewardesses. Her second was that she couldn't wait to lord it over Jesse Freidin, the airlines' well-heeled lawyer. She didn't actively dislike him, but she'd scored a victory and been proven right. She was planning out exactly how she'd gloat the next time she saw him when she learned he'd just died of a heart attack. She was shocked and saddened to hear of his death, but she could have cried with disappointment.

In tandem with the EEOC's deliberations, contract negotiations had been ongoing at American for months, and despite getting the company to agree to her wage increase, Patt and her colleagues hadn't managed to talk American into removing the age restriction. So the American Airlines stewardesses decided to make good on Colleen's threat from the congressional age hearings: they would strike. To strike was a last resort, an ultimatum, and a gamble that could lose them all their jobs if the airline decided to simply replace them. But they couldn't let the age restriction continue: too many of them were getting older. So they readied for battle. But in the nick of time the EEOC released its decisions, averting the need for the strike.

Negotiations between the TWU and American Airlines had been deadlocked for ten months, but when the EEOC's decisions were released, American caved. They could see the way the tide was turning, and the decisions, paired with the threat of a strike, secured the longed-for victory for the company's stewardesses. The new contract wording would read, "Marriage is not a cause for termination of employment. Pregnancy is a cause for termination of employment." The pregnancy restriction was in violation of other EEOC rulings on the right to maternity leave of absence, but the biggest obstacle to a stewardess's career was removed: she would no longer have to leave the job at thirty-two. And American agreed to reinstate stewardesses who had either been reassigned, like Ann Davis, or fired at the age of thirty-two when they refused reassignment.

The press, always happy to put a stewardess on the front page, went to town with the EEOC rulings, discussing them energetically and clearly enjoying inventing humorous headlines. "Do Women Age Faster on Airplanes?," "Stewardesses Can Now Wear Wings and Rings," "Demand Makes Sexample of Airlines," "Those Gals Who Fly High Get Their Guy AND the Sky," and "Old Plane Janes" were just a few.

The stewardesses had been waiting years, and they'd finally been vindicated. Even though the agency couldn't actually force the airlines (or anyone) to make immediate changes, EEOC decisions in their favor gave them powerful leverage to argue away these rules at the bargaining table as well as a strong foundation for taking their case to court. But the courts would not always see things the same way the EEOC did.

The process wasn't quite over. After the terms of a contract had been agreed in bargaining, the stewardesses still had to ratify the contract. This meant that the members of the bargaining team had to go back to their bases, explain the benefits and downsides of the new contract, and put the contract to a vote. Patt went back to Dallas and held a membership meeting, just as Kathy and Marge were doing at their bases. The stewardesses voted overwhelmingly to ratify the contract. Patt was flushed with success: what a feeling, to go to her members and tell them she had been able to get them what they wanted! This contract in particular was, she knew, a massive victory. The wage increase had an effect beyond just making everyday life easier for her colleagues. It turned the job itself from something you'd do just to travel cheaply for a couple of years before marriage to an actual career. And not only was there an immediate pay raise, but they had negotiated a big wage increase for stewardesses after they completed five years of flying. When the pay was terrible, sticking around after nineteen months or so was much less appealing; many people literally couldn't afford to stay on the job. With this new pay structure, there was much more incentive to keep working. And in the next few months, Patt was pleased to see, women who had been fired for getting older started coming back to work. Only one took the offer of alternate employment; she went to work in the reservations department. Everyone else went back to flying.

Though Patt was thrilled with what she'd come away with, not all of the contract provisions were wins for the stewardesses. First of all, while American would no longer fire women for aging or marrying, there was no sign that the company would make any effort to hire older women, or married women, or men. Pregnancy was still grounds for dismissal. As well, the agreement between the company and the union included a sneaky provision: it stated that stewardesses who had been employed on November 30, 1953 (and who had therefore never been subject to the age restriction, which was imposed afterward), would receive a severance payment of $6,000 if they voluntarily resigned before August 10, 1970. It was a not-so-subtle way of trying to get older women off the plane. Patt fully realized this, but they'd take, she thought, what they could get. It was far more than she'd expected.

Perhaps fortunately, Patt was unaware of Charlie Pasciuto's perfidy in these years. Much later, his secretary would tell Patricia K. Willis, a doctoral student writing about the stewardess battles, that her negotiating partner, the tough-guy vice president of personnel and labor relations, had held out on the age rule as a petty punishment. "She told me," wrote Willis, "that American knew it had to eliminate this discriminatory barrier when the 1964 Civil Rights Act was passed but purposefully put up obstacles to stewardesses who fought it . . . She told me that Pasciuto always intended to abolish the rule after the 1964 Civil Rights Act passed but he just wanted to make the flight attendants, whom he considered dissatisfied troublemakers, work hard to fight this paper dragon. She told me that he 'just laughed' at these flight attendants in their efforts."

"Dissatisfied troublemakers" was not inaccurate, but the dissatisfaction was hardly unjustified.

The defeat of American was hugely significant. The airline was one of the industry's giants, a major employer of flight attendants, and its vanquishing was a major landmark in the slow disintegration of no-marriage rules. Other, smaller airlines had struck their rules on age and marriage marginally earlier, thanks mostly to union pressure. And TWA had come to an agreement with the union that the company would eradicate the retirement age if four stewardesses who had filed a discrimination complaint with the EEOC would drop their claim for back pay for the years of work they'd lost. The union agreed—but one of the women did not. She quit her job instead. This concession on the part of the union, which set up an unfortunate precedent for relinquishing rights to back pay, had the side effect of diminishing stewardess confidence in the TWU. Its failure to protect its female members' wages was something that would come back to haunt it.

The essential ruling on the marriage ban in a court of law came with *Sprogis v. United Air Lines.* Mary Burke Sprogis had been fired in 1966 for having married. She'd filed a sex discrimination complaint with the EEOC, but the response had been put on hold while the EEOC conducted its stewardess hearings. In 1968, the EEOC authorized her to sue, and she took United to court.

The court followed the EEOC's lead, agreeing that United had failed to convince the judge that being either single or a woman was a BFOQ for the job of flight attendant. Any policy that targeted a group of employees because of their sex was sex discrimination, regardless of whether that policy only applied to some people in the group, like married women, and not to everyone (all women). It was the beginning of a shift in the way the courts looked at sex discrimination in the workplace, toward seeing it as a real problem, and demonstrated a willingness to use Title VII to fight it. And it was a groundbreaking decision in more ways than one: the key arguments from this case would be cited by the courts when they began to decide whether sexual orientation and gender identity could be included under the umbrella of sex discrimination. In the landmark cases of *Hively v. Ivy Tech Community College of Illinois, Evans v. Georgia Regional Hospital,* and others, the lower courts referenced the idea put forth in *Sprogis* that a policy didn't have to apply to everyone in a group to be considered sex discrimination. The Supreme Court, based on these building blocks at the lower court level, would ultimately hold that sex discrimination includes sexual orientation and gender identity—an outcome that was fueled in part by *Sprogis*.

By the time the legal judgment came down in Mary Burke Sprogis's favor, United had gotten rid of its termination-upon-marriage rule, although it had held on to the bitter end, outlasting even American Airlines. But the *Sprogis* decision—that marriage bans were definitively illegal—set a robust legal precedent for future marriage challenges, as well as demonstrating a heartening tendency for courts to include sex discrimination as a violation of Title VII. United had to give Sprogis her job back, the court ruled, along with all the back pay and seniority she would have accrued in the years since she was fired, and United had to pay her legal costs. *Sprogis* was the final decider on marriage, the first time the courts had found in the stewardesses' favor on the marriage rule. It was already 1971. And it wasn't the longest-lasting case, not by far: a class action suit, filed in 1970 by 475 United flight attendants who had been fired due to marriage in the previous decade, dragged on until 1986. United had to pay almost $33 million in back pay and reinstate any flight attendant who still wanted her job almost two decades later.

The staggered, slow, but final collapse of the age and marriage rules, so long fought for, was life-changing for stewardesses across the airlines. Now they could fly for decades longer, didn't have to remember to take off their wedding bands before coming to work, wouldn't have to find an entirely new profession in their thirties. The cases they'd brought to court, the pickets they'd held, the complaints they'd lodged with the EEOC, and the long, fraught negotiations with management had finally earned them something worth having. The stewardesses had taken a temporary job, a "training ground for future wives and mothers," and turned it into a career.

CHAPTER NINE

In and Out of Uniform

THE STEWARDESSES WERE far from holding all the cards, as Patt was well aware. By the late 1950s and the 1960s, advances in technology and safety meant that passengers took these things for granted; it was hard to run a marketing campaign on them. So in their continuing efforts to differentiate themselves from other airlines, each carrier was trying hard to establish a distinct "personality" that would entice businessmen, still the most valued customers, to choose it over its competitors. And these airline "personalities," execs decided, could best be expressed through new uniforms.

It had started with the "Air Strip" at Braniff, but the trend caught on fast at other airlines. At American, 1967 saw Patt in a navy blue mid-thigh dress with white trim, worn with white heels (knee-high white vinyl boots in inclement weather) and what the *New York Times*, in an article on the new stewardess fashions, would call "status gloves with a touch of fishnet." Patt immediately started wearing a pair of form-fitting shorts underneath; this quickly became popular. In early 1969, American introduced a frontier uniform of tartan miniskirts, matching vests, and "Daniel Boone"–style raccoon-fur caps. These were short-lived. The "Field Flowers" serving garment debuted in 1971: a ruffled white apron patterned with red and blue flowers that buttoned over the uniform. Patt found this humiliating and unflattering. She looked, she complained, like a football player in drag. The shift from the highly tailored, military-style uniforms of the early 1960s when Patt had started, to frilly wrappers that looked more appropriate for the bedroom, wasn't something that felt empowering.

No matter how many rights you win at the bargaining table, she thought angrily, it's hard to get people to take you seriously when you're serving dinner wearing a raccoon hat and a miniskirt. Or to get passengers to follow your orders in an emergency when your dress is so short they can see your underwear every time you raise your arms. The stewardesses had expended so much energy in the effort to be treated as professionals, but the airlines had still found a way to undermine their authority. Even as they were winning in the courtroom and at the bargaining table, the airlines were eroding their power by turning them into sex symbols. Patt had to admit, it was clever.

She'd almost stopped noticing suggestive remarks from male passengers. The cockpit crew were nearly worse; a passenger would get off the plane and she'd never have to see them again, but she had to keep working with the pilots and fleet service employees. Pilots were notorious for harassing the stewardesses. A pilot had told Kathleen's friend, Suzanne, also a stewardess at TWA, that he named the left breast of each stewardess (the captain always sat in the left-hand seat in the cockpit). And then there were the interactions on the ground. On one of Patt's first international layovers, she went out to dinner in Mexico City with another stewardess and four pilots, one of whom paid for her meal. He walked her to her room and tried to kiss her, saying she owed him for the dinner. It was one of the few times she was grateful that stewardesses had to share rooms; she was relieved to see the other woman coming down the hall. On another layover, in St. Louis, the copilot came into her room and forced her down on the bed; she managed to get rid of him by threatening to call the captain. Every stewardess knew about the "foot in the door"; after the crew went for dinner and drinks together, returning to the hotel with your colleagues often included a protracted debate at the entrance to your room, the pilot pushing to come in and the stewardess trying to politely decline.

Still, when she looked at her minidress and boots, Patt had to count herself relatively lucky. American's uniforms could have been worse. At Pan Am, management had upgraded its stewardesses from the "natural" look to a new look that included heavy makeup (with extra eye shadow) and false eyelashes. And Canadian Pacific Air Lines had turned their uniform redesign into a giant PR stunt. The new uniform included a midi skirt, one that reached below the knee to mid-calf in harmony with contemporary fashion trends, and was worn with patent leather boots. But male passengers hated the new look, sending hundreds of letters to the airline in protest. Where were the women's legs? they wanted to know. The airline decided to invite customers to take a poll: the new look versus the old miniskirt. When it seemed like the midi would win, the airline sounded the alarm in the press. The fact that a majority of flight attendants preferred the midi was disregarded; the mini was declared the winner. The lingering memory of the midi was preserved through a staged photo of a smiling stewardess triumphantly taking a pair of scissors to her midi.

Not long after this, another Canadian airline, Pacific Western, introduced the "Stampeder Uniform," worn mostly on flights that brought loggers to and from their camps. Western-style boots, a short-sleeved blouse, a fringed vest, and a miniskirt so short that red "bloomers" peeked out from underneath made up the costume. Two women refused to wear the uniform after a male passenger groped one of them in flight. They were fired, then reinstated but suspended without pay. They grieved the suspension, though, and won. After feminist picketing at the Vancouver office, the uniform was no longer required.

Southern Airlines made an attempt to buck the trend, trying to make a gimmick out of *not* dressing their stewardesses in sexy uniforms. The airline would "respect femininity," executives decided, and give its stewardesses "an outstanding look, while maintaining dignity." To do this, the airline commissioned designer Pierre Balmain to create a knee-length dress as the new Southern uniform; presumably dignity included being able to bend over without flashing the entire coach section. But it didn't last long. Three years later Southern gave in and switched to a tunic that only reached mid-thigh (wearing black vinyl pants underneath was optional); then in 1972 it abandoned all pretense and dressed the women in hot pants and short-sleeved shirts, worn with lace-up go-go boots.

The public was taking notice of the wardrobe changes. On June 8, 1969, the *New York Times* ran a full-page spread in its Travel section, titled "Which Stewardess Is the Girl on Your Flight?" It posted photos of stewardesses in their distinctive, newly chic uniforms and invited readers to guess which girl matched which airline, advising that there was no prize for successful guesses, "save the satisfaction that comes from keeping a sharp eye on the stewardesses on those dull business trips."

These uniform updates were sharing the page with news of a different kind. The end of the decade was a time of intense political and cultural change. In 1968, feminists demonstrated outside the Miss America pageant in Atlantic City. While bra-burning existed only in the popular imagination, the protesters did throw bras, curlers, high heels, and girdles (practically a full stewardess uniform) into a trash can, triumphantly crowned a sheep, and snuck a "Women's Liberation" banner into the auditorium for the final moments of the pageant. Florynce Kennedy, the activist and lawyer, chained herself to a giant Miss America puppet, protesting how a patriarchal society kept women enslaved to beauty standards. Two blocks away at the Ritz-Carlton hotel, a rival contest, Miss Black America, was being held in a pointed rebuke of the unvarying whiteness of the Miss America contestants, who, all white and none over the age of thirty, bore a striking resemblance to a group of stewardesses. Miss America would have its first Black contestant two years later, but the Miss Black America pageant kept going; in 1971, Oprah Winfrey was Miss Tennessee.

The Miss America protest had been organized by the New York Radical Women, a women's liberation group. Other women's groups were gaining members rapidly, channeling the rage many were feeling into radical action. Possibly the most outré of the groups was WITCH, the "Women's International Terrorist Conspiracy from Hell." Members performed a sort of subversive theater, casting hexes on Wall Street and leafleting bridal fairs with pamphlets that read, "Marriage is a dehumanizing institution—legal whoredom for women."

On the political front, the battle for the Equal Rights Amendment was ramping up. The ERA was a proposed constitutional amendment that would invalidate sex as a determinant of men's or women's legal rights. The EEOC made a decision in 1969 that made a difference. Much of the opposition to the ERA was based on wanting to keep protective laws in place. These were state laws, mostly sex-based, that ostensibly protected women from danger or hardship. In practice, they barred them from things like working late at night, or in bars, or in jobs that involved lifting heavy objects. The EEOC's declaration—that most protective laws were illegal and in conflict with Title VII—made this particular argument against the ERA null. And court cases that invoked the BFOQ as a reason to keep protective laws in place put the final nail in the coffin: ten years after Title VII became effective, it had become well established that the BFOQ defense could not preserve state protective laws. The next decade would see the ERA gain massive support. In 1970, the United Auto Workers, a large and politically active union, endorsed the ERA, and more unions and union federations would follow.

Seeing these advances in women's rights happening all around her, it often felt to Patt, bundled into miniskirts and leered at by passengers, that she was living in a time warp. As the '60s came to an end, the legal victories and EEOC decisions the stewardesses had won remained dwarfed by the reluctance of the airlines to treat them as equals. Each new right had to be fought for again and again, at the bargaining table and in the courtroom, each concession won with sweat and tears and time. The sultry stewardess image felt too powerful to fight at all. Even the new president had got into the act: on January 20, 1969, stewardesses—forty of them, wearing matching minidresses of silver sequins—welcomed guests to Nixon's inaugural ball as its official presidential hostesses.

One day, driving home from Love Field in her bronze 1966 Mustang convertible (she'd traded in her motorcycle, realizing that in Texas she needed something with air-conditioning), Patt spotted a fellow stewardess walking home.

Anna, all tumbled blond hair and smiling eyes, had been born in Germany, and had been a model in Milwaukee for the John Robert Powers School. Patt had become totally smitten with her. Patt wasn't out of the closet, not even close, but she noticed how beautiful her fellow stewardesses were, and her feelings for Anna, try as she might, couldn't be explained away as friendship. She pulled over and, heart pounding, asked Anna if she wanted a lift home.

Smiling, Anna hopped in the passenger seat, and Patt drove her to her apartment. Anna invited her up for a beer. Patt still didn't drink, but she accepted, parking the car and heading upstairs. Anna persuaded her to try a dark German beer. "You'll like it," she assured her. Patt couldn't resist. She had one. Then she had another. They talked, laughed, and then Anna leaned over and asked, "Would you like to kiss me?" And Patt said, "I would."

She would never have made the first move. But she was ecstatic. She pushed away her anxiety about going to hell, about other people finding out, about doing something so forbidden she'd never seen it on television or read about it in a book. She kissed Anna, and then she kissed her some more.

She found herself, as her relationship with Anna began to deepen, going through a crisis. She was in love with Anna, that much she knew, but she was struggling with the idea that she was gay. She and Anna continued to date, but they hid their relationship at work. Then they moved in together, but there was still no way they could tell anyone. It was just too risky. Patt had no one to talk to about it. In some ways it was fun, a secret love affair, but it was one buffeted by her own inner conflict. Being in a romantic relationship with another woman was a constant source of stress and self-questioning. When she and Anna were together, the questions went away. But as soon as Patt was alone, they came racing back.

The relationship didn't last. Anna, like Patt, had not come out to her mother, and feared disappointing her so much that she ended her relationship with Patt. It would kill her mother, she said, to know that they were together.

Patt was heartbroken. But this rejection had several unexpected results. Patt decided to go to a psychiatrist. Her relationship with Anna had been the first time she'd acted on her attraction to women. She was questioning herself constantly: Am I gay? Or was this just a one-time occurrence? Are my feelings for Anna something unique, or is this who I am? She agonized, unsure she would ever meet anyone again. Anna had rejected her; maybe she was just unlovable. So she finally went to therapy. She saw the therapist for a year. He was open-minded, never trying to convince her she was straight. He just kept asking her, "What do you want? What are your feelings?" She struggled with the answers. Finally, she told him, "Well, I guess I'm going to have to start dating a guy and see how I feel about it."

So she did. She'd met a man from Highland Park; he came from a well-to-do family. He shared her interests—aviation, boating, sports—and he really liked her. They had been dating for months when he told her he wanted to get married. That brought Patt up with a sharp shock. Her immediate reaction was one of sudden clarity: no, this wasn't what she wanted. She tried to come to grips with it, asking her therapist what she should do. He told her, "You have to make a choice here about who you think you are. I can't tell you who you are."

She was still trying to figure it out when she went to work one day, and there, on that flight, she met a new colleague, a stewardess just starting out on the line. For the first time in a year, those feelings of attraction came rushing back. She thought to herself: this is a test of who I am. How could I be instantly attracted to a woman if I really am straight? If being gay was a choice, she knew, she wouldn't be attracted to her. Okay. This was who she was. And there was no going back. She ended the relationship with the man from Highland Park and started dating the stewardess. Her year of self-doubt was over.

Patt's relationship with Anna had another long-lasting effect. Not long after meeting her, Patt decided to resign from her union position. She had been the head of the policy committee, head of the finance committee, head of the constitution committee. She'd negotiated the 1968 contract. She had been reelected for a second term as master executive chairperson. She had seen the age and marriage rules fall away, and she had fumed as the airlines doubled down on their sexist ads and uniforms. She had dedicated her whole self to working the line, and working for the union. But there was life beyond the cabin and she was determined to figure it out. She left in the middle of her term as chair.

The other result of the breakup with Anna was that Patt learned how to fly a plane. She'd inherited a grand total of $600 from her parents, who had died within months of each other, and she decided to put that money toward flying lessons. She'd always been interested in flying; if becoming a pilot had been an option for women in

1962, she'd never have applied to be a stewardess. A friend made her an appointment to learn with Benny Barton, one of the best pilots in the area. She was waiting in the flying school office on her first day when Benny walked in, chatting with another student and looking like a 1970s caricature: ducktail, exaggerated sideburns, aviator glasses, white belt, and white shoes. A cigarette hung out of the side of his mouth. Benny walked over to the owner and asked, "Is my next student here yet? That Patt Gibbs person?"

"Yeah," the owner replied, pointing to Patt. "She's right there."

Benny turned around and looked at her. "She?" he said. "You?" He shook his head. "I don't teach women. Nope. If God wanted women to fly, he would've sprouted wings on 'em."

A lot of convincing later, a truculent Benny took Patt out to the hangar. He opened the door of the Cessna 150 and got into the co-pilot's seat. Patt climbed into the pilot's chair. There was one immediate problem: she couldn't see over the nose of the plane. The cockpit had been designed with Patricks, not Patricias, in mind. The lessons proceeded, with Benny getting grumpier each time. Patt's takeoffs and landings weren't good, they were too bouncy— she couldn't easily reach the rudders or the pedals, and so the plane tended to plop down on the runway rather than smoothly glide to a

Patt and her plane, 1972.

stop. But she was dogged, coming back for lesson after lesson. She knew she had won him over when, just before her first solo flight, he went to the office and brought back two cushions for her to sit on. She'd come straight from work, still wearing her uniform blouse. He made her take off and land three times. When pilots soloed on a plane for the first time, it was a tradition for the instructor to cut off their shirttail, which they would keep as a souvenir. Benny did the same for Patt. The fact that it was her stewardess blouse Benny cut, and that she'd never gotten the chance to be a pilot for the airlines, wasn't lost on Patt. Throwing herself into flying the same way she'd thrown herself into union work, she got her private pilot's license in three months. A photo from 1972 shows her squinting into the sun, smile on her face, leather pilot's jacket half unzipped. Hair cropped short and scarf knotted at her neck, she's resting an arm contentedly on the tiny plane's propeller.

Part Two

Tommie

CHAPTER TEN

Flying Pianos

FOR TOMMIE HUTTO, it was the final assassination that did it. JFK's, in 1963, had been the first. Martin Luther King's, on April 4, 1968, the second. And Robert Kennedy's, on June 5, 1968, was the third. Tommie had been glued to the television for three days. Finally her roommate came in and told her she needed to shower. Tommie had been so excited for an RFK presidency, and so horrified by the news, she'd forgotten.

Tommie was about to turn twenty-two. She'd just graduated from North Texas State University (later the University of North Texas). She was from Big Spring, in West Texas, and the greenery and the rain in Denton had been brand-new to her. Tommie had started out as a journalism major—she'd edited her high school newspaper— but the head of the journalism department only addressed the men in the class, and never called on a woman. She had *heard* of sexism, but she didn't identify what was happening as sexism. She figured there was something wrong with her. After a semester, frustrated and helpless, she switched to sociology. She liked it, it turned out, and was planning to go straight to graduate school when a professor said to her, "Tommie, it's 1968. Get out there. Live! 'Cause things are about to change."

She decided he was right. She found a job where she could use her education, working at the Opportunities Industrialization Center. The center provided job training for people of color; it had been founded by the Reverend Dr. Leon Sullivan, the "Lion from Zion," who was a powerful activist in the movement for economic equality. Tommie was the first white person hired in the Dallas office, and her job was to go to companies in the city and convince them to employ the people the center trained. The very first corporation she talked into hiring their trainees was American Airlines. She got American to hire her people as baggage handlers, at least to begin with. She was flushed with success: they'd get on-the-job training, a chance to move up, union membership, pensions, health care.

She worked at the OIC for an eye-opening two years. Her family were Democrats, but southern Democrats; Tommie used to have such heated political fights with her grandfather in Louisiana that her mother would have to drag her out of the kitchen. Tommie was different. She'd had two progressive teachers in high school who inspired her; then the slew of assassinations had horrified her. Two years at the OIC showed her some of the injustices people of color were facing. She could see it even with the trainees American had hired; they were some of the first Black and brown people working for the airline, and they frequently quit after two or three months because of the way they were being bullied. And that's when she really started clashing with her family. "I want to get out of here," she thought to herself. "I need to get out of Texas altogether."

That was in the back of her mind when she made her next visit to American Airlines. She was in the personnel office, and they were telling her how somebody who she'd really, really thought was going to work out had quit. She felt depressed. One of the men there had a suggestion. He said, "You know, we're hiring stewardesses like crazy. You should go see the world. They're interviewing right down the hall." She'd never even thought about being a stewardess. But she was young, single, free from responsibility. And she wanted to leave Texas. She walked down the hall.

She was interviewed by a much older man. He had her stand up and turn around, get on the scale, show him her hands. He asked her some questions. Then he hired her on the spot. She was a known quantity; she'd later meet women who had been to three or four interviews. And she was white, slim, and educated. As she was leaving, though, he issued one instruction: "Remove the hair on your arms." Excuse me? she thought. The hair on my arms? She walked out to the parking lot thinking, "That was really weird." She assumed they'd remove the hair when she got to the stewardess college, but they didn't, and she didn't remind them. She arrived at the charm farm in January 1970, figuring she'd fly for a couple of years, maybe see what life was like living on the West Coast, or maybe try New York, and then get back to social justice work. She was twenty-three years old when she joined American Airlines. She'd be sixty-one when she retired.

She arrived at stewardess school prepared for the worst. She'd driven there with a group of other Texas women who were starting at the same time. They were taken to their dorm room, where she first realized she'd be rooming with three others. "Oh my God, I've gone backwards," she thought. It was like boarding school. But in spite of herself, she was impressed with the training. They learned about different aircraft, about handling medical emergencies, even a bit of maintenance. She learned how to jump out of a plane. All day long they trained, lifting exit doors, practicing hauling up passengers who'd fallen ill. You needed to be strong to do this work, although skilled stewardesses would be denied graduation and a job because they were a couple of pounds over their cutoff weight. Tommie watched as her fellow trainees who hovered close to their maximums were weighed morning and evening. It stayed with her, this constant measurement. Watching her friends being called out of class or the lounge to be weighed made her cringe. She felt their humiliation and embarrassment as if it were her own.

They took tests every day, some medical, others mechanical. There was a lot more to this stewardess thing than she'd thought. And the trainers were impressive, strong women who were good at what they did. Some, she discovered, were lesbians; none were openly gay, but rumors circulated about their relationships, and about the relationships between some of the instructors and men in management. For Tommie, who had thought she was going to be a writer or journalist, it was all intriguing.

She did have to hold her nose when she was being told how to apply makeup. False eyelashes were a requirement, but she'd often skip putting them on, risking admonishment from the instructors. And she rebelled when the order came down for them all to get the same short haircut. She pushed back, managing to engineer a compromise by creating what would become a popular style with other flight attendants—a kind of side ponytail. She'd done it shrewdly, first creating a relationship with the stylists, then pointing out that if her curly hair were cut short, it would just frizz outward. Ballerinas have long hair, she pointed out, and they just keep it in a bun. Couldn't she try it? It worked. From then on, the edict from the stylists was a resigned "Confine it, ladies, confine it."

When graduation neared, they were told they had to pick a graduation song. Her classmates wanted "Leaving on a Jet Plane," and Tommie, rolling her eyes, wondered how many classes before them had chosen the same tune. She refused to go to rehearsal: the training college might have looked like a school, but there were limits on how much she'd be made to feel like a child. Though she was, at twenty-three, one of the oldest in the class, they weren't Girl Scouts. Still, no one had made her remove her arm hair. That was something.

All of her dormmates were fellow Texans. Most of them were, like Tommie, trying out this new job for a lark. Only one of them had always dreamed of being a flight attendant: Melody, the youngest, who had an older sister who flew for Braniff. The women got a weekend off in the middle of the six-week training program, but when Tommie returned to school, Melody's bed was empty and all of her things were gone. Tommie knew that students could be dismissed for almost any reason, but Melody had *really, really* wanted to be a stewardess. Tommie went to one of the trainers, a woman she'd gotten to know, and asked, "What's going on? This is the one person that's going to be brokenhearted to be sent home. She wanted to do this more than anything. Where is she?" The trainer told her Melody had been dismissed for an infraction. Her sister, the Braniff stewardess, could give family members a card that entitled them to a percentage off the price of a flight. Melody had loaned her card to another student, someone flying home for the weekend. The check-in agent had questioned it, then reported the incident to American Airlines, which dismissed Melody immediately.

Tommie was furious. This was entirely unfair and wrongheaded—Melody hadn't known she was doing something wrong, she was just helping out a fellow stewardess. Tommie started a petition to bring Melody back, talking her reluctant fellow students into signing it, and then taking it to the instructors. She advocated for Melody, speaking slowly and calmly, but making her point. It worked. Melody was permitted to finish her course at stewardess college, and even ended up rooming with Tommie when they were sent to their first base.

Then Melody quit. She didn't really like the work. Tommie couldn't believe it.

It was her first time representing a fellow stewardess, but it would be far from the last. It was, however, a moment that would stay with her. She knew nothing yet about the labor movement, or the part the stewardesses were playing in it. But she knew it had been unfair to dismiss Melody, she had fought for her, and she'd got her back her place.

When Tommie graduated—lining up with her classmates on the famous staircase for a photo, singing "Leaving on a Jet Plane"—it was C. R. Smith himself who pinned on her silver wings. He was a tall Texan who reminded her of LBJ. He was courtly, smart, and seemed to like his employees. Tommie was no honeybun, but compared to the CEOs who would come after, C.R. was a gentleman. Tommie was sent to New York. She had hoped for a smaller base, perhaps Washington or Boston, but at least, she thought, she was getting out of Texas.

She reported to work in February 1970. It was scary, stepping off the plane. The airline paid for a single night in a hotel; after that they were on their own. Tommie moved into an apartment across from LaGuardia with a few of her fellow Texans from the charm farm. It was nothing fancy, a typical stew zoo, with two bedrooms for four women. The building was filled with flight attendants, pilots, and other aviation workers. But she didn't think she'd be there long. She planned to work out her six months' probation and then transfer to California. Her best friend was out there, working in Santa Barbara for the University of California. Soon she'd be tanning on the beach on her days off.

She watched as a number of her colleagues quit in the first six months, taken aback at how much work the job was. It wasn't nearly as glamorous as they'd expected. Tommie didn't mind that part, though. This was a good old blue-collar job, she thought. The hard work didn't bother her, and her colleagues were nice. Once she even ran into someone from her old job, a man she'd helped find a baggage handler position at American; he'd spotted her walking across

Tommie in her first year of flying. Photographer: Ken Sawyer.

the ramp in her uniform ("Hey, Miss Hutto!"). She could see that the appearance standards were absurd, but she could put up with them. After all, she wasn't going to make a career of being a stewardess.

She avoided wearing her girdle when she could, though she was subject to the "girdle thump" like everyone else—a smart flick of a supervisor's finger on her rear to make sure she was wearing it. And they'd run their hands down her back to make sure she was wearing a bra. The thing that bothered her most, though, as it had on the charm farm, was weight. She could see her fellow stewardesses flush with embarrassment and worry every time they had to get on the scale. "This is 1970!" she thought. "And we're being put on scales?" Tommie was never over the weight limit, but the issue was on so many stewardesses' minds it was impossible to avoid. It was a constant topic of conversation.

The job was intensely physical, she realized quickly. First of all, she was too tall, bumping her head on everything. Most stewardesses topped out at five foot seven; she was almost five foot ten. As the planes got bigger, her height became an asset, but at the beginning she was clumsy in the cabin. She'd work a flight from New York to

Chicago or Detroit or Toronto, the 727 carrying around a hundred people, all of whom were expecting a full meal on a trip that lasted around an hour. First she'd go through the plane, writing down everyone's name on a seating chart and asking what they wanted to drink. If they could, the stewardesses would start this before the plane took off, to save time, though she'd find out in later years that the minute the plane started moving they should have been belted into their seats, not rushing around the aisles taking drink orders.

Once the plane was in the air, it was time to hustle again. She'd deliver the cocktails first: "Here's your drink, Mr. X," set down with a smile. Passengers, of course, addressed her as Tommie, never Ms. Hutto. She started playing a game with herself, asking passengers sweetly, "I'm Tommie, and do you mind if I call you by your first name?" She always said it with a smile and they never said no.

Once cocktails were delivered, it was time to run out the meals. Each tray was preset with salad, dessert, a coffee cup, a napkin, and a glass engraved with the AA symbol, which the stewardesses always called "the roly-poly" because it would tip over so often. If they were really pressed for time, the stewardesses would send out the cocktails and the trays at the same time, putting the drink where the entrée would go, and running the entrées out later. Tommie would pull trays from the galley, plop the drink in the center, and rush them out to the passengers, two at a time—there were no carts—while the entrées were heating up. Then she'd pile the entrées high onto a tray and go through the cabin, picking up glasses and dropping the entrées one by one in front of the passengers, keeping an eye on the clock the whole time and cursing to herself if people didn't eat fast enough. Then it was hurry to the front of the cabin to start collecting the trays, as many as she could carry at one time, bringing them back to the galley and stowing them away before running back out for more. She'd be covered in sweat by the time the flight was over. American was notorious for sending out a flight staffed with all or almost all new stewardesses, some of whom would freak out from the stress. Tommie would tell them to sit down, and enlist a passenger's help with the trays. Once in a while she'd fly with a more senior stewardess, but it was unusual enough to fly with a "gold winger" that she'd come home and mention it to her roommates.

She quickly made friends. Bobbi (her real name was Barbara)

Lennie was blond to Tommie's dark hair, but they were the same height, and they immediately recognized each other as kindred spirits. Then Dana Olson turned up on one of their flights and the three of them became inseparable. Dana couldn't reach five foot four on a good day; she had long, straight blond hair and bangs, and was a musician—she was immediately nicknamed "Joni Mitchell." They started bidding together, flying the same flights whenever possible.

They were all young, enjoying New York life, going into Manhattan on their days off, visiting museums and walking their feet sore, and feeling on top of the world. Bobbi was closest to embodying that glamorous stewardess lifestyle that was so popular in the public imagination. She had been working longer than Tommie and, thanks to Patt's contract machinations, was making a decent wage. She earned enough to live on her own in Manhattan, two doors off Central Park West at 13 West 74th Street. It was a studio, but it was all hers. From the outside, she was living exactly the sort of life used to sell the job to a young woman: you can have your own Manhattan apartment, fly around the country, be free, independent. And she enjoyed it. When she got a bit more seniority she started flying to the West Coast: San Diego, Los Angeles, San Francisco. She was having a ball. And then, bit by bit, disquiet started to creep in. The way she was treated by the male passengers. The way she was treated by the female passengers, who often resented the stewardesses. When Bobbi met Tommie, for whom activism was a way of life, she was ready to be swept along.

The feminist movement was a thrum of energy that buoyed them up, energizing them more and more. Betty Friedan and Gloria Steinem were in the news talking about equality, women's groups were forming, rules were being broken. It was just as her professor had told her, Tommie thought. Things were changing.

> I propose that the women who are doing menial chores in the offices cover their typewriters and close their notebooks, the telephone operators unplug their switchboards . . . and everyone who is doing a job for which a man would be paid more—stop. Every woman pegged forever as an assistant, doing jobs for which men get credit—stop.

These were the words Betty Friedan used to call for a strike. It was fifty years after the suffragists had secured women the right to vote, and she was stepping down from the presidency of NOW with a headline-grabbing call to arms. The use of the word "strike" rather than "march" was significant: women were calling attention to their role as workers. The rallying slogan? "Don't Iron While the Strike Is Hot!" The Women's Strike for Equality took place on August 26, 1970, and while the New York event, which gathered tens of thousands of women, would be the most frequently remembered, other strikes took place in cities around the country, from Los Angeles to Detroit. Women held teach-ins to educate others about issues from unions to welfare, submitted petitions calling for the passage of the Equal Rights Amendment, and took action in their workplaces, including kicking men out of one of their bathrooms at the *Detroit Free Press*, where men had two bathrooms to the women's one. At the midtown march, Betty Friedan and Bella Abzug spoke, Abzug reiterating the three main demands of the strikers: free, accessible abortion in every state, free universal childcare, and equal opportunity in both education and employment.

Marching at the head of the parade, calling loudly for that equal opportunity in employment, were stewardesses. Four union leaders, all from Continental Airlines, carried signs that pointed to the immediate termination the stewardesses faced when they became pregnant: "Storks Fly, Why Can't Mothers?"; "Mothers Are Still FAA Qualified"; and "We Want Our Babies and Our Wings."

Tommie was inspired, her brain and her heart racing with new ideas, but other parts of her daily reality weren't all that different. The stew zoo was on the other side of a bridge from LaGuardia, a walk that didn't take too long. Her starting salary was low, and it would have been a waste of money to call a cab, so she always walked to work. Even for "zero dark hundred" sign-ins—what the crew called the early flights that meant waking up before dawn and getting to the airport before the sun rose—she'd put on her uniform and her heels and head out over the bridge. One still-dark morning she walked past a car and the passenger door opened suddenly, the light flaring. A man was sitting in the car, masturbating. She ran the rest of the way to the airport, praying the whole time that she wouldn't hear steps behind her. It happened four or five more times before she moved out. She'd share the stories with her fellow stewardesses, who were experiencing the same thing; apparently the stew zoo was known as a desirable location for men looking to get off. But it also happened in the subways and on the street. It was the uniform, Tommie always thought. Men just seemed to feel that they had the right. And the more commercials she saw starring flirty stewardesses, the more innuendo that appeared in magazine ads, the more she realized the airlines were telling them they had that right. Even off duty, if she was wearing her uniform, whether on the bus or walking down the sidewalk, men would tell her to smile. She felt more like punching them.

Still, it was hard to blame the men entirely. The idea that a stewardess was there to cater to a man's every need was built into the industry. A 1966 print ad from United was dominated by a photo of a neatly bobbed and smiling stewardess adjusting the flower on the lapel of a besuited businessman easily twice her age:

We hope you had a pleasant flight.
We tried to make it so.
It arrived on time.
You ate well.
You went to sleep after dinner. Why not? You work hard.
When the flight landed the stewardess smiled goodbye like she
really meant it. She does.
She even straightened your boutonniere.
You get this kind of "extra care" every time you fly with us.
Come back soon.

The "you work hard so you deserve this" theme echoed the famous words of Mary Wells, creator of the blockbuster "end of the plain plane" campaign. "When a tired businessman gets on an airplane," she'd announced, "we think he ought to be allowed to look at a pretty girl."

Another United ad ran along the same lines, with the tagline "The boys with the Friday night faces." The photo zoomed in on a

Come Back Soon

We hope you had a pleasant flight.
We tried to make it so.
It arrived on time.
You ate well.
You went to sleep after dinner. Why not? You work hard.
When the flight landed, the stewardess smiled goodbye like she
really meant it. She does.
She even straightened your boutonniere.
You get this kind of "extra care" every time you fly with us.
Come back soon.

*fly the
friendly skies
of
United.*   "I always fly United."

line of men in suits (much further from being boys than the stewardesses were from being girls) being welcomed onto the plane by a cheerful, smiling blonde. The copy emphasized how hard the men were working. "Every United stewardess knows a Friday night face when she sees one. It's the tired face of a businessman who's put in a hard week and just wants to go home." The copy goes on to enumerate the amenities that businessman deserves—sizzling steak, broiled lobster, a pillow for his back, and conversation if he's in the mood— and guarantees that his stewardess will deliver.

Sexism on the plane itself came from every direction, but relationships with the cockpit were often the most fraught. Tommie didn't get along with the pilots very well; she was known to be a feminist and that seemed radical. The captain was in absolute charge on board, and the stewardesses had to put up with whatever he dished out at work, though later, in Operations, they'd sometimes

The boys with the Friday night faces.

Every United stewardess knows a Friday night face when she sees one.

It's the tired face of a businessman who's put in a hard week and just wants to go home.

Maybe he wants to talk. Maybe he doesn't.

We'll feed him well. His favorite drink. Hors d'oeuvres. Sizzling steak. Or broiled lobster. Cornish hen, maybe.

A pillow for his tired back. Six channels of stereo and a movie to unkink the tensions.

Some people want to be fussed over. Some don't. Extra care is different for every passenger.

But they all get it.

That's why more businessmen fly United than any other airline.

They think the service is great.

We agree, but we think it's good business, too.

fly the friendly skies of United.

let him have it. Every once in a while there'd be a yelling match, shouts of "Who the hell do you think you're talking to?!," and supervisors would come running.

The pilots, who had mostly come to the commercial airlines from the air force, many after a stint in Vietnam, were by nature much more conservative than the stewardesses. They were often older, married, less adventurous when it came to spending time in a new city on a layover. There was also a huge salary discrepancy. Pilots made around five times as much as stewardesses. Even the mechanics made over 20 percent more, taking home salaries of between $8,380 and $13,100 while the average annual pay for a stewardess started at $7,200 and topped out at around $11,100. Kathleen Heenan, over at TWA, grew to especially resent the pilots who'd board the plane and, without introducing themselves, ask her to bring them coffee. It never occurred to a pilot to go to the galley and pour his own. On one occasion, with a full cabin and little time, she told a pilot to help himself to coffee. "But they'll think I'm a flight attendant if I help myself," he protested. They weren't all so offensive, but they were bewildered by the hostility from the women. Tommie always felt that the pilots taught the stewardesses a lot about sexism, especially those women who hadn't given it much thought before. Walking into the cockpit to see pages ripped from *Playboy* taped up on the wall would radicalize someone fast.

To Tommie, it became very clear very soon that seniority number was everything, and the smaller that number the better. When you went on the line, you were added to the bottom of the very long list, and the gold wingers, those with seniority numbers in the double or triple digits, weren't flying the short hops, going back and forth between New York City and Syracuse six times a day. They weren't trying to beat the clock getting the meal service done on an hour-and-fifteen-minute flight to Toronto. Bobbi Lennie, Tommie's new best friend, had run-ins with passengers who ate too slowly, at one point physically trying to pull a tray from a woman who didn't want to let the rest of her meal go. The passenger ended up with chicken in her lap, and Bobbi ended up dashing to her seat as the plane coasted to a stop, still clutching the tray.

The stewardesses found shortcuts. They'd open a mini bottle of vodka and use it to wash their hands when the lines for the bathroom were too long. For a while, on those short flights, Bobbi came up with what she thought was a smart workaround: she would open the doors to the lavatory and shove the used trays inside to save time, so that she could get back to her seat before arrival. Sliding each tray neatly back onto its shelf in the galley just took too long. The cabin service crew would come on once the plane landed and have a fit. Bobbi was told to quit it.

The huge new 747 had been introduced in 1970; it could fit eighty-eight passengers in first class, hundreds more in coach, and required fourteen flight attendants. You had to be specially trained to work the 747. Working first class meant setting up tables with tablecloths and silverware, serving a roast dinner, hot fudge sundaes, caviar, salmon. After the appetizers, the stewardesses would serve the salad, tossing it in front of the passengers before dishing it out. There was a credenza in front with a lavish buffet spread that included fruit and cheese; it had to be set up and taken down on each flight between the time the plane took off and when it landed. The upper level, the so-called Captain's Deck, was up a spiral staircase. It had its own cocktail lounge with a full bar. Carts would be sent up from the lower-level galleys in a dumbwaiter. Initially, a bartender was employed to mix drinks for the first-class passengers. Eventually, passengers were just told to pour their own. Before the wide-body planes had been introduced, there had been a two-drink maximum per person. Now that went out the window. Passengers would throw back too many cocktails and drop their cigarettes in the aisles. People fell down the spiral staircase all the time.

The newest idea, the most gimmicky way to attract customers, debuted in the back of the 747, in coach class. Rows of seats, around twenty of them, were removed and in their place appeared a lounge. The lounge had its own piano, an electric Wurlitzer. Any passenger was free to play the piano, to accompany themselves as they sang, or just bang out "Chopsticks" again and again. Other passengers could join in the musical revue from their positions at the stand-up pedestal bar or the comfy sofas. "Put a piano in a room full of strangers and something nice happens," intoned one television commercial featuring a young Henry Winkler. Drinks flowed. It was always the responsibility of one minidress-wearing stewardess to supervise the piano lounge and the off-key singers; it was not a job they vied for. The piano bar didn't last long; it added too much weight to the plane, and of course, the seats they'd taken away to make room for it meant fewer ticket sales. But the 747 was there to stay, though the pianos, stand-up bars, and living-room-style lounges for coach passengers gradually disappeared.

Running up and down the spiral staircase, slicing roast beef in first class, trying to look entertained by drunk passengers picking out show tunes on the piano: the stewardesses did all this dressed in the Daniel Boone uniform (the plaid skirts and raccoon hat) or the Americana collection (short dresses in red, white, or blue). This was Tommie's first uniform, and she added her voice to the fight for the right to wear shorts. When she'd reach up to get bags or blankets from the overhead bins, she'd see male heads swiveling toward her. At least it wasn't the hot pants and boots they had to wear over at Braniff, she thought; she might have quit if they'd try to put her in that outfit.

In 1972, American tried another whimsical idea, a sailor uniform—a jaunty white sailor's cap, navy dresses with white trim-

Tommie, on left, in sailor uniform.

mings, or a white V-neck sailor shirt with a navy ribbon that hung down the front like a man's tie. This one you could wear with pants; it was the outfit Patt wore most often, thinking it was the least absurd option. But she wore the short navy dress, too; before boarding the plane she'd sometimes pair it with a pair of khaki soldier's socks pulled up to the knee. They were a present from the crew, who'd taken to calling her Captain Gibbs or Sergeant Gibbs when she was in charge of the flights, a friendly nickname with a bite to it.

Tommie didn't yet know Patt Gibbs. But she discovered the same way of pushing back against the indignities of the job: she joined the union's base council. Though she was mostly happy, Tommie needed somewhere to channel her frustration at the weight restrictions, at the sexist ads, at the patronizing pilots. It was her first step into the labor movement.

Her dreams of transferring to California never materialized. She'd moved to New York in February, and by December she was living with the man who would become her husband. This wasn't part of the plan. But her very first weekend in New York, she took a big step: she went to a bar. Going into Manhattan and to a bar felt like something out of a movie. In Texas in 1970, there was no such thing as a neighborhood bar. Bars were private establishments, and women couldn't come in unescorted. She'd drunk beer in college, sure, but she'd never walked into a bar without a man. A fellow charm farm graduate had invited her and her roommate, Jane, to her apartment, introduced them to some off-duty crew schedulers, handed out drinks. What did they want to do, they were asked, this very first weekend in New York? They wanted, they said, to go to a bar. The group headed to an Irish bar on the East Side, Tommie and Jane walking in first. A man smiled at Tommie as she entered, uttering a gentle pickup line: "Took you long enough to get here." Her group sat at the bar, and Tommie ordered herself a rum and Coke with a thrill of excitement. The smiling man and his friend joined them, everybody talking and laughing. "Have you seen New York yet?" the man asked. Tommie, with her still-strong Texas accent, told him this was her first time going out, that she lived in Queens. He also lived in Queens, he said. His name was Al Blake, and he suggested that he come and pick her up the next morning; he'd take her to the Statue of Liberty and the Empire State Building. Sure, she said. She didn't think he'd actually turn up. When he did, arriving promptly at ten that Sunday morning, she was fast asleep. But she went. He took her everywhere, to all the New York sights, they covered the city. By December, her roommates had finished their probation periods and were heading to California, or back to Texas. She thought about her California plan. "Well, damn," she said to herself. "I think I'm going to stay." She and Al got a tiny apartment together in Manhattan.

He didn't tell his mother. She didn't tell hers. If they wanted to be happy, her family would say, they needed to be married. In a Methodist church. If she did get married, she thought to herself, it sure as hell wouldn't be in a Methodist church. They lived together for a year, then went home to West Texas and got married in her parents' living room. They wrote their own vows, toasted their union, then drove back to New York in her turquoise '67 Mustang.

CHAPTER ELEVEN

Pregnancy and Pursers

IN 1970, AT age forty-two, Sonia got married. She'd lived on her own until then, in an apartment in Arlington, Virginia, and, before that, in what was essentially a boardinghouse: the Meridian Hill Hotel for Women. She'd had a room there, one so small that in the summer she'd keep her winter clothes in the trunk of her car, and in the winter she'd swap them out for her summer things. She was perfectly happy there for over a year, until her mother, Hinda, came up from Florida for a visit. As Hinda and Sonia rode the elevator up to Sonia's room, Hinda noticed a sign: "No men allowed above the first floor." She turned and asked Sonia how she could possibly live in a place where men weren't allowed above the first floor. Sonia was embarrassed: her sixty-two-year-old mother was shaming her for not having enough sex! She moved to her own apartment soon after.

Still, it wasn't until she married her husband, Roberto Fuentes, that she bought furniture. It had been drummed into her by her parents that a single person did not buy furniture—when a couple married, they bought furniture for their home together. That was the way of things. So she'd rented the furniture for her single-person apartment for years; she was the rental company's best customer. Roberto was also a government employee, a biostatistician from Puerto Rico whom she met while on a blind date with someone else. He wasn't really interested in marriage or in having more children—he had had three with his first wife and considered that plenty—but Sonia was adamant: she'd wanted both of these things all her life. He gave in, but with a caveat: if she wasn't pregnant within six months of their wedding, they'd forget about having kids. They married, and, just days before the six months were up, she was pregnant. Zia was born when Sonia was forty-three and a half.

Sonia took six weeks off from her job at the EEOC to take care of the baby. She had longed for a child, and now she had one. She was miserable. She had been used to being in the office, going out to lunch, talking to people all day, going to the theater after work. All of a sudden she was at home all day every day, with a baby who couldn't keep up her end of the conversation, and nothing interesting to do. Roberto got up in the morning and went to work, just like before. People did come visit, to see the baby, and Sonia discovered she was supposed to make dinner for them. She'd never enjoyed cooking, wasn't particularly good at it, but suddenly she was looking after a baby all day and cooking dinner every night. After five weeks of listening to her complain, Roberto turned to her and told her she was going back to work on Monday. She had another week of maternity leave, she protested. Impossible, he said. Monday.

They drove to the supermarket and bought formula. And on Monday she went back to work. She was so happy she went out at lunchtime to Sterns Jewelers and bought herself a jade ring to celebrate.

This quick detour into the world Betty Friedan had laid bare in *The Feminine Mystique* was enough for Sonia. The life of a housewife wasn't for her, even with the difficulty of finding someone to take care of Zia (a succession of college students and housekeepers took turns at the job). One day, traveling for work, she met a forty-year-old woman who had married when she was twenty, and her kids had grown up and moved out. She told Sonia she was unhappy, didn't know what to do with herself. It was a shot in the arm for Sonia. She looked at the woman, listened to her, and made a resolution: I don't want to be in that position. She never forgot that housewife.

She had her husband, her daughter, and her job. But Sonia was getting restless at the EEOC. Charlie Duncan had left to work for D.C.'s Corporation Counsel, and she missed him. They had been close friends, always joking together, and she'd enjoyed lecturing him on women's rights. She'd hoped he'd take her with him when he left, but he couldn't, and the sound of her high heels walking down the hallway away from his office one final time stayed with her.

She began looking for a new job. The year before she left the

EEOC, Sonia published an article in the journal *The American Statistician* on Title VII and its effects. In her typical brusque style, she finished her discussion of how discrimination cases were being dealt with at the EEOC with a scathing commentary on systemic sex discrimination in the United States: "We don't need any further studies in this country to know that women are conditioned from birth to expect that their primary life role is that of wife and mother; that, if they work, they may expect to be relegated to lower-level, lower-paying jobs; and that they should not aspire to distinction in the arts, in the professions, and in politics. And yet—there are still areas where additional statistics—and the resultant additional knowledge—would be useful." She called for studies on the effects of testing and job interviews on the employment of women, pointing out that most interviewers were white men and that "since most people relate best to people like themselves, the effect of the job interview on women's employment may be considerable." She suggested an examination of attitudes, a study that wouldn't feel outdated or out of place fifty years later. "How can we get the American public to abandon the attitudes it grew up with and adopt new ideas suited to the decade of the 70's? How do we overcome the fears men have of competing for jobs and on jobs with women? How do we overcome the belief we've installed in women that they're inferior to men and must therefore always have lower aspirations? How do we educate the public to begin to live in equality?"

She also got prickly with the statistics professionals themselves, noting that "it would be anomalous for you to concentrate on esoteric research projects and overlook sex discrimination in your own backyard." She pointed out that the journal itself had published statistics showing that male statisticians made a median average salary of $14,900 a year, while female statisticians took home only $12,000. She suggested that statisticians develop high school programs for girls, and increase female representation in important positions in the American Statistical Association. She ended with a quote from the Bible ("Ye shall know the truth, and the truth shall make you free"), accompanied by a dry remark: "Statisticians are in a particularly advantageous position to help us know the truth. Perhaps you'll use that position to liberate us all."

As might have been guessed from the tone of her article, Sonia needed a change. After having her daughter and returning to work at the EEOC, she'd come to realize that her dream, becoming an EEOC commissioner, was not going to happen. She was too stubborn, too female, didn't have enough influence in higher levels of government. She could see no upward path at the EEOC, so she quit. She began applying to other federal agencies, but without any luck. One day she spotted an ad for corporate legal counsel at the GTE Service Corporation, formerly the General Telephone & Electronics Corporation. The job paid $30,000 a year. She had been making that at the EEOC, but her husband suggested she write to explain her qualifications and that she was looking for a higher salary. She got the job, senior attorney, at $40,000 a year.

She started work on June 18, 1973, in Stamford, Connecticut, the company's new headquarters. GTE was the second-biggest phone company in the country. Sonia was the highest-paid woman at headquarters, and the first woman in the legal department, just as she'd been the first female attorney in the office of the general counsel at the EEOC. On her first day, the security guard directed her to the secretaries' elevators. Preconceptions among the higher-ups were no different, she soon found out. They knew women had to be hired because attitudes were changing, but they were reluctant to let women into their sacred spaces, like the executive dining room. When the man who'd hired her, George Shertzer, told her he'd be bringing her to lunch there, he joked that she'd be "the Jackie Robinson of the dining room."

Working in the legal section, she quickly realized that GTE was firing female employees who got pregnant. GTE was being taken to court frequently for this, cases were popping up all over the country, but the company was fighting them all. Sonia was appalled. "Listen, guys," she said, "it's crazy that you're fighting this." The Pregnancy Discrimination Act wouldn't pass until 1978, but the EEOC had already ruled that firing women because they were pregnant was unlawful, and it was clear that stronger legislation was on its way. Nothing if not dogged, she kept trying. "It's costing you a fortune to fight all these cases!" she pointed out. "The law is about to change," she argued. "Stop it!" she ordered. They didn't pay any attention. They said, "We are interested to hear your views on this, but we're not going to do it," and sent her away with a pat on the head.

Their response echoed, almost eerily, that of men at the EEOC when she'd tried to bring up women's rights. GTE was bearing huge costs in litigation, but they wouldn't give in. When the Supreme Court finally upheld the EEOC's decision, the company had to concede. Sonia was vindicated, but no one ever pointed out that she'd been right all along.

A company firing pregnant women would not have been news to Patt. Stewardesses were still required to immediately inform American Airlines if they became pregnant, and they would be taken off the line posthaste. If a stewardess didn't tell the company she was pregnant—in writing—she would be fired. A pregnant stewardess, then, had two options: to quit, or to request maternity leave. One who chose to take leave would be required to pass a medical exam upon her return and meet her previous weight standard, no exceptions. She would not accrue vacation time, sick leave, or enjoy sick leave benefits while out on maternity leave.

Patt hated this, but she was losing her energy to fight. She had resigned from her union position, and though she still served on a few local committees, her enthusiasm had waned. The negotiating team had scraped a few wins out of the latest contract in 1971, but in Patt's opinion the TWU reps hadn't done their best to secure the things the American stewardesses wanted. She was fed up. Stewardesses, she felt, were still being left behind, getting the scraps after other, male workers had fed. And there were more stewardesses working than ever before. In 1960, there had been 63 million passengers a year. In 1970, there were 169 million. And there had to be women on board to take care of them.

Patt knew that the average baggage handler at TWA, also a TWU member, made 24.4 percent more than the average stewardess in 1972, although becoming a stewardess required more training and education. Union dealings had established this discrepancy; why wouldn't they fix it?

Having to fight their battles on two fronts wasn't new to the stewardesses. After all, they'd been pushing back against sexism from management and passengers for years. But the abdication of responsibility by their union was another story. Patt spent more and more time reflecting on this. They paid dues to this organization, she thought. It didn't seem like too much to ask that it should stand up and represent its female members the way it did for the men. It was hard to get away from the idea that sexism was, in some way, built into the union structure.

She was even more discouraged because she could see bold change happening in the outside world, where outrage was manifesting itself as action. In July 1971, Bella Abzug, Shirley Chisholm, Gloria Steinem, and Betty Friedan, among others, organized the National Women's Political Caucus, with the aim of getting more women into office. Two months later, Martha Griffiths, ever the fighter for women, spoke out at congressional hearings on discrimination against women. She pointed out that in 1970 in Virginia twenty-one thousand women—and no men—were turned down for admission to state schools. The same year, the Professional Women's Caucus launched a class action suit against every law school in the country that received federal funding, citing discrimination against women. Title IX, which made discrimination on the basis of sex in regard to any educational program or activity illegal, was signed into law June 23, 1972. As Patt saw it, the playing field was being leveled everywhere she looked. Except in the cabin, where the progress of the last few years seemed to have stalled.

Exhausted by the sheer scale of the problems, and tired of explaining to both the company and the TWU that women workers were struggling, she retreated. She mostly kept her head down and did her job. And she did it well. Along with the new wide-body planes, the DC-10s and the 747s with double aisles, American had decided to institute a new system of authority. Someone would be put in charge of the other flight attendants learning the ropes on the new planes. Other airlines, those that hired men, had long had this position—the men were called "pursers" and they made more money and had more responsibility than the stewardesses they supervised. On American Airlines flights, executives decided, this position would be called "First Lady." Patt did additional training and became a First Lady in December 1971. The flight attendants, to a woman, hated the term; they associated the word "lady" with sex workers, and complained that it was too close to "lady of the night."

They were already battling the oversexed stewardess image the airlines were peddling; being called a "First Lady" they considered an additional humiliation. Eventually they would win the title change to "first flight attendant" in bargaining, and in the end it became "purser."

Downcast as she was, there was one legal victory that gave Patt hope. It all sparked from the position she'd just taken on: purser. And it would turn out to be a landmark case in the history of Title VII.

CHAPTER TWELVE

The Case of Mary Pat

IT WAS ANOTHER case of stewardess versus airline. Northwest Airlines had, a few years before, eliminated its age and marriage rules, and had opened up the purser position to women. It was a new age for women at Northwest! At least that's what the new contract said. The purser jobs, available on overseas flights only, comprised supervising the stewardesses and dealing with paperwork and customs when flying abroad, and they paid more than the flight attendant positions. In the past these jobs had been handed out to men without regard to seniority. It was infuriatingly common for a woman to be bossed around by a man who had less experience than she did, and was getting paid more money to boot.

Mary Pat Laffey was the stewardess taking on the airline. It wasn't the first time she'd stood up for rights, hers or other people's— she was one of the stewardesses who had appeared at the age discrimination hearings in front of Congress, and she'd attended the first EEOC hearings on stewardesses, full of hope.

Mary Pat had worked the line for years, starting when she was just twenty years old. Like Patt, she was active in the union, and she'd even been one of the negotiators for what she referred to in her own mind as the "liberation contract"—the one that had eliminated age and marriage rules at Northwest. Now, she decided, she wanted to become a purser. But it turned out that Northwest had other ideas. Though it had removed the men-only rule from the contract, it tried to get out of hiring women for the job by not posting bids. This was how jobs were advertised. The company would post the openings, and then employees would have the opportunity to "bid" for the jobs.

Instead of posting the bids for the new purser positions, the airline simply hired five young men with no airline experience whatsoever, "off the street," as Mary Pat put it. Mary Pat, furious to have missed her chance, called the director of labor relations. "Where are the bids?" she asked. She cited the new contract. He posted the bids. Mary Pat put in her bid.

The next step would have been to interview her for the job. Northwest prevaricated, saying they were coming up with a new test that all pursers would have to take; it would determine "supervisory potential." Six months went by. Finally, Mary Pat was permitted to take the new test. She got the highest score. The airline had run out of excuses. She became Northwest's first female purser. She was over the moon; finally, a chance to make more money doing essentially the same job she'd already been doing. And she wouldn't have to be bossed around by some young man who'd only been on the line a few months.

She had been a stewardess for a decade when she got her promotion. But the airline put her at the bottom of the purser seniority list, below even the men they'd recently hired who had no experience. The twist was that Northwest did employ some men as flight attendants, and when *they* were promoted to purser, they brought their seniority with them. But the union hadn't negotiated this—that stewardesses promoted to purser would retain their seniority—into the stewardesses' contract. She protested, again. The company agreed to give her the same level of seniority as the five most recently hired men, even though she had ten years of experience and the new hires had none. Then she discovered that her new salary was lower than what she'd made as a stewardess. Mary Pat persisted. She went to the union. Didn't the collective bargaining agreement say that accepting a purser assignment was not to be accompanied by a reduction in pay? It did. She got a raise. But since she had no seniority, she was assigned to the worst trips, thirteen-day military airlift command flights in and out of Vietnam during the Tet Offensive, even when shelling was going on. As a stewardess with so much experience, she'd been able to pick and choose her schedule. But those ten years suddenly didn't count.

After two years of this, the final straw was a strike by Northwest's ground workers, which meant a reduction in flights. Everyone on the purser list with low seniority was demoted; Mary Pat had to go back to being a stewardess. When flights resumed, Northwest began rehiring. But because she'd lost her decade of seniority when she became a purser, men with seven years less experience than her were being called back to purser duties before she was. Mary Pat had had enough. She called a lawyer.

Gil Feldman, the attorney who'd won Patt her job back, couldn't take the case, but he suggested she call Michael Gottesman, telling her "he's a genius at labor law." Mike immediately saw the potential for a class action suit: women were clearly getting paid less than men. They filed in 1970, citing violations of both Title VII and the Equal Pay Act, and went to trial in December 1972.

Mike threw himself into the case with enthusiasm. He loved the Northwest flight attendants; he thought them delightful and very smart. And they schooled him quickly about the inequalities on board. But as he prepared his arguments, some of the details of their working conditions struck him as truly bizarre. Why did the women have to be a certain height? he wondered. The company executives explained that if the stewardesses were short, when they reached into the overhead bins, too much leg would show. Mike deposed the company's vice president and asked how he had determined this. "We did a study," the man replied. Who had done the study? Mike wanted to know. The VP said he had done it himself. How? He'd brought in women of varying heights and had them reach up to the overhead compartment while he sat and watched. He decided when he was seeing too much leg and when he wasn't, and so the minimum height requirement was born.

The VP wasn't the only one who reacted badly to Mary Pat's efforts. The male pursers at Northwest had formed a "Purser Defense League" in 1971, upset about the legal actions their female colleagues were taking against the airline. Now they bruited it about that Mary Pat was going for the job out of sheer greed. One purser described her as "stealing the shoes for my children." Their comments got back to Mary Pat, but she carried on. Eventually, the airline executives told everyone to back off; they were just making her discrimination case stronger. After that she was ostracized by some of the pursers. They'd ignore her completely, just look right through her.

As the trial went on, Mike exposed a pattern of discrimination at Northwest. Women were being blocked from promotion. They received fewer benefits. Female flight attendants couldn't wear glasses, but men could. Women had to purchase a specific brand of luggage to use while in uniform; men could use whatever luggage they liked. Weight monitoring applied only to women, not men (the company claimed it monitored the men "visually"). Men got hotel rooms to themselves on layovers, but women had to share. The list went on.

Although no one in Northwest's management said it out loud, Mike suspected that the reason Northwest gave men single rooms was that most of the male flight attendants were gay, and in the atmosphere that prevailed in that era, Northwest feared there might be danger in allowing them to share rooms. Still, Mike thought, that wasn't a reason for forcing female flight attendants to share. During the trial, he brought it up. The VP testified that "we know that women in restaurants like to go to the women's room together, so we decided women liked to be together for their own security and that's why we put two of them into each room."

Under fire from Mike, and the testimony of stewardess after stewardess, Northwest did its best to argue its side, rehashing the same arguments the airlines had made in front of the EEOC commissioners during the BFOQ hearings. (The EEOC filed an amicus brief on behalf of Mary Pat and the stewardesses.) First, it argued that the duties of purser and stewardess were wildly different. This was easily disproved; the duties were almost identical and in many cases the pursers had an easier time of it, serving the smaller, slower-paced first-class cabin, while the flight attendants were rushed off their feet in coach. It was revealed that in many cases, the pursers were asking the stewardesses to do the purser duties anyway. Then Northwest pointed to the physical demands of the job: lifting cargo, working in the galleys. When Mike asked why and how these things got done on flights that didn't have pursers, there was silence.

Northwest protested that Asian (they used the word "Oriental") passengers, flight attendants, and officials both expected and were more comfortable dealing with male leaders than female. And, like so many airlines before, it argued that the high turnover rate of stewardesses made it more sensible to hire men because they were more "career oriented" and would stay longer with the company. Northwest, like its fellow airlines, had, of course, created that very high turnover on purpose with its age and marriage rules.

For Mike, it was an easy case to argue. The airline was so obviously in the wrong. And he could tell that the judge thought Mary Pat was sensational and found the whole case fascinating. Her story—just a woman trying to get a job, and the increasingly ludicrous lengths to which the company had gone to avoid giving it to her—was a compelling one. Mary Pat was soft-spoken and charming, but she had an iron will when it came to this issue. She had rallied the other women to join the case, and she won over male flight attendants too; they testified on her behalf about how the purser job and the stewardess job were almost exactly the same.

On November 12, 1973, the court decided in favor of Mary Pat. The purser and stewardess jobs were so similar, declared the judge, that the company was in violation of both Title VII and the Equal Pay Act. The wins were huge: stewardesses now had to be paid on the (higher) purser pay scale, and they'd receive back pay that was equal to the difference between their salary and that of a purser with the same seniority, going back five and a half years. The weight chart had to go, and those who had been suspended for weight were to receive back pay for the periods of their suspensions. Women were to be allowed to wear glasses. On layovers, the female flight attendants were to get single rooms, an issue that flight attendants at American were gearing up to do battle over. The total amount of money awarded to stewardesses was more than $20 million.

That win helped cement the enforcement of Title VII. The *Laffey* case was one that could be applied to working women in nearly all professions, helping to abolish the distinctions between "women's work" and "men's work," something that would have important ramifications for women in the decades to come. It also kicked off a series of deals that the country's biggest employers scrambled to cut with the EEOC, rather than wait to be taken to court the way that Northwest had. AT&T, General Electric, General Motors, and others all paid out huge amounts of money to aggrieved workers, and devised affirmative action plans to move women and minorities up the chain of command.

Though the decision in Mary Pat's favor launched rapid change at companies around the country, Northwest dug in its heels and appealed again and again. The case dragged on until 1984, with Mary Pat continuing to fly the whole time, though Northwest got rid of the purser role in the early 1970s. The job title became "lead flight attendant" and it went to the senior flight attendant on each flight, whether they were a man or a woman.

The final appeal was held in front of three judges: Ruth Bader Ginsburg, Robert Bork, and Kenneth Starr. When Mike learned who would be hearing his case, he was terrified: after nearly fifteen years of work, the final word would end up coming from a panel that included two notorious conservatives. He was comforted when, halfway through a point that his counterpart, Philip Lacovara, was making on behalf of Northwest, Bork interrupted, saying, "Mr. Lacovara, if you had a client who wasn't so obviously guilty, these arguments might have greater merit." Mike also faced a moment of indecision. Ginsburg had urged him to go out on a limb and make feminist arguments that he knew would annoy Bork and Starr. But he reined in the "women's lib" talk, trying not to be too aggressively pro–women's rights for fear he'd lose Bork and possibly Starr. It worked. They won everything Mary Pat and her fellow plaintiffs wanted. Ginsburg wrote the opinion; Bork and Starr concurred.

Thanks to compound interest and further awards from judges, the payout for Mary Pat and her fellow stewardesses totaled $63 million. It was the largest monetary judgment in Title VII history. Mary Pat continued to fly until she retired (Northwest changed the job title back to "purser" in 1985, after the case was settled). Her career lasted forty-two years. Her efforts had established case law that benefited women working at the biggest companies in the United States. Still, as Patt knew all too well, the airline industry was different. Although things had to change at Northwest, that didn't mean that life would improve at any other airline without a fight. But something was about to happen at American that would help Patt make real change: men came on board.

CHAPTER THIRTEEN

Men on Board

AS WITH SO many of the rights the stewardesses fought for, getting men on board took a legal decision. Celio Diaz was the plaintiff; he applied for a job at Pan Am in 1967, and was denied on account of his sex. He took Pan Am to court, where the airline argued that most men would be unable to adequately perform the duties of a flight attendant (they brought in a psychologist to testify that "feminine" traits, including benevolence and a genuine interest in the comfort of others, were essential to the job). After one loss and one appeal, Diaz won his case in 1971: the definitive barrier for hiring only women as flight attendants had been broken. The court's decision hammered home the point that a BFOQ exception to Title VII must prove that all, or substantially all, of one sex were unable to perform the job "safely and efficiently"; Pan Am's arguments that men couldn't do that were unconvincing. Treating the sexes differently, the court decided, could only be justified with a business necessity, not a business convenience. And using customer preference as an excuse for hiring only women (Pan Am had argued that their customers wanted female flight attendants) was prohibited, in line with EEOC guidelines.

The *Diaz* decision, along with the *Sprogis* decision, which was issued the same year, became case law. Employers taken to court in Title VII lawsuits would find, after *Diaz* and other flight attendant cases, that their ability to justify sex discrimination on the basis of the BFOQ would be much more restricted. As more flight attendants brought cases and the courts continued to agree with them that the BFOQ exception, as Sonia had suggested, was to be interpreted narrowly, companies were forced to open up new jobs to women, and to eliminate conditions (marriage, children, lifting heavy things) that had been used to bar or limit their employment.

Though Celio Diaz's suit was successful in forcing the airlines to hire men, he suffered the fate of so many women flight attendants over the years: he'd aged out of the job. When he'd applied in 1967, he was already thirty years old. Pan Am's cutoff age for applicants (occasionally waived for those with "outstanding qualifications"; it would not be waived for him) was twenty six.

The *Diaz* case was the end of the all-female cabin. Before *Diaz*, just a few of the almost forty airlines operating in the United States hired male flight attendants; in 1966 fewer than eight hundred out of eighteen thousand working flight attendants were men— although all the pursers were. Now men leapt at the opportunity to climb aboard. Pan Am's first class of trainees in 1972 was half male. The stewardesses, for the most part, welcomed them. When American started hiring men to crew domestic flights in 1973, Patt was excited. *Now*, she thought, we'll get things done. She foresaw using men as leverage to gain more concessions from the company; she had a list of longtime grievances that she planned to win by showing sex discrimination. Finally, she figured, the stewardesses would see some real changes.

Indeed, they'd gradually stop being called stewardesses, though there was no single moment when the title was formally changed to "flight attendant." After men started working in the cabin, "stewardess" was no longer all-encompassing, and "stewards and stewardesses" was long and awkward. The word "stewardess" had been coined by Steve Stimpson, who was credited with inventing the job in 1930 (along with Ellen Church, the very first to hold the position). Alternative names he'd debated and discarded included "courierette," "airette," "attaché," "skipperette," "attendant," and "escort." It was time for a final name change. From now on, they'd mostly use the gender-neutral "flight attendant," though as a joke some stewardesses started referring to male flight attendants as "ball bearings."

Brian Hagerty was one of the men who felt an unexpected urge to become a flight attendant. He was a chemistry student at the University of Texas, in Austin. It was 1973, and he was lying on a campus lawn reading *The Daily Texan* when he saw an ad for Eastern

Airlines. They were accepting male and female interviewees. He had a job already, working part-time for the IRS while he finished college, but being a flight attendant suddenly seemed like more fun. He interviewed and was hired, but had qualms; Eastern mostly just flew up and down the East Coast. TWA, he thought, was where he'd rather be. He was hired there, too. He decided to take the job. He'd worry about finishing his degree later.

At Breech Training Academy, TWA's Kansas City stewardess school, he was one of seven men in a class of fifty-five. Less than 10 percent, but still a not insignificant number. The men didn't have to go to the women's classes on makeup, or learn to walk in high heels; they had their own grooming classes and rules. Beards weren't allowed, but Brian had shaved his off before he got there. Mustaches had to be parallel with the upper lip. Nails should be neatly clipped. Manicures weren't feminine, they were told—"Wall Street traders get manicures." The men would sit around buffing their nails and cracking jokes. They'd laugh at the lessons, but had to pretend to take them seriously; if they snickered too loudly they'd be kicked out. Brian thought the whole thing was hilarious, especially watching the men he knew were fellow homosexuals trying to "butch it up." "Half of these guys are queens," he thought to himself, "but they behave like frat rats with the girls." On the weekends the trainees would go out to bars in Kansas City. Walking into a bar with seven women, he found, was a quick way to get men to buy you a beer; they hoped you'd introduce them to the stewardesses.

They learned tips and tricks of the trade. The best way to get the lint off the dark uniforms was to grab one of the strips of tape that were stuck onto the catering carts ("36 beef," "36 chicken," "36 pasta") and use them to pull off the fluff that seemed to accumulate constantly. Don't throw your coat in the overhead bin when you're working; hang it up on the back of the cockpit door so it doesn't get wrinkled. Make sure you take lip balm with you; there are boxes of it in Operations. They absorbed all the little things that added up to a professional appearance. TWA wasn't as strict as American; when men started training at the charm farm they were told to use makeup to cover up their five o'clock shadow.

Brian graduated, got his wings, and was sent to San Francisco.

He had just signed a lease on an apartment downtown when he

ran into trouble. It was one of his first nights on reserve, but he'd been fifteenth on the list, which meant the chances of his being called to crew a flight were practically nil; they'd have to call fourteen others before they needed him. But one morning, as he raced back home after an assignation with an American Airlines ticket agent he'd met in a bar, he was called. He heard the phone ringing as he unlocked his door and raced across the room to answer it, but they'd already hung up. Shit, he thought. He was fired. His new life as a flight attendant was already over.

He went back to work for the IRS, in an office on the nineteenth floor of the agency's Golden Gate building. He sat there all day long looking out the window at the airplanes taking off. After about five days, he said to his boss, "I can't do this. My heart isn't in paperwork. I'm going back to Austin to finish my degree." Still, he thought he'd take one last shot at a flight attendant job before he left San Francisco, interviewing with Pan Am. He'd likely be sent to London in the summer, they'd told him. Fantastic, Brian thought, thrilled at the idea. But as he arrived back in Austin, Pan Am withdrew their offer; the OPEC oil embargo had thrown everything into chaos. It went on all winter and into the spring of 1974, with lines at gas stations growing longer and the price of a gallon skyrocketing. Brian moved in with his partner, Paul. He finished his degree. He was interviewing for office jobs when someone told him American Airlines was hiring. He went straight to his car, drove out to the Dallas airport, and was hired on the spot. By September 10 he was at the charm farm; by October he was living in New York.

Tommie was sitting in Operations one day looking through the heap of file folders in her lap. This was union work, grievances she was taking with her on the flight she'd be working in an hour. It was late afternoon, and she'd be flying what they called a "three-hauler," a trip with three flight attendants in total. Dana was on this flight, too, flying the "number one" position, which meant that when they arrived at the hotel, Dana would get her own room and Tommie would be sharing with the third flight attendant. She looked up and saw a male flight attendant signing in. "Shit," she said. She put the folders down on the chair next to her. "Fuck." She stood up and strode away, heading into the bathroom and banging the door behind her. The man looked at the stewardess who'd been sitting next to Tommie. "Is it the single-room thing?" he asked. "Yes," she said. "But don't worry about Tommie. She'll get over it."

That was the first time Tommie met Brian. The stewardesses had always hated sharing rooms, but after men came on board it took on a whole new dimension. If there was an odd number of female flight attendants on a trip, at least one woman could count on having her own room, on not having to bunk with a stewardess from her flight or, worse, having to share with a complete stranger from another flight. Tommie especially hated that: arriving at the hotel, getting assigned a room, and then being told there was already a stewardess in there. She loathed having to go knock on the door, smile, and say, "Hi, I'm Tommie," and enter knowing full well the other woman had been hoping to have the room to herself. When the crew arrived at the hotel, it was infuriating enough to watch the pilots go off to their luxurious solitude, but to watch a man who'd been serving drinks with you, who was junior to you, saunter off with his own key—it made her blood boil. Tensions ran high. Brian was getting used to this hostile reaction. He tried not to take it personally, but it made things unpleasant.

Once they got on the plane, Tommie became friendlier. They were in the galley heating up trays at the same time, trying not to bump butts with each other every time they stooped down to get the trays out. They started chatting and Brian told her about getting fired by TWA. "That was you?" Tommie asked, her interest piqued. She'd heard the story through the union grapevine. Quick to sense an opportunity, she suggested that he come to a union council meeting. They swiftly became friends. Brian was a born storyteller, full of hilarity, and with the ability to make everyone laugh. He had shiny brown eyes that gave him an impish look, making you wonder what he was up to. He was also, as Tommie quickly discovered once she'd convinced him to do union work, a great researcher. If she asked him for paperwork, she could count on every detail being correct.

It took almost everyone some time to get used to the new normal, stewardesses and passengers alike. A *New York Times* article about the ingress of male stewards began with, "Tired businessmen flying home after a long day have come to expect a sweet, feminine smile from a stewardess at 35,000 feet as sort of a constitutional right as much their due as a safe landing. But soon they will look up from their newspapers to hear increasingly a masculine voice saying: 'Would you like a cocktail before dinner, sir?' "

The journalist went on to interview a newly minted Pan Am steward, who positioned the change as a win for equal rights: " 'Male passengers have always had somebody to flirt with, but that left out lots of single girls who travel,' said Barry Shelby, a 25-year-old Michigan State University graduate who started work this week as a steward for Pan American World Airways. 'Now the women will have somebody to flirt with,' he added . . . Mr. Shelby, the Pan Am steward from Michigan State, is a former Fulbright scholar who speaks Japanese and German. He said he had applied for his job largely because it offered a chance to travel, but he said a fringe benefit was being 'the only man among a lot of pretty girls.' 'When people, kid me about my job,' he said, 'I say this is man's liberation.' "

A full six years later, writing in the same paper, reporter Anna Quindlen interviewed a business traveler about the influx of male flight attendants. He still hadn't got used to it: "It wasn't until I saw my first steward that I began to take seriously the fact that these people are there for public safety and not just for drinks and decoration. And I'm still hesitant about asking a steward for something when there's a stewardess around." (Quindlen would continue to write about stewardesses for years, cheerleading them in their battle against weight regulations and other sexist work rules.)

Having men on the plane was, as Patt had envisioned, useful to the stewardesses at American in pushing back against the most infuriating appearance rules. For starters, men were leveraged to get rid of high heels. The men's uniform, newly designed by Bill Blass, was a white shirt, Tattersall jacket, and a wide navy, red, and white tie, with flat lace-up shoes. Heels, three inches high, were required for women, and multiple grievances had been launched about them without result. Now that men were doing the same job in flat shoes, the flight attendants took this issue to arbitration: they could clock up to eight miles of walking in a single flight, and heels were not only uncomfortable, they were impractical and caused back problems. Comfortable shoes for people who were on their feet for hours at a time didn't seem like a big ask. They won it. With this, Patt thought, as with so many other indignities, the fact that they had to go as far as arbitration was farcical. It is absurd, she thought to herself, that we have to negotiate to be treated equally and like human beings.

Still, she was actively making the most of having male colleagues. Every stupid rule that she'd hated, if she could find a sex discrimination angle, she filed a grievance about it. One was about nail polish, which was required for women. The airline said that colored nail polish, in management-mandated colors, was essential because it would hide any food the women might get under their nails while serving on the plane. This was mostly okay with Patt; she didn't love having to keep her nails polished and chip-free, but she understood. But once the men came on board, she started thinking, "Wait a minute. They don't wear fingernail polish. Why do we have to wear fingernail polish?" In fact, men were specifically forbidden from wearing it. She wrangled a meeting with Stu Peak, the base manager, and pointed out that men also got food under their fingernails. Stu knew he couldn't concede right then and there— management frowned on giving even an inch too quickly—and time passed, but right before the deadline for escalating the grievance, she was notified that she'd won. American put out a bulletin that colored nail polish was no longer required. Nails had to be neatly trimmed and polished with clear polish, but that was it. And the regulation applied to both men and women.

Dana, Tommie's good friend, found wearing makeup the most onerous of all the rules. It seemed minor, but women would be disciplined if they didn't make themselves up in accordance with regulations, getting C-314s for not having false eyelashes on. And if you got three of those, you were fired. Occasionally the union could get a malefactor her job back, but only if she promised to wear makeup from then on. Dana just couldn't stand it. She was a laid-back beach girl from Long Island, and the makeup rule was, for her, intolerable. Supervisors came and went frequently, and every time she got a new one she had to have the whole makeup discussion again. When the men came on board, she had the perfect excuse: they don't have to wear makeup, so why do we? "I don't think they're inherently better-looking than we are, so why do I have to doctor my looks?" she'd ask each supervisor. They'd usually go quiet and then wouldn't bother her about it anymore.

Dana wasn't on New York's union council, like Tommie, but she helped out occasionally, and one day she got a call from the union: there was a flight attendant who had gotten in trouble for not wearing makeup. Would she go to the airport and be the union witness? Dana balked. She didn't like drawing attention to herself, and always preferred working behind the scenes, but there was no one else to go. The woman was about to have the meeting with her supervisor and she was panicking. So Dana went. She wasn't supposed to say anything, she was just there as a witness, but she couldn't stop herself from asking a couple of questions. She felt nervous, but she probed little by little, mentioning men and how they didn't have to wear makeup, casually dropping in the word "discrimination." Management retracted the C-314.

Men also came in handy for finally getting rid of the dreaded girdles, and their accompanying "checks." Women had long been subjected to not just girdle and bra checks, but slip checks, too—having to lift their skirts for their supervisors to prove they were wearing one. It was humiliating, and the girdles were suffocating. The rationale behind bras and girdles was the supposed need for support: the airline didn't want any moving parts ("Patricia, you jiggle!"), everything had to be taped down. Dana had a friend who was five foot five and weighed under a hundred pounds; she couldn't find a girdle small enough. Patt filed a local grievance, again using men to point out the unreasonableness of the requirement. If support was so important, why weren't the men required to wear jockstraps? She wasn't the only one pushing back on this—it was happening across American, and at other airlines—and she won, one of a series of grievances the stewardesses filed that eventually got rid of the requirement.

Patt wasn't just leveraging her new male colleagues in various fights to spare women the wardrobe rules. She fought for the men, too. Robert Crandall, the senior financial vice president who would become CEO, was known to have a thing about hairy arms; Brian heard that he'd once declared: "I don't want anybody with hairy arms serving me a coffee." No passenger, he believed, would enjoy seeing a hairy arm hand over their dinner tray. So male flight atten-

dants could wear only long-sleeved shirts, no matter how warm the
plane or how tropical their destination. This was another control
issue, thought Patt. Any way management could cement their power
over their workers' bodies, they would. The union filed a grievance
and took it all the way to arbitration. They collected hundreds of
photos of anonymous forearms, men's and women's, and challenged
management to identify which belonged to which sex. They won
the arbitration, and short-sleeved shirts were added to the men's uniforms, but it was ridiculous, Patt reflected, that they'd had to spend
any amount of time doing that. Everyone knew some women had
hairy arms and some men didn't.

With the advent of male stewards, the percentage of homosex-
ual flight attendants went up. The gay men got along well with the
stewardesses for the most part. One reason, Tommie speculated, was
that the women recognized that these men also suffered from prej-
udice and unfair treatment. Brian found many of the most senior
women to be homophobic, though, and the pilots almost universally
so. Some pilots didn't want to work with male flight attendants at all;
they didn't even want a male flight attendant bringing them their
meals. The captain of the plane had significant power, and some of
the captains used it to rejigger crew schedules to avoid working with
male flight attendants. Others would simply avoid meeting their eyes
in crew briefings. In later years, when the AIDS epidemic was growing, some wouldn't touch plates male flight attendants had handled.
The cabin-cockpit relationship was often strained. "The Republicans
in the cockpit and the Democrats in the cabin," was how Tommie
always described it, succinctly summing up their differences. Most
of the men who began working as flight attendants fit in beautifully,
politically at least, with the cabin "Democrats." That disdain from
the cockpit was something the stewardesses recognized. It helped
bond them with the men, and they became a cohesive group. For the
most part, they thought, it was fun having men on board.

Brian found it easy to tell when another flight attendant was gay,
and as the planes got bigger and more men were hired, the chances
of there being more than one male flight attendant on board went

up. If there was another gay man on a trip, Brian would often meet up with him at the hotel and they'd go to dinner, or head to a bar. It depended on the city; sometimes there was a place to go and sometimes there wasn't. They wouldn't go out with female flight attendants all that often, but every once in a while one of the women would overhear them making plans and ask if they minded if she tagged along. Then they'd find out she was gay. Homosexuality was rarely spoken of in the cabin, but as work environments went, it could have been worse.

The general opinion, among the female and gay cabin crew at least, was that the straight men were the worst flight attendants. They were lousy workers, they were lazy, and they thought they were better than everybody else. They exuded a sort of hearty, frat-rat attitude, Brian found, particularly the ones from Dallas, and he referred to them collectively as "Joe Popular." Second to the pilots, they were the least sought-after coworkers on the plane.

Joan Dorsey, American's first Black stewardess, saw that male privilege playing out starting as far back as the interview stage of hiring. She was off the line now, working in recruitment, and she found that two out of three of the men she'd interview would at the end of the interview ask something along the lines of, "We get paid more than the female flight attendants, don't we?" She'd pause, letting silence fill the room. Then she'd say calmly, "Why do you think you'd get more money because you're a man?" And she found that they had no answer. "No," she'd go on, steadily pushing her point home, "you make exactly the same. If you add trips to your schedule, you can make more money that way. But you're not paid more. You're on the same salary as a female flight attendant." No sooner would she explain this to one candidate than another would come along and ask the same thing, and she'd think, "Oh, here we go again."

While there might have been a growing gay subculture, management executives weren't shy about their homophobia. In a 1969 New York State suit brought against the airline by a man who wanted to become a flight attendant, Lloyd Wilson of Pan Am testified that gay employees would be fired: "If we are aware of homosexuality as a trait or characteristic of an individual that can be made to stand up in a labor hearing with our union, there would be immediate dismissal." Delta's CEO, Tom Beebe, it was reported in the book

Delta Air Lines: Debunking the Myth, declared that the airline would "no longer hire any more male flight attendants, because they get restless and restlessness creates unions. Besides . . . they are gay as a three-dollar bill and we don't need any fags in the Delta family."

After Anna broke her heart, Patt had been convinced she'd never fall in love again. It had taken her a long time to recover, a period of self-questioning and lots of time alone. But then she met Kathy Williams, a flight attendant who was working her way through a PhD, and her feelings came rushing back. She and Kathy, who paired big earrings with an even bigger grin, flew together for a month, and they were sharing hotel rooms, which worked in Patt's favor. They started dating. Patt called her "Dr. Williams"; she called Patt "Captain Gibbs." They were together for months, but Kathy wasn't fully committed; she was dating a man at the same time. Then there was Miriam Sherman, another flight attendant. She and Patt dated for about a year, and even lived together for a short time, although Patt always kept her own place; after Anna she was wary about going all in. While she was in a relationship with Miriam, Patt got to know Shana, another union organizer. They had met playing softball. Patt offered her a ride home, just as she'd offered Anna a ride home all those years ago, and one thing led to another. Patt spent the night. Shana was married but had left her husband, and Patt started staying over at her cottage. She finally told Miriam, and they split up.

She and Shana got serious. They bought a house together in Teller. They both worked part-time for Shaklee, a multilevel marketing company, and they sold vitamins to other flight attendants on the plane. Patt was good at it; she made enough to get the down payment for the Teller house. They kept saving and bought a building on Becker Boulevard in Fort Worth, opening their own vitamin store.

Patt, while not officially "out," was coming into her own as a lesbian. She would never date a man again; that was something that seemed to belong to another age, another person. And the world was catching up around her. At the end of 1973 the American Psychiatric Association removed homosexuality from its official list of mental illnesses. Patt, certainly, was no longer questioning her sexuality, or if she'd ever fall in love again. She was empowered: finally doing on the outside what she'd long wanted to do on the inside. She felt hopeful. It might have been this new energy and confidence that propelled her back into union work.

CHAPTER FOURTEEN

Go Fly Yourself

ALONG WITH INCREASING numbers of men and gay employees on the planes, people of color were finally coming aboard in more significant numbers, though by 1972 still only around 6 percent of flight attendants were nonwhite, with Latinx and Asian Americans making up around half of that.

A few days after Martin Luther King Jr. was assassinated in 1968, President Johnson signed the Fair Housing Act, which mandated equal housing opportunities for everyone regardless of race. The Black Panther Party was at the peak of its power and influence. Still, in the world of the airlines, Black stewardesses remained second-class citizens. Discrimination was rife among stew zoo landlords who owned buildings near the airport; though they filled their apartments with airline employees, they often didn't want to rent to Black people. On layovers, when the crew arrived at their hotel, receptionists would sometimes house the Black women away from the rest, despite airlines' policies of keeping everyone—the women in particular—in rooms close to each other. Racism among the crew made itself known as well. Pilots would occasionally refuse to be served by Black flight attendants. And they made little attempt to keep their opinions hidden.

Cheryl Stewart had been jubilant to start her career as a flight attendant, but her first trip tempered her expectations. As the plane was landing in Arizona, the pilot called the cabin from the cockpit, and Cheryl picked up the phone. "Look here," he said, "you gals bring any other clothes with you?"

"Yes," she replied. "We brought clothes."

"Great," he told her. "I'm gonna take y'all to a meeting tonight. It's for the John Birch Society."

Cheryl had never heard of it. She'd go, she thought. Why not? He seemed friendly. When the stewardesses walked into the hotel, the captain was in the lobby—the cockpit crew got off the plane first, and their car had already arrived. He took one look at Cheryl, turned around, and said, "Girls, look here, we're not going to this meeting today. Y'all go have dinner or something." Cheryl didn't think much of it until she got to her room and called her boyfriend. "John Birch?" he asked. "Don't you dare go. They will hang you from a tree."

That was her first experience with the cockpit. From then on, she knew she'd have to be careful.

Sharing hotel rooms with white stewardesses was also fraught. Even if the senior woman was entitled to the single room, she'd sometimes give it to the Black stewardess, so that a white woman wouldn't have to share with her. If they did share a room, a Black stewardess might notice the white woman racing to use the shower before her, or skipping it altogether rather than use it second. Not long after the John Birch incident, Cheryl watched as a colleague, realizing that she'd have to share with Cheryl, asked the lead flight attendant if she could share her room instead. The lead flight attendant refused; her boyfriend was coming over. The other woman looked at Cheryl and said, "I'm not used to sharing a bathroom with a colored girl."

"Good," Cheryl told her. "Get your own room."

She didn't. Cheryl made a point of using the bathroom first.

The implementation of the Civil Rights Act had been the catalyst for a big recruitment campaign. Airlines had advertised in publications aimed at a Black audience, and searched for potential employees at historically Black colleges and universities. Even Afros were eventually permitted, although they were restricted to three inches. One day at work, Cheryl was pounced upon by a supervisor carrying a ruler. When the woman tried to place the ruler on her head, Cheryl, startled, asked what she was doing.

"I have to measure your hair," the supervisor told her. "Your hair has to be three inches."

Cheryl stared at her. "If it's not long enough, what are we going to do about it? And if it's too long, what are we going to do about it?"

"Um . . . I just have to record it," the woman told her.

"Fine," Cheryl told her. "You can put the ruler in it but you can't put your hands in it."

Her supervisor wrote down three inches.

Cheryl had gotten used to this by now. At the charm farm, during the standard end-of-school interview, her supervisor had asked—instead of the usual questions about whether she'd enjoyed her time there—"How does it feel to be colored?"

Cheryl asked her to repeat the question. When she did, Cheryl replied, "Well, tell me which color you want me to be and I'll tell you how it feels."

"What I mean is," the instructor amended, "you're the only Black girl here."

"Really?" asked Cheryl, the sarcasm dripping from her voice. "I never noticed."

Sharon Dunn also realized early that she needed to have her guard up. She was at the charm farm when she met another Black student, Brenda, in the hallway—they were two of the handful of Black trainees. They were both from Queens, it turned out, and they'd both endured the same questions from their white classmates—mostly not malicious, they'd tell each other, just uneducated. What did they use to wash their hair, things like that. There was a Black instructor at the charm farm by this point, a woman named J.J. Robinson, but she wasn't an ally. Sharon would sometimes try to catch her eye when something particularly egregious happened, like the stylist's utter failure to make her hair look like everyone else's, but J.J. was on the management track and never responded. Fine, thought Sharon. I'll just bite my tongue until I get out of here. When she met Brenda, they decided then and there that when they went on the line, they'd always bid together. Flying together was a strategic move: it meant they would never be the only Black crew member on board, and it gave them someone to vent to when, as often happened, the pilots would walk right past them without a word and go introduce themselves to the white flight attendants. Sharon and Brenda ended up bidding together for forty-one years.

Kat Clements, too, was getting a lot of practice at keeping her mouth shut. Kat was from Chicago, and she'd figured she'd become a flight attendant for a few years, pay off her student loans, and then go to grad school. She arrived at the stewardess college to find only one other Black woman in her class. Kat was biracial, with long curly hair and light skin—people often thought she was Puerto Rican—but she never felt at home in the campus beauty salon. Before arriving, Kat had been trepidatious, assuming that the company wouldn't know what to do with Black hair and skin . . . and they didn't. No one knew how to style her hair; she had to do it all herself. All the makeup was for white skin tones, the foundations half a dozen shades too light, the lipsticks a bright pink, the eye shadow an even brighter blue. She looked, she knew, ridiculous when she put it on, but the supervisors were oblivious. When they handed out beige panty hose, she almost laughed. But that was all there was. She wore her clown makeup, put on the beige panty hose, and kept her mouth closed. She just had to graduate and then she could escape.

Although the airlines were making efforts to diversify their ranks, flight attendant unions took few pains to integrate, or to use their power to open up the job to nonwhite applicants. In the mid-1960s, after the Civil Rights Act had passed, some added race non-discrimination provisions to their contracts, but this was a largely symbolic gesture. Sharon came from a union family—her grandfather had started the groundbreaking Brotherhood of Sleeping Car Porters union with A. Philip Randolph—and she stopped by a couple of American Airlines union meetings in her early years on the job. She came away with the distinct feeling that no one would be voting her into office anytime soon. If she were lighter-skinned, maybe. But probably not even then.

If you were a Black woman flight attendant, life wasn't easy, especially when you were dealing with the cockpit. At TWA, Kathleen Heenan would listen to the pilots, who mostly lived out in the wealthy white suburbs, complain that Black people were lazy, that the race protests and marches were uncalled for. Kathleen watched with pleasure as, over the years, the Black flight attendants she worked with pushed back against racism, becoming gradually more militant, refusing to let slights and racist remarks go by without a word.

And despite the industry's increasing recruitment of nonwhite cabin crew, attitudes at the top hadn't changed much. United's ads celebrated flights to Hawaii with a photo of two stewardesses beaming at a man in a suit. His face was turned away from the camera; no smile was required from him. In bold print under the photo was the line "The natives are friendly."

BOAC, which would become British Airways, ran an ad with a close-up of a smiling Asian stewardess, with copy that read:

> Stewardess Lancy Lee is an artist. When she's not flying, she's painting and writing poems on bamboo. Or studying Chinese abstracts. Or teaching children how to draw. Whether she's decorating a house, or cooking Moo Goo Gai Pen, the result is always beautiful. If Lancy's aboard your next BOAC flight to the Orient, watch every move closely. She's an art in herself.

Another BOAC print ad was mostly taken up with a photo of an Asian stewardess coyly biting a piece of paper that read, "Yasuko Nakamura." The text assured passengers that they wouldn't have to learn how to say it:

> Can't pronounce her full name? Try "Suki." Suki's more than beautiful. She speaks Japanese and English fluently. Understands modern jazz and customs forms. Can serve you sake, sushi, and teriyaki steak with ancestral grace, and say thank you so nicely you'll know she means it. She does.

The racist reference to "ancestral grace" aside, "Suki's" charm lay in the genuineness of her feeling. The "you'll know she means it" was no accident.

From the minute they set foot in the airport, the stewardesses smiled. Smiling was a nonnegotiable job duty. Sociologist Arlie Russell Hochschild wouldn't coin the term "emotional labor" until 1983 (when she did she was referring to stewardesses), but the performance of welcome, warmth, and friendliness was perhaps the most important part of the stewardess's work, at least according to the airlines. And the key element of the stewardess smile was its authenticity. Airline ads emphasized that their smiles were *real*. Another United ad showed a stewardess testing the warmth of the milk in a baby's bottle by shaking out a drop onto her forearm. "Enjoy your-

The Natives are friendly

We know you don't fly just to be smiled at.
So we add efficiency.
We have schedules that are convenient for you.
We fly more jets to more U.S. cities (and carry more passengers)
than anybody else.
And United Air Lines is the only airline that connects with every other U.S. airline.
We add extra care for your creature comforts, too.
"Extra care" is doing things nobody tells us to do, or maybe even expects us to do.
We prepare your meals ourselves, coast to coast,
which is something no other airline does.
We pay top prices for steak, and we have European-trained chefs
with a proper respect for beef like that.
And we never forget that you like to be smiled at, too.

"We've got a great movie today, Mr Bryant"

fly the friendly skies of United.

Stewardess Lancy Lee is an artist.
When she's not flying, she's painting
and writing poems on bamboo.
Or studying Chinese abstracts.
Or teaching children how to draw.
Whether she's decorating a house,
or cooking Moo Goo Gai Pen,
the result is always beautiful.
If Lancy's aboard your next BOAC flight
to the Orient, watch every move closely.
She's an art in herself.

Fly direct to Tokyo and Hong Kong from San Francisco or Honolulu on Rolls-Royce 707 fan jets.
And if you want to continue on to Singapore, Bangkok and around the world, BOAC will take you.
See your Travel Agent or call British Overseas Airways Corporation. Offices in all principal cities.

ALL OVER THE WORLD

B·O·A·C

TAKES GOOD CARE OF YOU

You may meet BOAC Stewardess Yasuko Nakamura when you fly from New York,
San Francisco or Honolulu to Tokyo and Hong Kong by Rolls-Royce 707 fan jet.

Can't pronounce her full name? Try "Suki."
Suki's more than beautiful. She speaks Japanese
and English fluently. Understands modern jazz
and customs forms. Can serve you sake, sushi, and
teriyaki steak with ancestral grace, and say thank you
so nicely you'll know she means it. She does.

All airlines are alike. Only people make them different.

ALL OVER THE WORLD

B·O·A·C

TAKES GOOD CARE OF YOU

Call your Travel Agent or British Overseas Airways Corporation

No floor show
just a working girl working

This is for real. No model. No put-on
smiles. Her name is Carol Koberlein.
But it could be Virginia White. Or Linda
Epping. Or any one of the other 1724
stewardesses who work for Delta. In her
new chic outfit, she looks like anything
but a stewardess working. But work
she does. Hard, too. And you hardly

know it. Even when she spreads Delta's
new eight-course, 1200-mile first-class
meal before you. Or a Tourist meal that
seems anything but economical. Next
trip, come see our working girls work.
It's no floor show. But it's funny how
you get to feel like
a leading man.

ＡDELTA

Delta is ready when you are!

self," the copy read. "And watch her smile. When our gals smile, you can easily tell that they mean it. We've got 2,769 of these bright-eyed young ladies. And not one of their smiles is pasted on." Pacific Southwest Airlines ran a television commercial in which a "smile inspector" walked down the line of flight crew, finally choosing one of the stewardesses to receive the "Smile of the Day" award. Even the nose of the plane had a smile painted on.

Delta, always resistant to selling sex, decided instead on an ad centered on a cheerful blond stewardess beaming her way down the aisle with a tray, above a tagline that read, "No Floor Show, Just a Working Girl Working." Her smile was genuine, Delta insisted. "This is for real. No model. No put-on smiles. Her name is Carol Koberlein." Delta would soon launch an entire campaign based on the "authenticity" of its stewardesses, using the names and photos of the "working girls" to drive home the point. Carol, the ad specified, excelled at working without seeming to: "In her chic new outfit she looks like anything but a stewardess working. But work she does. Hard, too. And you hardly know it."

The less being a flight attendant seemed like legitimate work, and the more the stewardesses seemed to enjoy doing it, the easier it was to convince passengers (and airline executives) that it wasn't what anyone would call a "real" job. Look how much fun the girls, in their short skirts, with their ear-to-ear grins, were having! The campaigns were doubly successful: propping up the demand for the emotional labor necessary to treat each customer as if they were the only one on the plane, while simultaneously convincing those same customers that the job was an easy one. And why would these girls, having such a good time for the few years before they married and settled down, want to be bothered with things like pensions, health care, and maternity leave?

National Airlines had the dubious honor of being the first to run a campaign that sparked serious action on the part of the stewardesses. The "Fly Me" campaign launched with a print ad that displayed a photo of flight attendant Cheryl Fioravante, all gamine haircut and smiles, looking straight at the camera. The big, bold headline read, "I'm Cheryl. Fly me." Other ads featured other women, all real working stewardesses, who also invited the viewers to "fly" them. The campaign was a massive success. It had a theme song, and merchandise that included mugs and T-shirts with the famous slogan. The airline even painted the names of the female employees on the outside of the plane, so you really could fly Donna or Linda or whomever.

The campaign infuriated the stewardesses. They hated these ads with a passion. Grinning male passengers began asking them, "Can I fly you today, baby?" The stewardesses joined the almost equally angry members of NOW who were picketing outside the office of the New York advertising agency that had created the slogan. Marching in circles, they sang at the top of their lungs, "I don't have propellers and I don't have wings. I don't have none of those mechanical things. I'm only a woman, and as you can see, I can sure be walked on, but you can't fly me." Their picket signs read, "Go Fly Yourself." The agency owner, Bill Free, tried to quell the protests by handing out bouquets of roses to the marchers. New signs were made. They read, "I'm Bill—Fire Me."

NOW also picketed National's ticket offices in New York, Washington, D.C., and Philadelphia, and asked its members to write letters to the airline. It didn't stop the airline from running the ads; the campaign had paid off in spades. National had a 19 percent increase in revenue per passenger mile in less than a year. The agency created a follow-up ad, starring Cheryl again. This time, the headline read, "Millions of people flew me last year."

Getting the message across to people about sexism was the hard

part. In some ways, the fight for equality was everywhere you looked: Shirley Chisholm was running for the Democratic party's presidential nomination and Ruth Bader Ginsburg was creating the Women's Rights Project at the American Civil Liberties Union, focused on dismantling, as far as possible, sex discrimination. But people still had to be educated and it seemed to be all women doing the educating. Carin Clauss, who would become the first female solicitor of the Department of Labor, was working as a DOL lawyer when she flew to a meeting in Paris with colleagues. A few of them were wearing the "Fly Me" T-shirts. "That's sexist," she pointed out. But they just couldn't see it. To them it was normal. These were men committed to writing and enforcing the laws against discrimination; it was in their very job description, just as it had been for the commissioners at the EEOC whom Sonia had pushed, desperately, to take on cases for women's rights. A situation where a factory would pay its male and female packers a different wage, they understood as sex discrimination. But wearing a "Fly Me" T-shirt—what was wrong with that?

CHAPTER FIFTEEN

Stewardesses
for Women's Rights

ON SEPTEMBER 20, 1973, ninety million people watched Billie Jean King beat Bobby Riggs in a tennis match billed as the "Battle of the Sexes." Patt was on a layover, and all the stewardesses on the flight crowded into her hotel room to watch, eyes glued to the television. When Billie Jean won the third straight set, they cheered and whooped, elated. She was, they felt, proving their point: they could do anything men could do. The women's movement had made them feel more empowered than they ever had before. And Billie Jean was scoring point after point, it seemed, just for them.

Tommie was watching too; everyone was. She was with Dana and Al, and she was scared to death Billie Jean would lose. It felt to Tommie that Billie Jean was carrying all womanhood on her shoulders when she walked onto the court. This is what it must be like to watch your kid play sports, she thought: feeling excited for them, but terribly nervous that they'd fail. But she could see that Billie Jean seemed to be enjoying herself and was full of confidence, and that was, in its own way, exhilarating. Billie Jean was a passionate campaigner for women in sports. Earlier that year she'd threatened to boycott the U.S. Open unless they paid the women's tournament winner the same as the men's, a fight for pay parity to which stewardesses could relate. Her advocacy got results: the U.S. Open became the first major tournament to equalize the prize money for men and women. Still, even though she was a world-famous tennis player earning more than $100,000 a year—and supporting her law student husband—Billie Jean couldn't get a credit card unless it was in her husband's name.

The early 1970s in the United States were a period of startling contrasts when it came to women's rights, a maelstrom of liberating legislation and pushback against the advance of feminism. At the beginning of the decade, women who wanted to buy property could be required to provide their husband's or father's signature on the contract. Divorced women had trouble getting credit cards; a woman applying for one would often be asked if she planned to have children. In North Carolina, only a virgin could charge a man with rape. On average, a woman needed a college degree to earn more money than a man with an eighth-grade education. But 1973 was also the year of *Roe v. Wade*, the Supreme Court decision that legalized abortion on the federal level, striking down state laws that banned it.

Texas had been one of those states where abortion had remained illegal even as other states, like New York, legalized it (New York made it legal in 1970). Young women in Texas who needed abortions would come up to New York on charter flights to get one; even before she'd moved to New York, Tommie and her friends had pooled money to buy a friend a plane ticket.

Tommie was feeling the push and pull of the times. She and Al moved to Bronxville, a town about fifteen miles north of Manhattan, in 1973. A few months later the apartment next door opened up and Dana moved in. Bobbi still lived in the city, but she frequently hopped on the Harlem line and came up to visit. Al was working for the Bank of New York, in its still-nascent computer department. He and Tommie took trips with her free travel passes, went to parties, had an active social life, Tommie usually in her bell-bottom jeans, Al in corduroys and a flannel shirt. They discussed having kids, but Tommie wasn't ready for her career to be over. And her activism had found a new outlet.

Bobbi, Dana, and Tommie were all working the same flight the day *Ms.* magazine published its first issue. As often as possible, they'd bid for the same schedule so that they could fly together; it was more fun that way. It was the summer of 1972, and they had spotted the magazine on a newsstand and bought a copy to share, poring over it when they could snatch a free moment in the galley. The next day Tommie was heading off on a three-day trip, but no one was willing to give the copy up. They went back and bought two more.

They weren't the only ones mesmerized by the magazine. The

first issue sold out in eight days. The editors received over twenty thousand letters. Twenty-six thousand people subscribed. Gloria Steinem and Patricia Carbine, the cofounders, had long been activists, but with *Ms.* they cemented their place in feminist history.

Tommie read every word of that first issue of *Ms.*, down to the classified ads. Articles included a comparison of Nixon's and McGovern's views on women's issues, instructions on "de-sexing" the English language (using "police officer" rather than "policeman," or changing "stewardess" to "flight attendant"), and a satirical article titled "I Want a Wife!" about women who wanted the kind of support that housewives provided to men. Here, finally, was media coverage of issues that mattered to *her.*

But the thing that changed her life was a tiny ad, tucked away at the very back of the magazine. It was a notice about a meeting, to be held in a church basement in the Village. Women, it announced, were invited to attend to discuss the founding of a new group, to be called Stewardesses for Women's Rights. "Oh my God," thought Tommie. "We have to be there." When the day came, she, Bobbi, and Dana walked in, clutching the brown bag lunches they'd been instructed to bring, dying of curiosity. They spotted a couple of women they knew in the group of thirty or so stewardesses already there. But their eyes were drawn immediately to the woman sitting at a table with long hair parted down the middle. It was Gloria Steinem.

This was one of the "click!" moments that the women's movement (and *Ms.* magazine) were always talking about, those moments of recognition and change that suddenly shifted how you saw everything in the world. Patt had had her share, maybe more; Tommie hers. But this moment—meeting a group of like-minded women, stewardesses from other airlines and from theirs, who were sick of the status quo, not to mention the added glamour of the support of the world's most famous feminist—was another. *This* was empowerment: sisters who didn't need you to explain *why* it was humiliating to be forced into a miniskirt, women with enough rage in them to take action.

Sandra Jarrell was the first speaker. She had been a stewardess for Eastern, and had been fired when she gained weight. It had been her idea, along with Jan Fulsom, who had quit when a drunk passenger had torn off her skirt and the captain had simply laughed at her, to form the group. They had been the ones who posted the ad in *Ms.* Sandra talked about the hot issues, the discrimination problems they were all ready to say goodbye to. Her frustration with the airline and her anger at her own powerlessness were obvious. Sandra, it was clear, had had enough. It was time, she said, to form an organization that fought for the rights of stewardesses. Tommie found herself nodding along without even noticing she was doing it.

Gloria asked everyone to sit in a circle, a move that would become a Gloria trademark, as well as a standby of women's consciousness-raising groups. No one sits at the head or the foot, everyone is equal. Then Gloria spoke. She made a point at that first meeting: the stewardesses could do their own part for the women's movement. "Why didn't we think of this before?!" she cried, only half joking. "You're the ones that fly congressmen in and out of Washington! You're articulate, you've been trained to speak in public. I can't believe that it's taken us this long to realize that you guys are an unbelievable vehicle for women's rights."

She was organizing.

(It was true that flight attendants had unique access to politicians. Dusty Roads often flew with congressmen, her friendliness opening conversations into which she might drop a reference to the plight of the stewardesses. Once, Richard Nixon offered her a ride from the airport into Washington, D.C. When they got to her hotel, Nixon got out and opened the door for her. "Thank you, Mr. Nixon," she said. He replied, "Any time, Dusty.")

When it came time, toward the end of the daylong meeting, for everyone to share their stories, Dana was moved to speak up. She was in shock, she began. She told the group that when she had first started flying, she didn't really want to be identified as a flight attendant. The popular image of a stewardess was of a dumb sexpot, and she didn't fit that image and didn't want to. So she had isolated herself a little bit from her coworkers; she would sit and read instead of joining in with the other stewardesses' conversations. Dana had been in this meeting for a full day, and all of a sudden, she told the room, she had realized that by acting like they were beneath her she was doing to all her coworkers what she didn't want anybody to do to her. She'd spent hours listening to all these incredibly bright women who were flight attendants and realizing, "Holy shit, there's a lot of really cool people here." Gloria sat there listening, and nodded her head in agreement, as if to say, "Yes, I get it, I get what you're saying." It wasn't really a click, Dana thought to herself afterward. It was like a big clonk on the head. And it was one she never forgot.

Tommie, Dana, and Bobbi walked out of the meeting exhilarated. They knew they wanted to be part of this. It was what they had been waiting for.

Stewardesses for Women's Rights, quickly shorthanded to "SFWR," rapidly became official. It wasn't affiliated with any union or any airline; it was open to all stewardesses. Not all stewardesses would be interested (some groups, like the Texan stewardesses Tommie referred to as the "Dallas dollies," embraced the weight and appearance regulations, thinking it was a good idea to "get the fatties out" of the business), but the work SFWR did would go on to affect all of their careers.

Tommie, Bobbi, and Dana were already members of NOW, attending local meetings and chairing occasional committees, rallying to its slogan "Womanpower, it's much too good to waste." The trio had even gone to a NOW convention once, but Tommie had hated it. The women there, she thought, were completely divided. There were the old-school feminists, what she thought of as "the Friedan party," as in Betty. There was the younger, white, lesbian group. And then there were the women of color. "It's the National Organization for *Women*, people!" she thought to herself. "Get it together!" SFWR, on the other hand, was a smaller group, more cohesive, and a fount of camaraderie, somewhere it was clear she could make a difference. She was energized, not enervated, which was the way she'd felt at the NOW conference. Still, she would come to appreciate NOW's assistance with SFWR projects as the years progressed. Some NOW leaders would attend SFWR conferences. They'd offer the wisdom of NOW's advising council; they even helped picket the airlines. But NOW's agenda was general, enormous. Stewardesses for Women's Rights could make change right here, right now, in Tommie's life.

Word spread fast. Filled with passion, Tommie, Bobbi, and Dana couldn't stop themselves from mentioning SFWR to every stewardess they saw. Then, in January 1973, *Ms.* ran a feature on SFWR titled "Stewardesses Against Coffee-Tea-Or-Fly-Me" (Shirley

Chisholm was on the cover). As word of the new organization made it to stewardesses in other cities, women started reaching out. Letters flowed in from stewardesses who had read the article and wanted to know more about SFWR. In these letters, often written on hotel stationery, they shared their stories of various indignities, copied out the addresses of other women they thought might be interested, asked if there were local chapters they could join. They made general comments on men's attitudes ("Some men do not acknowledge a woman's authority, either in her job or in the home"), complained about executives who refused to allow slacks as part of the uniform ("because of his own personal preferences. He won't even let the women in his dept. wear pants to work"), and cheered the airlines that let them wear trousers ("I saw the new uniform. It's great—pants, a dream come true. I'm telling the pilots to get a good look at my legs now because when we get our new uniforms it's going to be a privilege to see my legs.")

They shared their fears, enthusiasms, questions. One woman had received four anonymous letters in her work mailbox accusing her of being a lesbian; she believed them to be from pilots. Some wanted to "strip away all these ridiculous, arbitrary rules and regulations, and make this job professional the way it should have been in the first place." Others wanted to join but were too afraid of retaliation from their employers.

That the union didn't take their concerns seriously was a constantly recurring frustration. Some complained that their representatives were too weak, or had too close a relationship with management, or refused to protect them when their jobs were threatened because they'd gained weight. Letters referenced instances where they felt the union couldn't or wouldn't help, or had even connived with management against them. The TWU's multiple vice presidents, women reported, were more concerned with issues like retirement benefits for the mechanics than with getting flight attendants single rooms or taking a stand against sexist advertising. When stewardesses turned up at union meetings, they found the leadership quick to dismiss their concerns, telling them their complaints were irrelevant and unimportant. The idea, still radical to many, of running for union leadership positions themselves was broached: "If we could get Stewardesses for Women's Rights active, then we could vote our own ideas in, vote equality into the unions, it's not an impossible thing . . . What does it take to run for union representative? It's nothing but saying I wanna run as a union representative."

One new member proposed a revolutionary (and prescient) alternative: abandoning the traditional, male-run union structure altogether. "Perhaps," she wrote, "we could ultimately arrange the withdrawal of all F/A's [flight attendants] from all 3 unions and form our own by about the time we have someone groomed to head it. This seems to me to be the only alternative to a rotten, self perpetuating oppression from labor unions. Maybe it's a dream, but then you need one to start with!"

The problems they described were deeply rooted, but Tommie took heart from these letters. She was optimistic about making changes in the union and in the airlines. Now she could really see just how many of her sisters felt as she did. Together, she thought, they could do it.

SFWR felt, to Tommie, at once clandestine and gloriously empowering. They weren't doing anything wrong, but it *felt* as if they were. Even the mundanity of answering the letters offered the possibility of change. How could they educate other women not to fear the feminist movement? women wrote in to ask. How to convince the young stewardesses, who "feel that Prince Charming is gonna come so what difference does it make and they don't get involved," to start taking action to improve working conditions? Tommie knew these women, the ones waiting for Prince Charming. They were the ones sharing the galley with her, the ones who thought of the job as a way to travel on the cheap and put in a fun year or two before settling down. Still, the letters coming in to SFWR showed her that there were other types of women out there.

Something had shifted. Discovering one another, scattered as they were throughout the various airlines, was a catalyst for action: there were other women who felt just as strongly that the weigh-ins were unjust, who objected to being called "girl" by the pilots, who dreaded the stares of the male passengers as they conducted safety briefings in go-go boots. For Tommie, walking into a meeting to find kindred spirits was something that seemed to soothe the soul and gird the loins at the same time. Being in the same room, hearing similar stories, reading the same articles, coming together from cities across the country—it was powerful. And power was, she thought, something they'd been short of for a very long time.

The mission of SFWR expanded with each additional member, but after much discussion they decided on their primary goals. These were: to force improvements in health and safety, primarily in regard to radioactive cargo; to shame the airlines and advertising agencies out of exploiting the "sexy stewardess" image; to move more women into leadership positions, both in the union and in airline management; and to help stewardesses feel empowered as professional working women. To Tommie, it all seemed gloriously possible.

Her enthusiasm was buoyed by the luminaries who'd appear at their meetings. Gloria Steinem was the undisputed figurehead of the women's movement and she was coming to their basement lunches! Florynce Kennedy, the lawyer, mesmerizing speaker, and provocative activist (she was the one who had chained herself to the Miss America puppet at the 1968 pageant protest), came to a meeting, and Tommie, Dana, and Bobbi shared a cab with her afterward, sitting like worshippers at the feet of a deity, struck entirely dumb with excitement. Margaret Sloan-Hunter turned up; she was a *Ms.* editor as well and a founder of the National Black Feminist Organization. With the help of these women, and each other, what couldn't they do?

They agreed that Sandra should be the national coordinator—SFWR had been her idea, after all—and everyone else pitched in as necessary. New York became the official headquarters, and chapters opened up rapidly in Chicago, San Francisco, and other cities. Any member could contribute ideas and items to the meeting agendas. National conferences, they decided, borrowing the idea from NOW, would be a way to bring together stewardesses from around the country.

Losing no time, they scheduled their first national conference for March 1973. The entrance fee was just $5. Around a hundred stewardesses filed into the Washington Square United Methodist Church in New York to meet fellow members, find a sympathetic audience for their anger, and hear from a formidable lineup of speakers: Gloria Steinem, Margaret Sloan-Hunter, Betty Southard Murphy (a feminist lawyer who would advise SFWR on legal matters for free), and Kathie Sarachild, an activist in the Redstockings, a radical feminist

group. These women were at the vanguard of the feminist movement, women who could express succinctly and convincingly the
reasons why the stewardesses could and should push back against
their employers. Tommie, Bobbi, and Dana were enthralled.

Union leaders, though, were noticeably absent. When Sandra
Jarrell gave the keynote address, she explained why. "Perhaps the
most obvious tool available for remedying the injustices we are subject to are the unions," she said, adding drily, "unfortunately, unions
do not have the reputation of representing the interests of women at
the bargaining table."

The two-day conference neatly balanced the external—
explaining the tangible ways a stewardess could fight injustice at
her company—and the internal, encouraging self-examination
through voguish ideas such as consciousness-raising. With a flour-
ish, the organization's new symbol was introduced. The pictograph
for "female"—one vertical line crossed by another and topped with
a circle—had been given wings stretching out to the right, in the
same style as the wings that were pinned on stewardesses when they
qualified. But with a decidedly feminist twist.

Tommie loved it. The symbol was immediately added to the
organization's newsletters and other materials, printed on T-shirts
that they wore when they were doing informational picketing and
weren't permitted to wear their uniforms, and turned into pendants
for necklaces. Wearing this necklace when on duty was against regulations, but as soon as Tommie took her uniform off, she put her
necklace on.

In June 1973, SFWR received an unexpected windfall: a $25,000 (around $153,200 in 2021 dollars) grant from the Stern Family Fund, a small New York foundation that supported organizations trying to bring about social change. The women were over the moon; this was a fortune. They designated $9,000 to pay for a full-time executive director position, which meant the organization became more hierarchical. That decision didn't sit well with the more collective-minded, grassroots-inclined members, who had embraced the 1970s tendency toward more horizontal group structures. But the grant bestowed a thrilling sense of legitimacy on the organization and its members.

Another stroke of luck was the unexpected opportunity to open an office in Rockefeller Plaza, the luxury building in midtown Manhattan known colloquially as "30 Rock." They got it cheap, through a friend of a friend, moving gleefully into a mezzanine space with five rooms that seemed enormous for a fledging organization. They cobbled together furniture, constructed a lounge. They filled a library with materials on the women's movement, the airline industry, alternative careers, and travel, inviting off-duty stewardesses to come and browse. Thumbing their nose at the corporate stylings of their 30 Rock neighbors, they added potted plants, colored candles, low tables, and comfy chairs. In January 1974, filled with excitement, they threw an official office opening party. Al, Tommie's husband, was the party's bartender; he'd been informally designated the "first husband" of SFWR.

They planned out the guest list carefully, inviting colleagues they thought might be interested, and reporters, of course. And they decided to invite airline management, both their supervisors and company executives. It felt reckless, inviting these people to a party celebrating an organization that was set up to oppose so many of the airlines' policies, but they were filled with daring. The address was impressive and they knew that showing off a little would make management take SFWR more seriously. Upper management instructed the flight attendant supervisors not to attend; SFWR was, they said, a dangerous and subversive group. They showed up anyway, dying to satisfy their curiosity. The women in management who had once been flight attendants and then moved up in the ranks were especially eager to see what SFWR was about; they arrived in mink coats that showed off their new status, which Tommie thought was ridiculous. On occasions when the flight attendants picketed in front of American headquarters, calling attention to their working conditions, a flight attendant would sometimes show up in a fur coat if it was a cold day. "Go home," Tommie would always tell them. "Your salary could not pay for that."

"My boyfriend gave it to me!" they'd protest.

"It's inappropriate," Tommie would point out. And she'd send them off the picket line. It was that kind of education of other women that she, learning from Gloria and Florynce and Margaret, found herself employing to good effect.

The press also accepted their invitations with alacrity. Reporters came from *Women's Wear Daily* and the *New York Post*, suffused with curiosity to see what these young stewardesses were up to. Dana was interviewed by a young journalist who asked her about makeup. Dana, per usual, wasn't wearing any. She told the reporter that she had to battle each new supervisor over the makeup issue, and point out that the men didn't have to wear it. If she had to, Dana told her, picking up steam, she'd take American to court! The reporter, Anna Quindlen, reported it faithfully.

Plunging ahead and newly energized by their Stern grant, SFWR held a second national conference the same year, this time in Chicago. This conference had two themes: the stewardess image and job advancement. Discussions were held about how they could carve out individual identities in an industry that wanted them to look identical. One airline ad in particular epitomized this problem. Delta, the most prudish of the airlines, avoided overtly selling sex. Instead, their ads reflected the interchangeability of the women. A print ad featured a photo of a blond stewardess laughing with a male passenger as she holds his coat. The copy read:

Delta is an air line run by professionals. Like Rose Wynne, Stewardess.

Rose beat out 24 other fine applicants to enter Delta's rigorous training program and passed with flying colors. She loves being part chef, part wine steward, part mother, part sweetheart and part hostess. And the nice part about it is we have 3,800 Roses.

Other ads featured "4,000 Christas" and "2,200 Anitas." The sop to their identity as workers ("professionals") didn't mitigate how all these Roses loved being part mother and part sweetheart. Captains and other male employees were also featured in the campaign, but as individuals, not one of thousands in a matching set, and there was no mention of their attractiveness.

The energy crackled. Tommie was in her element: being thrown together with a bunch of new people, sharing stories, trying workshops. (A panel titled "Ourselves" was convened to talk about the psychological effect the stewardess image had on the workers—were they really just one of 3,800 Roses?) No one had much money, they shared hotel rooms and snacks, but they all had the same hunger to make change and every moment was interesting. They created task forces (for health and safety, membership, public relations, fundraising), elected new officers, proposed bylaws. Tommie came home exhilarated.

The Chicago conference was Cindy Hounsell's first. She went alone, the only one from Pan Am to attend. She was more of a loner than many of the other, more gregarious stewardesses, but the camaraderie at the conference was irresistible. One woman approached her in the lobby and asked if she wanted to share a hotel room to save money; they stayed friends for years afterward. The psychological focus spoke to her; and when the speakers discussed the pressure from employers to smile and give themselves emotionally as a part of the job, it resonated.

The attendees all stayed in the same hotel, adding to the feeling of kinship, and they forged connections over shared realizations. Cindy listened to a woman break down in tears as she spoke about how she'd fight with her boyfriend every time she got home from a flight. And then other women spoke up; the same thing happened to them. The psychologists at the conference helped them to understand that their mental health was compromised by their job and it was not their fault, and that the desire to push back against the expectations of the airlines and the public was not in fact some kind of defect. With the airlines exerting such exacting control over their appearance and behavior, it was common for the women to feel that there was something wrong with them if they didn't want to wear makeup, or take amphetamines to stay under 120 pounds. In Patt's inelegant metaphor, they had all, to some extent, been plugged into the airlines' umbilical cord. But now the conference was helping women realize that the problem was not self-generated. The rage they felt had strong parallels to what Betty Friedan had described in *The Feminine Mystique*. And the panels, which gave practical advice on how to change the public image of a stewardess, deal with pilots, and counter misconceptions about the feminist movement, gave them the tools to channel that rage into change.

Cindy, well-spoken, with prematurely salt-and-pepper hair that she refused to dye, had taken a couple of years to get active in the union. She had marched at the women's strike and had joined NOW's New York chapter right away, but it wasn't until several years after she'd started flying that she became involved in the labor movement. She'd been enjoying the perks of working for glam Pan Am: she'd frequently fly to London, eat at wonderful restaurants, see Judi Dench in a West End production; she saw so many world-class plays that it ruined theater for her ever after. How many young women get to do this? she asked herself. Even the work itself had an air of class that other airlines couldn't quite match. Pan Am dished up *real* food, big trays of coq au vin, or Wiener schnitzel, depending on which country they were flying to. Passengers knew they could ask a Pan Am stewardess for a recommendation on where to buy a handbag in Milan, or where to find the best bistro on the Left Bank. All the stewardesses spoke at least one foreign language.

She started small, joining the health and safety committee, which didn't meet very frequently. Gradually, she'd been getting angrier about working conditions, and the union, she thought, was the place to do something about it. She joined more committees. She scaled up at SFWR, too, becoming a regional coordinator, and the head of the New York chapter.

Cindy felt herself growing more and more frustrated over the fact that many of her fellow stewardesses couldn't have cared less. As she became more active in the union, fighting for benefits like maternity leave, she'd encounter bewildered stewardesses who wondered out loud why she cared when she wasn't even married. The majority of stewardesses weren't feminists, but, she thought, they were quick to take advantage of the rights feminists had fought for. They'd ask for special "lines for mothers," so they could fly just on the weekends. They'd ask if the union could get them off a trip when their babysitter canceled. Cindy would smile and nod, thinking to herself, I could kill you. At Pan Am she was especially lonely, which was the reason she joined SFWR. She came to the second meeting, held in the same church basement in the Village. SFWR could at times feel dominated by American Airlines stewardesses—they were the majority—but Cindy sympathized; they did seem to have an especially hard time. At Pan Am, when she'd bring up SFWR's conference on safety, or their campaigns against sexist advertising, people would look at her and say, "Well, that has nothing to do with us." Cindy dragged a couple of friends along to meetings, but they would never have gone on their own. Some stewardesses would cheer SFWR on—"That's great, there's Cindy and her group on TV"— but never joined in. Even the appearance standards didn't seem to bother her colleagues that much. They'd shrug them off, blaming those over the limit for their weight problems, and assuming that if the company suspended someone, it must be for a good reason. "If I had to organize these people into a union," she thought, "I never would have got them in."

She didn't get much sympathy from the newly minted businesswomen who began flying in the early 1970s, either. When she started seeing women in business class, she was thrilled. But they didn't treat her like a fellow career woman. She'd enthuse about how wonderful it was to see a woman in business class; they'd thrust their coat into her hands and open a magazine.

Recruiting became Tommie's passion. She made extra certain to wear her SFWR necklace on layovers when the crew all ate dinner together. Someone would be sure to ask her about it; she'd explain, and always just happened to have the latest newsletter in her flight bag and would they like to read it? She'd try identifying potential members on the car ride from the airport to the hotel, or in Operations, picking out women she thought might be interested and approaching them. One of those, as it happened, was Patt.

They were both working hard for the union by this point. Patt, reinvigorated, was plunging ahead with using men's incursion into the cabin to gain more rights for women, while Tommie was looking at bigger and bigger leadership roles in New York. Patt had decided to run to become a negotiator, a position elected by the membership, and the ballot count was being held at the union's New York headquarters. Tommie, who was on the ballot committee, was one of the vote counters. Patt lost. Afterward, when Tommie ran into her in the hallway, she blurted out, "You're the infamous Patt Gibbs!" Patt's reputation had preceded her.

Tommie knew their styles were polar opposites: Tommie would solve problems by talking and communicating, while Patt was known for going bullheaded at something and refusing to back down. It was a friendly meeting. Tommie sympathized over the lost vote. She handed over a newsletter and invited her to an SFWR meeting, telling Patt she should think about getting involved. She knew Patt was a feminist. And Patt went. She had a free night in New York, and why not? Gloria Steinem was there and Patt was duly impressed, but she decided not to get too invested. She had union work to do.

The membership of SFWR, although open to all, was almost entirely white women. A few stewards joined as the months went by, but the leadership was always female. In stark and oft-noted comparison to the unions, women were making the decisions here. In October 1974, the membership totaled 551, from twenty-one different airlines, although American and TWA had by far the most members. It was a numerically insignificant amount—there were around forty thousand working flight attendants in the United States—but SFWR got press befitting an organization a hundred times the size.

As union leaders well knew, organizing flight attendants came with some built-in difficulties. Bobbi realized quickly that getting people together was going to be a problem—the stewardesses were based all over the country, flying schedules that changed every month. She'd schedule a meeting but people wouldn't show up because they were working. And their salaries weren't high enough to allow them to take many days off, or pay for hotel rooms. Thirteen local chapters, in cities around the country, were now operating, but the nature of the job made the establishment of effective networks difficult, and recruitment an uphill battle.

Tommie, Dana, and Bobbi became editors of the monthly newsletter, though they experimented with getting rid of the "editor" title altogether and just using "staff"—it felt more egalitarian, and less likely to put someone's nose out of joint. It went out each month, painstakingly typed, the three of them clacking away in the glass-walled room dedicated to the newsletter at 30 Rock. Bobbi took some of the photos for the newsletter; she was taking a photography course at the New School.

The newsletters were an essential communication tool for a group of workers scattered around the country, and whose work schedules weren't fixed. Bringing in women to the warm circle of SFWR had to be done by mail, packing the pages full of things like shared stories, often humorously told, about the discrimination they encountered at work; practical tips for challenging a supervisor; contact information for government agencies charged with enforcing antidiscrimination laws; conference details; and updates on court cases initiated by fellow stewardesses.

The newsletter's "cold cup of coffee" prize was a regular feature, awarded to those who had been particularly egregious in their sexism, whether public figures, airline management, or, on one occasion, *Business Week* magazine, for publishing a joke about "squeezing the stewardess." The newsletter suggested that members gather up the on-board copies of *Business Week* and hide them so passengers couldn't read them. Contributors wrote angry articles with titles like "The Myth of the Great Playmate in the Sky." And they collected and published sexist quotes from airline industry professionals. One United Airlines executive: "We need more Indians than chiefs. It'd be hard to keep a lot of high-powered career girls in line. So we need the ones who are going to drop out and do something else after a few years. It's only natural."

The newsletters were sent to any stewardess for whom they could get an address. The TWU wouldn't share its list of members' mailing addresses; that was a closely guarded secret. When SFWR members started becoming more active in the union, the higher-ups at the TWU fretted that they would misuse the list of mailing addresses they could now access, perhaps using the list to build more support for SFWR instead of building the union.

Correspondence between SFWR officers was signed "In sisterhood." And they were, truly, in the language of the women's movement, sisters, embodying the kindness and generosity that the word implied. Stewardesses living in cities where the conferences were held offered up their guest rooms to those flying in on a pass. They got together to organize SFWR fund-raising events. The San Francisco chapter sold corn on the cob at a "Women's Suffrage" fair; they reported back that they'd "answered many queries from people who were shocked that their favorite sky bunny might be a feminist."

They tried new ideas to bring in members. Recruitment mailings got inventive. One included an SFWR luggage sticker along with a special version of the newsletter, printed to look like a newspaper with a photo of Gloria Steinem speaking at an SFWR conference on the front page. Gloria was a clever marketing tool, not only because she was so outspoken on behalf of the stewardesses but also because she was generally acknowledged to be a beauty. Stewardesses who might have been turned off by the "radical" element of the women's movement, who enjoyed the stewardess image and took pride in their looks, could see in Gloria's flowing hair and willowy figure a role model they could relate to. She could have passed, they thought, for a flight attendant. It was the biggest compliment they could give.

Famous and well-connected, Gloria was always traveling, and stewardesses got a thrill whenever they'd spot her on their flight. She made herself available, would speak at their events, attended whatever conferences she could. They loved her. Cindy thought she was "just wonderful . . . nobody can say anything bad to me about Gloria Steinem." To have an ally like this, when so many people refused to take them seriously, made all the difference. Tommie learned (and would never forget) that Gloria hated two things: the term "women's libber," which she considered a media-invented putdown, and the word "suffragette." "It's like 'actor' and 'actress,'" she told the stewardesses. "We're not 'suffragettes,' we're suffragists!" One flight attendant confided to Gloria that she'd had Phyllis Schlafly, the infamous antifeminist and opponent of the Equal Rights Amendment, on one of her flights, whispering excitedly, "I put her in a middle seat!"

More financial help came in, this time a loan from Stewart R. Mott, an eccentric philanthropist who was famous for donating money to unconventional causes. Then SFWR was offered funding from an unexpected source: Playboy Enterprises. They briefly considered it, weighing the good they could do with additional funds against the repulsion they felt at an organization built on the exploitation of women. They hashed the question out, but ultimately decided that, as Dana put it, "it wouldn't look right."

SFWR also helped stewardesses who wanted to take their employers to court. Kathleen Heenan, the TWA stewardess who had hated the paper uniforms so much, joined SFWR. She was happy to help direct women to the EEOC, and energetically assisted them in filing complaints with the New York State Human Rights Commission. Betty Southard Murphy, a lawyer in the Department of Labor who was on the verge of being appointed chairman of the National Labor Relations Board (and was maid of honor at Sonia's wedding), gave them free legal advice, as did Kathleen Peratis, who worked on the Women's Rights Project at the ACLU. When new legislation passed, Peratis would come to meetings to explain how it would affect women, generously giving her time to help the stewardesses understand what their rights were under the law.

Tommie, in the little spare time she had, attended some of the consciousness-raising meetings that were being held all over the city in women's apartments. Pioneered by Kathie Sarachild, the prominent feminist who'd spoken at SFWR's first conference, "CR" groups were springing up around the country. Women were on a quest to increase their awareness about their position in a patriarchal society, and in these meetings they discovered, much as the women in SFWR had, that their experiences and traumas were not unique. Tommie's groups (she belonged to two) would discuss assigned reading, query their own assumptions about gender, and share personal histories. A much-used text by Verne Moberg, titled "Consciousness Razors," invited readers to interrogate their own and other people's ideas about the differences between the sexes, posing exercises such as counting the aprons in children's picture books and seeing how many were worn by women and how many by men, or writing down every degrading comment about women you heard on TV and then calling your local station to complain. Cindy was a fan too; she and Tommie belonged to one of the same groups. Tommie found these sessions life-affirming. They were helping her, she realized, become more exhilaratingly awake to injustice than ever before.

SFWR's third conference was held in San Francisco, in another Methodist church (Methodist churches were good about giving them free space). Though some SFWR members were as active in their union as they were in SFWR, the flyer for the conference didn't hold back: "As long as a union's overall good intentions can be sacrificed to the self-interest of its male members, the woman worker is being short-changed for her union dues. The hopes of the future lie in dovetailing the efforts of the woman's rights movement and the labor movement."

With panels staffed by a psychiatrist, a physician, a pharmaceutical rep, and a neurologist, the focus of this conference was health and safety—issues that were of increasing urgency for flight attendants. The job was fatiguing: flight attendants could walk miles in the space of a few hours, then have to turn around and do it all again without a proper rest or the chance for a meal that was more than the leftovers from a passenger's tray. Shared hotel rooms and frequent time zone changes meant sleep was often interrupted. Pregnant flight attendants had higher-than-average miscarriage rates.

SFWR's primary concern was the transport of hazardous materials. At the San Francisco conference, members decided to take action. In 1973, one out of every ten planes carried radioactive cargo, and it was estimated that an astounding 90 percent of this cargo was improperly packaged, thus exposing crew and passengers to high doses of radiation. Repeated exposure was hazardous: Ozark Airlines carried more radioactive cargo than most, and in 1972, out of ten stewardesses who became pregnant, five had miscarriages and one had a baby born with birth defects. Ralph Nader was concerned about this; his Aviation Consumer Action Project tried to find out more, even distributing leaflets to passengers in an attempt to get the word out. Nader carried his own Geiger counter when flying. The transport of radioactive cargo, much of which was for medical use, was mandated by the federal government, but the airlines profited and the goal was to remove it from planes that also carried passengers. SFWR partnered with Nader's organization to form a coalition called Safe Transportation of People (STOP). They discovered that the Federal Aviation Administration was ignoring repeated violations of safety regulations, that it had colluded with the airlines to cover up the violations, and that in many cases inspections weren't even happening. The financial penalties imposed were low, so it was easier for airlines to take their chances and just pay the fines if they were caught. The FAA was neglecting its duty to passengers, they realized; it was focused on protecting airline profits.

SFWR went all out on getting press, emphasizing to reporters the impact on the health of the traveling public, and organizing a country-wide day of informational picketing at JFK, LaGuardia, O'Hare, and other airports. The airlines were always nervous about their public image, and the women were afraid they'd be disciplined if their employers could identify them. So Tommie, Dana, and Bobbi swapped places with other stewardesses, marching in front of TWA, not in front of American. Employee Relations staff from American, sent by Charlie Pasciuto, came down anyway, and brought cameras, getting right up into their faces and snapping photos. Still, they kept going. Tommie waylaid passengers heading into the airport, asking them, "Do you know what else is being shipped on your plane?" Rather than try to get their sympathy for the impact on the steward-esses, Tommie had learned to talk instead about the impact on the public; that was a much more effective way of grabbing a passen-ger's attention. Plus, she knew to be friendly, smiling widely as she stepped up to chat with someone entering the terminal. She'd seen pilots and maintenance workers picketing plenty of times, but they'd just hold signs, lined up in military fashion. The flight attendants sparkled; they could get people to stop, engage them in conversation. The same outgoing personalities the airlines required were put to good use in the service of activism.

It worked. In February 1975, the FAA decided that only radioac-tive pharmaceuticals, properly packed, could be sent on U.S. flights, and no other radioactive cargo was to be carried. Fines for violations were significantly increased. It was a major victory.

CHAPTER SIXTEEN

We Really Move
Our Tails for You

STEWARDESSES FIGHTING FOR women's rights? It was just as compelling a hook now as it had been a decade before when Dusty had staged her "old bag" stunt. SFWR's safety campaign was covered by the *Chicago Daily News* and by CBS. The office-opening party made it into the *New York Times*. Columnists waded into the debate, opining on the nature of the stewardess job: who should do it, how they should look. SFWR's campaign against sexist airline advertising earned column inches in the *Chicago Tribune*, the *Christian Science Monitor*, and the *Daily News*. One of the first stories about SFWR appeared in the *L.A. Times*, where Sandra told the reporter she'd been "pinched, fondled, leered at, asked out on dates and propositioned" more times than she could remember. "The airlines gear you into being a sex object," she said. "They brainwash you into accepting it and expecting it. You lose your self-respect. You become cynical. And you begin to hate people—while you're smiling at them—because you know they don't respect you. People don't consider you a professional, so you don't think of yourself as one."

Sometimes the media attention was the wrong kind. Joan Rivers made stewardesses the butt of joke after joke, referring to them as prostitutes, and calling them "tramps" on *Hollywood Squares*. She drove both Bobbi and Cindy crazy, constantly promoting the very image of the stewardess that SFWR was trying to combat. They joined a massive letter-writing campaign to get her to apologize, which she eventually did. Harry Reasoner, host of the ABC News program *The Reasoner Report*, and one of the best-known anchors in America, mentioned SFWR on his show. "I don't want a sex object in a narrow aisle," he said. "But I don't want a surly union member either. I want someone youthful and illusory who looks like she thought flying was fun even if she knows more about emergency evacuation of airplanes than I'd like to think about." He quoted "another male chauvinist" on stewardesses: "They should remain patches of color in the business of flying. They should be there for a few years and then, like the clouds outside windows, be replaced with soft and fluffy new ones."

SFWR went wild, blitzing ABC with letters and telegrams telling Reasoner in no uncertain terms where to get off. Dana, by this time the Northeast regional coordinator at SFWR, sat down and typed out a letter that she sent directly to Reasoner, telling him, "I certainly do not appreciate being referred to as a non-human, non-thinking, soft, fluffy thing, which can and should be replaced, and I imagine anyone would be offended by such a reference. Such a statement is as ridiculous as suggesting that you are becoming too old for television broadcasting and should be terminated to make room for the younger, more attractive and virile looking men in your industry." That was a trick she'd learned from Gloria Steinem and Florynce Kennedy, that when a sexist remark was made they should turn it around and fling it back at the offender. It worked—Reasoner went on the air and retracted his statement, mentioning Dana's letter specifically and even conceding that she might have a point.

Celebrities denigrating their profession was bad enough, but soon Tommie, Dana, Bobbi, and the other SFWR members were watching in dismay as new, ever more outrageous ad campaigns were launched. "Fly Me," it turned out, had only been the beginning. Airlines, which had previously been happy to portray the stewardesses as endlessly accommodating, always smiling wives-in-training, now went all in on the Playboy-bunnies-in-the-sky hard sell.

Pacific Southwest Airlines, Tommie decided, was one of the worst offenders, its ads making the most of the uniform—bright pink and orange dresses that barely covered the women's bottoms. One ad read, "Pssst, Stewardess Watchers: P.S.A.'s new Lockheed 1011 TriStar jetliners will each carry 8 lovely stewardesses (and up to 300 happy passengers)." It noted, farther down, "And 2 wide aisles for watching the most beautiful girls in the sky go by." A TV spot didn't even pretend that beauty wasn't the most important quality in a stewardess. The commercial showed nine women parading past an announcer, each wearing a pageant-style sash that identified her not by name, but by one of Pacific Southwest's destinations: "Miss Long Beach," "Miss Los Angeles," "Miss San Diego."

Domestic airlines didn't have a monopoly on this new strategy. Air Jamaica debuted an ad in 1974 that illustrated its slogan, "We make you feel good all over," with photos of stewardesses in bikinis and resort wear (along with copy that advertised "free Rum Bamboozles"). Air France asked with a wink, "Have You Ever Done It the French Way?" Finnair created print ads featuring a topless woman with the airline's route map printed on her back; she looked over her shoulder at the camera with a smile on her face. The copy

Take a good look at Finnair's summer routes
(they're not hard to take)

FINNAIR

read, "Take a good look at Finnair's summer routes (they're not hard to take)."

Southwest was particularly egregious when it came to turning flying into flirting. The airline aired a commercial that was simple but effective: just three long-legged women, dressed in the uniform of hot pants and knee-high white boots, striding across the tarmac to board the plane. One turned just slightly toward the camera to ask, "Remember what it was like before Southwest Airlines? You didn't have hostesses in hot pants. Remember?" That was the entire ad.

Southwest's "Somebody Else Up There Who Loves You" campaign debuted in 1971 and ran for years. The airline operated from Love Field, the main airport in Dallas until DFW opened in 1974, and went all in on the "love" theme. It was a new airline, and its brash and unapologetically sexual approach included calling its ticket machines "love machines," having stewardesses strip off their dresses to reveal bright orange hot pants once the plane took off, offering passengers "love potions" (cocktails) and "love stamps" (free drink coupons), and telling the stewardesses to wave passengers off the plane with a smile and a cheery "Don't forget who loves you!" Southwest milked this campaign for all it was worth; even in 1979, it was still advertising its abundance of flights from Dallas with posters that blared, "We Make Love 80 Times a Day." Southwest dug its heels in on hiring male flight attendants, too: its branding as the "love airline" necessitated young, female flight attendants, execs claimed. A federal court finally forced it to hire men in 1981.

Discussion of these ads at SFWR meetings had been fast and furious, and the members were at the boiling point when word came of a new ad from National, which was already notorious among stewardesses for its universally hated "Fly Me" campaign. Now it was doubling down. The new ads, the airline proudly announced, would feature stewardesses in swimsuits, with the tagline "I'm going to fly you like you've never been flown before."

SFWR snapped into action, calling their press contacts to register protests, which promptly appeared in papers from the *Chicago Tribune* and the *Christian Science Monitor* to the *Daily News* and the *Detroit Free Press*. Angry stewardesses always made for good copy. At SFWR headquarters, Tommie and her crew resuscitated the old slogans, making new buttons that read, "Don't Fly Me. Fly Yourself"

(Dana pinned hers on the underside of her uniform's lapel so she could wear it at work), and producing bumper stickers that declared, "National, your fly is open." NOW joined forces with the stewardesses to file complaints with the Federal Communications Commission and the National Association of Broadcasters (NAB). They protested the offensiveness of the ads, but worked another, more technical angle at the same time: pointing out that the ads were misleading because the stewardesses were not in fact piloting the planes. The NAB agreed, and issued new requirements: the stewardesses would have to wear more than just bathing suits, and National would have to include other aviation employees in the ads.

It wasn't hard to draw a line from advertising to an increase in the leering, groping, and heavy-handed flirting they'd encounter on the plane. Stewardesses constantly struggled with maintaining authority. Bobbi was always butting heads with male passengers; she'd ask them to fasten their seat belt, and they'd respond with, "I've been flying since before you were born." Credibility was already hard to come by. Erotic novels about the lives of stewardesses flying around the world (with titles such as *Coffee, Tea or Me*) had been published, and advertising's increasing emphasis on the "easy" stewardess was making their job more difficult by the day. When combined with the scanty uniforms, it became impossible for the stewardesses to escape being painted in the public view as sex objects who were on the plane to look pretty and catch a husband, not to save lives in case of emergency. That view came from the top down—from the management personnel who addressed them as "girls," to the supervisors who instructed them to glue on their fake eyelashes and weighed them on a whim, to the pilots, cockpit crew, passengers, and public. For Bobbi, seeing her job reduced to a stereotype in the popular media was bad enough, but to see that stereotype promoted by her own employer! It led to a sense of defeatism. And danger, too. On one flight, Cindy had a plane full of passengers who'd gotten food poisoning from a flan (Pan Am had been testing out a new menu). She went to the cockpit for help, but the pilot called her a "hysterical broad," and none of the cockpit crew would come back to see just how serious the situation was. More than ten ambulances had to meet the plane when it landed. Cindy later heard that one person had died en route to the hospital.

The stewardesses' pleasure at beating National was short-lived. Continental Airlines quickly launched an ad that was just as egregious. Its new slogan: "We Really Move Our Tails for You." Airline execs claimed that no innuendo was intended; it was merely, they declared, a natural extension of Continental's seven-year-old tagline "The proud bird with the golden tail." But the campaign had in reality been inspired by the massive success of "Fly Me." When Continental's stewardesses protested, pointing out that passengers would ask them, "Why don't you move your tail for me?" the airline's only response was to suggest a couple of comebacks, such as a cheeky, "Why? Is it in the way?"

SFWR had had enough. They decided they'd make a commercial of their own, what they called a "counter-commercial." It would be about the dangers of promoting the "bimbo" image of the stewardess. One story that circulated widely through the galley grapevine was of a stewardess who had been in the middle of conducting an emergency evacuation when a male passenger picked her up and carried her off the plane, declaring, "You shouldn't be here." The perception of stewardesses as sex objects was literally, they argued, putting lives at risk. The more passengers thought of the stewardesses as decoration, the less they'd be inclined to follow orders in an emergency. The group had already tried raising this issue with the airlines. It was hard enough, they'd point out, to convince a belligerent passenger to put up his tray table when you were dressed in hot pants and vinyl boots, but trying to evacuate a plane wearing a button that said "Fly Me" was too ludicrous to imagine. "I don't think of myself as a sex symbol or a servant," said one stewardess. "I think of myself as somebody who knows how to open the door of a 747 in the dark, upside down and in the water."

This had been the reasoning behind the flight attendants' decades-long fight to become licensed as safety professionals. The airlines had always resisted, not just because licensing would have improved the status of the stewardesses, but because safety was something airlines never liked to mention. No airline ad boasted about safety records for the reason that even hinting at the idea that air travel might not be 100 percent safe terrified potential passengers. If flight attendants became known as safety professionals rather than airborne cocktail waitresses, the thinking went, the idea that one might *need* safety in the air would put fliers off. But they did need safety in the air: hijackings were becoming more common throughout the 1970s, and on Pan Am Cindy was hearing about bomb threats more often than she cared to. If someone called in to say they'd planted a bomb on the plane, the airline would tell the crew during the preflight briefing. This eventually happened so frequently that Cindy and her fellow flight attendants would make jokes on the jumpseat about how if the plane was going to blow up, they hoped it would happen before they had to do the meal service.

But the stewardesses used a technique unions had wielded successfully for decades to build support. Playing on the safety of the public, just as they'd done in their campaign against hazardous cargo, was, they found, a much more effective way to get what they wanted than talking about the personal safety of flight attendants. And it was certainly more attention-grabbing than complaining about women's rights in the abstract.

Around a hundred SFWR members, wearing blue buttons that read, "Stewardesses are people too," crowded into the 30 Rock offices. It was a big event: reporters had been invited to watch the commercial debut, and they had responded with enthusiasm. The film was a simple one. A professional actor, posing as a stewardess, spoke to the camera: "Sure I serve coffee, tea and milk, as well as breakfast, lunch and dinner, but my primary function is the enforcement of federal safety regulations. I receive exhaustive training in all phases of emergency procedure, be it the in-flight birth of a child or the ninety-second evacuation of a jetliner. And I undergo frequent reviews and tests by the Federal Aviation Administration to maintain my proficiency in these seldom-used but terribly important skills. I'm a highly trained professional with a serious job to do. Should an emergency situation arise, I urgently need the respect, confidence and cooperation of all my passengers in order to minimize danger and accomplish what must be done." The ending was solemn: "Fantasies are fine—in their place—but let's be honest, the 'sexpot stewardess' image is unsafe at any altitude! Think about it." The commercial got a good amount of press, including another Anna Quindlen article, and coverage on three television networks (one was on a feminist show called *Woman Alive!* on New York's WNET).

The next newsletter featured the text of the commercial displayed prominently next to the membership form.

It wasn't just the airlines that had discovered that putting a stewardess in their ads could move product. SFWR launched letter-writing campaigns and boycotts against any company that put out ads demeaning stewardesses. And there were plenty. Hanes stockings were a target, as was Close-Up toothpaste, and Johnson & Johnson baby oil. The companies always responded defensively at first, but gradually the ads disappeared. Firestone, though, which produced an ad that showed a stewardess sensibly buying snow tires, got a thank-you note from a flight attendant, and a promise to tell her friends to choose Firestone in the future.

Airline VPs and advertising executives weren't the only ones who needed to be convinced these ads were sexist. Bobbi's husband was a social worker, and he'd get irritated when people ignored him in favor of asking Bobbi eager questions about her job. Just the word "stewardess," she could see, got them excited. The image of a stewardess had such power that it completely informed people's perception of her. She found it bizarre, and offensive. Cindy Hounsell tended to feel more disrespected socially than she did on the job. Her husband was an economist and it was clear his friends thought it was titillating that he'd married a stewardess. They didn't pay attention to the fact that he taught two days a week and she could arrange her schedule to work the same, so they had abundant time off together, and great vacations with free flights, all thanks to her job. She grew tired of defending her profession to people who considered her frivolous.

Even her mother didn't get it. One day she'd called Cindy, full of excitement, and told her she'd been hanging clothes out to dry when one of the airplanes National had named after its stewardesses flew overhead: she'd seen "Cindy" zoom by and she was delighted. Cindy, who spent her spare time picketing outside advertising offices and airline headquarters, was saddened. Her mother would never understand. When SFWR had been encouraging everyone they knew to write and complain about Joan Rivers, Cindy had sent one of the form letters to her parents. They'd dutifully signed it, but they didn't make the connection.

For many flight attendants, SFWR filled a role the union did not. Comradeship, a dedication to making women's lives better, a willingness to fight for issues the unions had let fall from the bargaining table—SFWR was a godsend when it came to providing these things. But Tommie, much as she loved the excitement and the thrill of feeling the women's movement expand around her, was learning that real power, the power to make tangible changes to the flight attendant job, was in the union. SFWR, though it garnered headlines, got the stewardesses' stories on television, and supported legal cases where it could, had no power to push back against the airlines on pregnancy rules, appearance standards, single rooms, or pay—those things were the remit of the labor union. SFWR excelled at publicity, raising awareness, and education. Their protests made people think for the first time about why an ad featuring a seductive stewardess might be sexist. They could even get a company to take a commercial off the air. But they didn't have a seat at the table.

"If I really want to make change and I really want to face off with management and I really want some kind of power," Tommie decided, "I have to run for union office."

She tried to convince her SFWR comrades of her revelation. "We've got to get involved with a union," she told them, sometimes climbing onto a chair in the middle of a meeting to make her point. "Stewardesses for Women's Rights is wonderful. Look around—in this room, we have stewardesses from Pan Am, TWA, Eastern, American. But we need to be in the union. We need to be elected officials." They'd had a great time doing what she, using one of her few lingering Texas expressions, called "hootin', and hollerin'." But what, she asked them, have we really achieved other than publicity? She was seeing other unions—maintenance, pilots—achieving real results during bargaining. They were moving ahead with higher wages, better work rules, more benefits. And the stewardesses were fighting for the right to be a parent, to have a hotel room to themselves, to not have to get on the scale at the whim of a supervisor. SFWR, Tommie thought, was not going to achieve the bigger goals. They couldn't demand to meet with management; they had no standing with the companies. The stewardesses were being left behind. They had to get on the negotiating team.

So she ran for office. Donna Forloine, the president of ALSSA, had been pushing her to run for base chairperson of New York, even when Tommie had protested that she didn't have enough experience. "I know you can do it," Donna told her. And Tommie won. She was still involved with SFWR, as were Bobbi and Dana, but she pulled them onto her council as well. In Tommie's mind she would occasionally hear the voice of Dusty Roads. Tommie had once heard her say, "Oh, Stewardesses for Women's Rights is just fluff." Dusty was a unionist through and through and had little patience for things like consciousness-raising. SFWR did serve as a sort of training camp for stewardesses moving into union leadership positions; they'd gotten a crash course on organizing and internal politics. Cindy Hounsell, at Pan Am, was running between SFWR meetings and union meetings. But she, too, was realizing that there was a limit to what SFWR could get done. The members were spread across different airlines, which made organizing difficult. Cindy was working as a shop steward (a worker who serves as liaison between a group of workers and the elected officers) at the same time. It was glaringly clear to her on which side the power lay.

"If I'm going to stay in this business," Tommie thought to herself, "this is where the power is—being involved and being elected to office so that you can sit at the table with your management counterpart and try to really change the rules." Her enthusiasm for the strength and potential of the labor movement, like the women's movement, was intense. Her coworkers encouraged her. Even before she became an official union rep, she'd doled out advice to people who had been, she thought, unfairly discharged, or she'd go in and represent them in a grievance. Management had started to refer to her as "the social worker." It was hard, maybe impossible, for her to keep her mouth shut when she saw something that wasn't right. Through a combination of happenstance and determination she moved up the union ranks fast. A position opened up on the executive committee; she got that, too. But she wasn't the only one who had gone after it. Patt Gibbs had also wanted that job.

At SFWR, though, Tommie was still fighting an uphill battle to convince the others that the change they were seeking would come through the union. Many of them felt strongly that unions, as Sandra Jarrell had stated way back at the first SFWR conference, "do not have the reputation of representing the interests of women at the bargaining table." Sandra had put her hopes of getting rehired, after being fired for weight, in SFWR instead. Tommie had tried to talk her out of this, asking her if she'd lodged a grievance with her union, warning her not to put all her eggs in the SFWR basket. "You're not," Tommie had told her, "going to *embarrass* Eastern into giving you your job back." Sure, SFWR would educate the public, but it was the union and the grievance process that would get her employed again. Sandra didn't listen, and never got her job back. That was yet another reason Tommie was determined to move up in the union.

Other flight attendants continued to complain about the uselessness of their unions. The letters from frustrated stewardesses who wrote to SFWR revealed the depth of betrayal they felt. There was, one wrote, "every reason for me to doubt that the Transport Workers Union of America is working for the interests of the stewardesses who have given their dues (mine for 10 years) to protect our job and improve working conditions. If they are selling out to Pan American on small issues, they certainly must be selling out on large issues at contract negotiations." Despite being just a small percentage of the flight attendant workforce, men dominated union meetings, another wrote. The men tried to intimidate women who attended the meetings, a third complained, and laughed at them behind their backs. The unions were too concerned with money, she went on, sacrificing the health and working conditions of the flight attendants for the sake of a few more dollars, despite the fact that 72 percent of the membership wanted working conditions to be the number one issue during negotiations. SFWR member Liz Rich gave an interview to the *Chicago Tribune* where she stated things even more baldly: "The unions to which we stewardesses pay dues are a male-dominated establishment just like the airlines. The union has bargained away our rights, time and again."

It was also becoming clear that the men at the highest levels of the TWU found SFWR activity threatening. On occasion, they'd stop SFWR from stuffing flight attendant mailboxes with their mailers and recruitment materials. There was a general feeling of uneasiness infecting the TWU leadership: not just that these upstart women were grabbing more headlines than the union ever had, but that they were potentially a threat to the union's power. As they'd soon find out, they weren't wrong.

CHAPTER SEVENTEEN

First the Commies,
Then the Feminists

AS BASE CHAIR, Tommie now worked at American Airlines' union headquarters, at the pleasingly fitting address of 747 Third Avenue. American's union actually shared its offices with TWA's; both airlines were headquartered in New York. In early 1974, the Air Line Stewards and Stewardesses Association had broken up. The same airlines were still affiliated to the TWU, but now instead of clustering under the ALSSA umbrella with its extra level of officers, each airline had its own local under the TWU. TWA became Local 551, and American Airlines flight attendants belonged to Local 552. Moving into airline-specific locals would, the stewardesses hoped, give each local more autonomy. If you were an American flight attendant, now you could concern yourself only with what other American flight attendants wanted. What the pursers at TWA were doing, for example, was now none of your business.

Tommie's passion for union work only accelerated as she learned more about the labor movement and its possibilities. Always a relationship builder, she knew that good relations with management and the TWU would mean that flight attendant problems would get fixed faster. She could take care of things at the grievance stage, rather than watching issues progress to arbitration, which could take a year. She was just twenty-nine, but she was adept at making friends with men twice her age who held the power in the TWU.

These men had much in common. They came from union families, they were mostly Irish American, their wives didn't work outside the home. Tommie befriended Ernie Mitchell, who'd been a mechanic and only had one arm; his nickname, the "one-armed bandit," was always spoken with friendliness. She didn't encounter as much resistance from Ernie or other TWU higher-ups as other union leaders did, but she gave some of the credit for that to her height. She would augment her five-foot-nine frame (topped, when not on duty, by an exuberant head of curly hair) with the highest heels she could walk in, so she could look down on most of the people who had more authority than she did. She towered over Charlie Pasciuto. (Patt, by contrast, was just five foot three, but anytime she got off the stage at a meeting someone would come up and exclaim, "I just thought you would be taller!")

Tommie, when representing flight attendants who'd been disciplined, listened and observed carefully, and tried to resolve the problem calmly. Yelling and loud arguments would distress the women she was representing—their jobs were at stake, and swearing and table-banging just made them more afraid. A fact-based argument was Tommie's best weapon. She settled case after case, impressing the labor lawyers. "It's because I know the rules," she'd tell them. "This is *my* company." On occasion Tommie would really have it out with someone, but it was rare that she lost her cool. She always preferred a peaceful resolution. Still, one issue always brought her close to losing her temper: weight.

Although the stewardesses were fighting for things that *sounded* more consequential—wage parity, benefits, respect from passengers—they were continually undermined by something that outsiders never seemed to take seriously. But it dominated their lives. It was always there in the background, a never-ending source of stress. For management, it was an easy way to maintain control, or to yank somebody back in line when they got too active in SFWR, or in the union, or spoke out too loudly. Being put on "weight check" and sent to the scale, usually in public, was a highly effective humiliation technique. Once a stewardess was determined to be over her max weight, she'd be disciplined, given a weight loss schedule with targets to meet, and required to get on the scale before each trip. A couple of pounds over? She could be pulled off the flight right there and then.

While the feminist movement was embracing new ways for women to look—long, unfettered hair; jeans worn everywhere; no makeup—in the cabin appearance regulations were still inflexible. It was an easy way to increase turnover. Thanks to the vanquishing of age and marriage restrictions, flight attendants were staying on the job for years longer than they had just a decade before, and they were aging in place. And now their toughly negotiated contracts called for wage increases the longer they worked. As a way to keep flight attendants young and to get the senior, better-paid ones off the line, weight checks were ingenious. If you couldn't fire someone for turning thirty-two, you'd just fire them for putting on a few pounds instead. As flight attendants scored more wins in the workplace, the airlines had started tweaking weight maximums downward. At Pan Am in 1968, for a woman five feet six inches tall, the limit went from 136 to 132 pounds. In 1970, United, which had previously relied on supervisors to exercise weight regulation at their discretion, suddenly began removing flight attendants from flights for failing to meet their weight requirement. A year later the company revised its weight program to make monthly weigh-ins mandatory and to eliminate weight *minimums*, announcing this change with a celebratory note in the flight attendant newsletter: "weight minimums are GONE. You can now be 5'9" and weigh 89 pounds." At Braniff, a program of putting overweight stewardesses on a "reducing schedule" had given the women some leeway and support while trying to meet the weight requirement; they could keep flying as they tried to "reduce." Then in 1972 management implemented a harsh new policy that called for immediate suspension of any female flight attendant over the limit. American created new weight charts, but they still relied on "frame" as the basis for their maximum allowed weight. A male flight attendant had a weight allowance based on a man's "large" frame, while the women's max weight was based on a woman's "small" frame. Eating disorders became more common.

Now that the birth control pill was widely available, and pregnancy was still for the most part a fireable offense, many flight attendants were on the pill, and they'd often gain weight. And as they aged, their metabolisms slowed down, and sticking to the weight standards became even more difficult. They took boxes of methedrine, the same pills Patt had been taking back in the 1960s, from the company doctors, who handed them out to anyone who wanted them. Speed killed the appetite; it was an efficient way to lose weight.

Tommie found the issue enraging. When a stewardess was disciplined for extra pounds, Tommie would jump in, helping her to file a grievance, then taking it to arbitration—anything to keep the woman on the line. As long as you were physically fit and could pass the emergency procedure test, she'd tell arbitrators, there was no reason you couldn't do the job! Being skinny didn't make you a better flight attendant. In fact, she pointed out, putting on a few pounds might make it easier to lift out the window exit and toss it over the seats. The arbitrators, though, would often find a way to rule in favor of the company and blame the individual flight attendant. Didn't meet the weight standard? Too bad. They'd argue that they couldn't enforce something that wasn't in the contract. "Don't try to arbitrate what you can't negotiate" was the refrain. Get it in the contract and come back to us, *then* we can rule in your favor. She got sick of hearing it. But somehow changing the weight standard, no matter how many flight attendants were taken off the line, was never the TWU's top priority at contract negotiation time.

It didn't matter for men. Brian had a friend, Rocky, who stood five foot eleven and weighed around 190 pounds. On occasion a supervisor would throw out a passing "watch your weight, Rocky." But there was never a question of him being suspended for being over the max. He was never even weighed.

One incident brought Tommie in direct opposition with Bob Crandall, future CEO. Dolores Simpson, one of American's still-too-few Black flight attendants, had been suspended for weight. She was a true professional, had won every flight attendant award for her work, and was generally acknowledged to be stop-you-in-your-tracks beautiful. Tommie brought her, dressed in her uniform, to a meeting. It was one of the annual occasions when Crandall would show up to address employees and take questions. After he gave his spiel, Tommie raised her hand. "What do you want, Mrs. Blake?" he asked. He always addressed her as "Mrs. Blake," which she suspected he did on purpose to rile her. She got to her feet, pulled Dolores up next to her, and told her story. Then she ended with, "I just want everybody in this room to try to fathom that you could lose your job when you look like this and are a fabulous employee." There was an audible gasp from the room, whether at Tommie's audacity or Dolores's beauty Tommie didn't know. They both sat down, and everyone went quiet. Tommie could feel Crandall's animosity from across the room. He snapped out something about the weight issue not being on the day's agenda, and swiftly moved on. Confabbing in the bathroom when the meeting was over, Tommie and Dolores were besieged by other women, all chiming in with support. Some of them weren't even flight attendants; they were management or ticket agents. It was a moment of solidarity that Tommie never forgot.

Sandra Jarrell had lost her job for being over her weight maximum, though she'd spent month after month waging a battle against the scale. Still, she hadn't put in more time monitoring her weight than her airline, Eastern, was putting in monitoring everyone else's. Memo after memo came from Eastern management, revealing the astounding amount of thought and energy being exerted in controlling the women's weight down to a pound or two (as with Rocky, no one weighed the stewards). Eastern was always changing the rules. Stewardesses found to be over their weight limit were put on weekly weight checks; they'd be removed if they hit five pounds over the max. Then it was announced that stewardesses who had made it past probation would no longer be required, as previously, to lose two pounds a week, but they must show some progress toward their weight standard. A concession was made: weight checks wouldn't be performed while a stewardess had her period. Were the amounts of weight, mostly just a few pounds, worth spending all this time on? For the company, it seemed, they were. Having built up its business on the promise of slim stewardesses, the airline was duty-bound to keep that promise. It built profits, and offered a singularly simple way to keep its workers in line at the same time. The effect on stewardesses like Sandra, who agonized over meals, went on all-liquid diets, and popped amphetamines to stave off hunger pangs, was immaterial. But the women were starting to push back. Stewardesses continued to file dozens of EEOC charges against the airlines in regard to weight. Sandra had started SFWR.

Some women took the airlines to court, where the judges often found in their favor. But even when these individuals got their jobs back, the weight standards at the airlines remained unchanged. The leash grew tighter, while the dissonance between the airlines' requirements and the increasingly powerful women's movement got louder and louder as the 1970s went on. Months would go by with a flight attendant trying to lose just a few pounds, stretches of time during which she would get repeated written and oral warnings, have to have discussions about her weight with supervisors, endure deep dives into her medical history and medications, sit through conversations about her attitude. After all this, her lack of progress would often be attributed to "noncompliance" rather than the sheer physical difficulty of meeting an unrealistic standard.

SFWR collected application forms for various airlines that highlighted the increasingly archaic requirements. The forms still asked if an applicant was married or single, and the appearance standards remained stringent. At American, a five-foot-seven stewardess could weigh no more than 135 pounds, with a hip circumference no larger than thirty-seven inches. A five-foot-seven male flight attendant, though, could weigh 25 pounds more, and was not required to meet a hip measurement target. National's 1971 application asked for bust, waist, and hip measurements. TWA's application asked if applicants were missing any teeth, what their natural hair color was, whether they had any visible scars, whether their parents approved of them becoming a hostess, how many brothers and sisters an applicant had and where she/he fit into the birth sequence, if they had a steady boyfriend, and if they had a savings account. A recruiting pamphlet for TWA, though, mentioned none of this. Instead, using bright colors and cheerful cartoons, it informed potential stewardesses that "you can combine flying with marriage. As long as you don't have any children and you're willing to locate where we ask you to locate, you can fly. You can be married when you enter training. Or you can get married any time thereafter." This trumpeting of a change the airlines had been forced to make, and the pointed mention of the fact that mothers were not welcome in the cabin, was not something the women of SFWR were inclined to celebrate.

The tension between the TWU and Stewardesses for Women's Rights had been growing for months when things finally came to a head. The TWU leadership was threatened by SFWR, suspicious of it, and worried that SFWR members were encroaching on their territory. It only fanned the flames when the director of flight attendants at Pan Am, where Cindy worked, invited SFWR members to a meeting to voice their dissent about various company policies. As far as the TWU could see, SFWR was competition: they were grabbing headlines, making waves, and now meeting with the company over policies that the TWU considered its own to negotiate.

In November 1975, paranoia mounting, Bill Lindner sent out a bombshell in the form of a letter. Lindner was a TWU vice president, a man in his fifties who'd gone from a mechanic's job at American Airlines to becoming one of the TWU's top dogs. He was the director of the air transport division, which meant he was in charge of keeping an eye on the stewardesses. The letter he wrote charged SFWR with one of the labor movement's cardinal sins: raiding. Raiding meant stealing members and wasn't to be taken lightly. The AFL-CIO, the labor federation to which the TWU was affiliated, had kicked the Teamsters out under accusations of raiding (and corruption charges). Lindner accused SFWR of being a rival union to the TWU, and of trying to steal its members. He pointed to mailings that SFWR had distributed, and denounced their work on health and safety, wages, legal rights, working conditions, and other areas he considered to be exclusively the province of the TWU. "Dual unionism," or organizing a rival union, was a serious accusation, and one that showed just how much the TWU leadership was threatened by SFWR. Even at its peak, SFWR never had more than around twelve hundred members, but its influence was out of all proportion to its size.

SFWR members balked. They weren't a union, they weren't trying to organize a union, they had no plans to become a union, and while most of them didn't have many good things to say about the TWU, plenty of their members, including Tommie and Cindy, were also union leaders. Lindner's letter had ordered a purge: he declared that any TWU officers or representatives who were also SFWR officers were to be removed from their union positions without delay. Cindy got a copy of the letter and was furious. She immediately took the letter to Kathleen Peratis, the ACLU attorney who often advised the stewardesses on legal matters. Kathleen helped Cindy compose a response, listing the laws Lindner had broken by sending this letter out. She never heard back.

Not long afterward, Lindner followed up his letter with a stunning display of temper. Tommie was attending a meeting of the joint executive committee. It was a sizable group, made up of base chairs from cities across the country, plus officers from the TWU. Tommie walked into the room and saw that Bill Lindner was there, too. Tommie wondered why. One or two representatives would always turn up at these meetings, but it was unusual for someone so high up in the TWU to show themselves. Lindner had taken a seat at the top table, and was staring down at paperwork spread out in front of him. Tommie, curious to know what he was studying so intently, took a few steps forward to see what it was. It looked, she suddenly realized, like the SFWR newsletter. The one with her name on the masthead.

The meeting began and business was proceeding as usual when Lindner abruptly stood up. He began speaking, addressing the room but looking directly at Tommie. "Uh-oh," she thought. She had met him before and they didn't like each other. It had been clear that he thought her a radical. She, for her part, had found him frustratingly reactionary, someone whose values and belief system had been frozen in time by the Cold War, and whose priorities never seemed to include his female members. He launched into a diatribe. "I want every one of you to listen to me," he said, raising a finger and pointing it at Tommie. "I want her off this committee. I want her removed! I'm charging her with dual unionism." Tommie, he said, couldn't sit at this table as an elected representative of the Transport Workers Union because she was involved with Stewardesses for Women's Rights. He worked himself into a fury, spittle flying. Finally, he stuck his finger right in Tommie's face and shouted, "In the '50s we got rid of the Commies and in the '70s we'll get rid of these feminists!"

There was a shocked silence. The AFL and CIO had participated in a Cold War–inspired purge of Communists and their allies back in the 1950s, and Lindner clearly hadn't forgotten. That to him a group called Stewardesses for Women's Rights was as much of a threat as Communism was a fascinating, and disturbing, revelation. But the room didn't stay quiet for long. Voices rose up, telling Lindner off. Tommie sat back, almost smug, and watched him get shouted down.

That day she gained many friends around the table. She took advantage of the situation, audaciously handing out SFWR membership cards. Lindner, furious and paranoid, filed a formal complaint of dual unionism against her. But it went nowhere. And his outburst had backfired. To many TWU representatives, the accusation seemed ludicrous. SFWR was patently not a union. And they were delighted that Tommie was throwing her abilities and her popularity behind the TWU. She was not removed from her position.

Tommie took full advantage of the resources available, resources only there because the American Airlines local was under the TWU umbrella. The TWU was affiliated to the AFL-CIO, the largest union federation in the United States, which had just opened a Labor Studies Center near the D.C. Beltway. Tommie used the center to learn as much about organizing as she could; it was one of the benefits, as she saw it, of being part of a larger labor organization. The AFL-CIO had more than 14 million members. At the Center, she made a lifelong ally—Becky Kroll, a stewardess from Dallas with a sparkling sense of humor. Becky was a union rep; she'd gotten into union work when her sister had been, she believed, unfairly fired from the airline. She joined SFWR at Tommie's behest, but the union was her priority, and she excelled at training other reps. Becky would tell the SFWR members, "You may not think your union works. But it's the only thing that will work."

With the time she was spending on union work increasing on what felt like a daily basis, Tommie decided to step back from her responsibilities at SFWR. She still paid her dues and did her best to convince younger flight attendants to join ("You'll have fun!" she would promise), but she gave up her newsletter position and took less of a leadership role. As more members began spending their free time on union work, Stewardesses for Women's Rights started losing momentum.

It wasn't just the general movement toward the union. There was dissension in the ranks. People in local chapters felt that the New York leaders weren't transparent enough about where the funding was going, that they made decisions without consulting those farther away, that the plans and budgets were barely defined.

Cindy, though a dedicated member and a regional coordinator, suspected that what she thought of as a certain "stewardess mentality," that is, an attraction to glamour and image, was hindering the leadership. They don't want a bare-bones operation with twenty thousand members, she thought; they want the prestigious office and the glittering cocktail parties and the important titles. "Where are the members?" she'd ask as she marched into the office each month. "When is the newsletter coming out? How many members do we have now? How many more do you think we're going to get?"

The San Francisco chapter sent a letter to the SFWR board members. It expressed many of the feelings of members outside New York. The signatories complained that the organization had abandoned its grassroots beginnings, was too multidirectional and unfocused, that the 30 Rock address was elitist and would attract "joiners," whom they defined as passive people who only wanted to associate themselves with the group without a real commitment. They said the address turned off those "committed to feminism, unionism and change." And they proposed breaking the organization into cells around the country, moving away from the centralization that had made New York the group's hub. They suggested establishing "principles of unity," taking defined positions on political issues like the Equal Rights Amendment, and supporting unions in fighting management. "Where there is a stand to be taken," the letter said, "we should take it."

Tommie, Bobbi, Dana, and Kathleen were among the list of

Bobbie and Dana, winter 1975.

respondees to the letter. They argued that excluding or discouraging anyone from joining SFWR, even "joiners," well, *that* was the elitist position. They noted that dissolving the national office would leave stewardesses without a central place to seek information or direct their questions. They dealt with the issue of the address by pointing out that it appealed to many members, both radical feminists and conservative stewardesses, and asked, "What does the address represent to our enemy? They fear that we may actually be a real threat. We say right on!"

It soon became a moot point. Membership dues could not sustain the organization once the Stern grant ran out. Even though they were getting a good deal on the rent at 30 Rock, they were still paying more than they could afford. They moved to 57th Street and a one-room office with a single phone line. Cindy and Kathleen, die-hard members, were still volunteering their time, but they spent more time dealing with bill collectors than moving the mission forward.

The differences of opinion, combined with the financial problems, were beginning to feel insurmountable. The organization had only been in existence a few years, but it started to become clear to Tommie that SFWR was running out the clock. Maybe, she thought, its time was over.

CHAPTER EIGHTEEN

The Single Rooms Contract

BY 1976, IT was possible to look back on the last decade with a sense that hard work had paid off. Significant gains had been made. Over half of all stewardesses were married. Fifteen percent had children (the rules about this were slowly changing) and were still flying. And the average seniority was now six years, which meant better flights and higher pay. But problems—wages, appearance standards, weight—still remained. There was one issue in particular that, like weight, seemed petty to outsiders but dominated flight attendants' agendas: single rooms.

The fight over single rooms on layovers was a battle royale. Not only did it grate that pilots—not to mention male flight attendants—got rooms to themselves, but sharing had other adverse effects on stewardesses. Everyone had different sleep schedules, some covering their heads with a pillow to block out the noise from a roommate who was on the phone or watching TV. Stewardesses would sleep on the bathroom floor to escape a snoring companion. If their roommate's flight arrived late, they'd have to wait in their room, unable to bolt the door. The public thought stewardesses were party animals, dancing and drinking and flirting until dawn. The reality was more like reading a book in the bathtub all night when you couldn't sleep, so the light wouldn't bother the woman in the other bed. Everyone was jet-lagged, always tired. Enough was enough, the women finally decided. Either everyone gets single rooms or no one does.

Contract negotiations were about to begin at American Airlines, and the Local 552 officers were surveying the membership to see which issues they wanted to address in this contract. Single rooms was the number one. The stewardesses had had it.

Negotiations began. Bill Lindner, the TWU VP, wanted to try something new for this contract. He had come to an agreement with the management at American: management had agreed to a standardized salary increase if the workers would cut their list of demands, thus expediting bargaining. And management required the TWU to negotiate all the contracts at the same time, including those for fleet service, mechanics, and flight attendants. Lindner sent out a letter to the leaders of these locals. Let's keep our list of issues short, he said. The United States was going through a period of high inflation, and the usual lengthy bargaining period would mean that the value of any raise they negotiated would go down as time passed. The TWU wanted the three groups of workers to stand together during this bargaining period, believing they'd have more leverage. That meant that single rooms were not, Lindner decided, up for debate. The flight attendants would just have to lump it.

Lining up the contracts was a good strategy, one that unions often used—the pie gets bigger for everyone when you have unity. But the problem was this: the flight attendants were miles behind the other groups in terms of wages, work rules, and benefits. They'd been fighting against sex discrimination, for things like the right to become mothers—not for their pensions, like the ground workers. They'd planned on using this contract negotiation to catch up with the other groups, and getting single rooms like the pilots was top of the list. Patt, part of the local Dallas committee, knew the flight attendants wouldn't go for lumping it, and she told Donna Forloine so. Donna, the union president and lead negotiator, passed that on to Lindner, but he held firm. Although the stewardess negotiators, led by Donna, pressed hard for single rooms, Lindner overruled them. He cut a deal with management, and ended up with a contract that didn't include single rooms. Still, the management team, led by Charlie Pasciuto, was confident. The flight attendants had never voted a contract down, Charlie reminded Donna. They wouldn't vote this one down. "Just you sit back and watch," she said.

Before the vote, there would be what they called a "roadshow," the union leadership traveling around the country to the different bases, explaining to the flight attendants why they should vote to approve the contract they'd negotiated, telling them the great benefits they'd secured from American. If the membership liked the new contract, they'd vote "yes" and it would go into effect. If they didn't—this was purely theoretical; as Charlie pointed out, the flight attendants had never voted a contract down—the union and management would have to start bargaining all over again.

Out went the roadshow. The TWU leaders traveled from base to base pointing to all the gains they'd scored for flight attendants in the new contract. The flight attendants voted. Tommie was on the ballot committee and helped with the count. She could barely contain her glee when she saw the results. They had voted it down.

Charlie was incensed. He blustered, threatening to sue the union for bargaining in bad faith. American, he declared, would not be "blackmailed" into giving single rooms because the stewardesses had voted the contract down. Everyone went back to the bargaining table. The TWU negotiators were focused on wages, benefits, better work rules, but single rooms was not on their list. Donna, at the table with the TWU higher-ups, lodged a protest: "If I don't bring back single rooms," she told them, "this contract is going to go down again." They didn't listen. A new contract was drawn up. The company had offered more money, but still no single rooms, and the TWU had agreed to it. Tommie snuck into Operations at LaGuardia and broke open the glass doors securing the union bulletin board, which was used only for announcing meetings or general news. She took down every notice and pinned up her own handmade sign: VOTE NO.

The TWU went out on the road again with the second version of the contract. This time Charlie insisted on coming along. He'd decided to try himself to convince the flight attendants to accept the new contract. Donna tried to tell him the stewardesses wouldn't like it, but he overrode her concerns, confident that he could convince them to vote yes. Tommie knew it was a bad idea. Management had never come to a ratification roadshow before; that alone was enough to make her, and everyone else, suspicious. It felt uncomfortably like management was poking into their private affairs. Still, Charlie was determined, so she figured she'd enjoy watching him try to talk the stewardesses into accepting the contract.

New York was the first stop on the roadshow, and the meeting was held in a big hotel conference room. Tommie, Dana, and Bobbi, all wearing their SFWR T-shirts, made sure to arrive early to grab seats in the front row. The room was packed full of flight attendants, hundreds of them. When she turned her head, Tommie could see that some of them were holding signs demanding single rooms.

From her front row seat, Tommie eyeballed Charlie and his cronies, who were sitting in a line at a long table at the front of the room, facing the audience and studiously trying to ignore the sign-waving. The show started. Charlie, trying to connect, walked out from behind the table. He addressed the room like he was giving the annual report. He talked industry numbers, what was ahead for the airline, the state of the economy. Single rooms, he declared, were too expensive. A rumble moved through the room. His arguments were not having the effect he'd wanted.

Charlie sat down, and the flight attendants in the room stood up. Woman after woman took her turn at the mic. They told stories of having to share a room with someone who had the flu, of being unable to sleep because a roommate was snoring. Charlie listened, but Tommie could see he was unmoved. These stories, she thought, are not going to change his mind.

"When are you guys going to get it?" Tommie said, more to herself than to the executives. "You've got to give us single rooms. Case closed." She got to her feet. She raised her voice. She talked about the male flight attendants and their single rooms. She pointed out that the pilots had always had single rooms. She asked for explanations. She used the word "discrimination." She called him Charlie. She pointed out what should have been obvious: "This is the single rooms contract, Charlie." And she took it one step further. "This," she said, "is a strike issue."

She could see him wondering: Who *is* this woman?

The two men Charlie had brought with him, flanking him at the top table, were former crew schedulers, men who had worked very closely with the flight attendants. Tommie could see them register immediately what she was saying, that the flight attendants weren't kidding around. And Charlie was cowed. He ran out of bluster. The meeting ended. Years later he'd complain to Tommie that she'd humiliated him at that moment. "Well," she'd tell him, "you shouldn't have been there in the first place."

The roadshow moved on to Dallas. New York was full of radicals, Charlie thought. Dallas would be different. Becky, who had been one of the negotiators on the contract, sat at the front with the rest of the team, next to Charlie and his men. Again, Charlie made his pitch, this time talking up the salary increase and the concessions the company had made. But anytime he said anything about not giving in on single rooms the flight attendants started stomping their feet. They stomped so loud they drowned him out. Becky kept looking down, trying to hide her smile. Charlie didn't do any more roadshows. He caught the next flight back to New York.

The flight attendants went to the polls a second time. A few days later, Tommie was back at union headquarters, counting the ballots again. They were in the middle of tallying the votes, surrounded by stacks of paper, when the door burst open with a bang. In stepped Charlie, accompanied, as always, by what Tommie called his "goons." He was there, he announced, to observe the union's ballot count.

There was an uproar. The line between company duties and union duties was clearly demarcated, and ballot counts were always, always for members only. Tommie was outraged. It was totally out of order for the VP of Employee Relations to push his way in and demand to watch the count. This was intimidation, pure and simple. But she panicked. She didn't think they were in physical danger, not really, but this was so unorthodox she wasn't sure that Charlie and his cronies wouldn't find a way to misrepresent the results of the vote count. Tommie made a quick decision, rushing to the phone and calling Al. "Can you come down here?" she asked. "They're trying to intimidate the ballot committee; they're suggesting that we're not counting the votes right!" Al was a tall guy with an imposing frame that belied his peaceful nature. He came right away, bringing a couple of friends. They did nothing, just stood there, observing the observers. Just in case.

The votes were tallied. The flight attendants had voted the contract down.

Charlie Pasciuto wasn't the only man at American angry about the way this contract was going. Bob Crandall, the senior financial VP and future CEO, had no respect for the flight attendants and they knew it. He frequently flew from base to base, and especially loved going into the cockpit and chumming it up with the pilots. Some of them liked him and were thrilled that Bob Crandall was riding with them. Others were less so. Brian heard a story that Crandall had been in the cockpit complaining to the pilots about how the flight attendants wouldn't let the single rooms issue go. Crandall had put it bluntly, Brian was told, saying that "those dumb broads back there are going to bankrupt the airline trying to get single rooms." (The flight attendants had also heard that he loved using the word "cunt" to describe them.) The captain had turned around and retorted, "Why don't you get the hell out of here? Because one of those dumb broads back there is my wife."

This story did nothing to bolster Crandall's reputation with the stewardesses.

Back at the bargaining table, after the second "no" vote, it was clear that things had changed. Management had expected the flight attendants to acquiesce as they had in previous years, to ratify the contract and say, "Thank you so much." That hadn't happened. American, finally, gave up. Single rooms made it into the contract. Management tried to save face. "We didn't add a single dime," they pointed out. "We just rearranged. You ended up losing other stuff to get single rooms." The flight attendants didn't care. They had got what they wanted. When the results of the third vote were tallied, they'd ratified the contract by an overwhelming margin.

The process had taken months and months. The flight attendants had, from the very beginning, been up front about what they needed. But neither the TWU nor management had listened to them.

Later that year, Tommie ran for president of Local 552. She'd moved rapidly up the leadership ladder, joining the local's board in January. Donna Forloine had had her first child and stepped down; Tommie stepped up. This was her opportunity, she thought. She could make real change, put all those hours of consensus-building and listening and cooperation to good use. She didn't run unopposed, though. As soon as men had come on board in 1973, they'd started running for office, having clearly decided that their lack of experience was no obstacle. Three men ran against her for president. Tommie was appalled. It was obvious, she thought to herself, that they wanted to tell everybody a man could do a better job. But she won, sending a message with no room for misinterpretation: the women were not going to support that idea. When they'd counted the votes, none of the men had come anywhere close. And Becky Kroll, the woman she'd met at the AFL-CIO's Labor Studies Center, was elected as her VP. The future looked bright.

Now Tommie was in charge, the head of the union. She saw a path forward to a seat at the TWU top table, to bringing more women into the upper ranks to fight for all flight attendants. She was the leader of a local that was fifty-five hundred members strong. Power, she thought, would come. But there was a flaw in her plan, although she didn't know it yet. Its name was Patt Gibbs.

Part Three

Patt and Tommie

CHAPTER NINETEEN

Stay or Go?

WHEN BRIAN HAGERTY needed extra cash, as he often did, he'd take a bus down Second Avenue and go into the company offices. He could add another $80 to his paycheck each month by helping to sort through American Airlines' customer service forms. These were tucked into seat-back pockets on each flight. Customers were invited to fill them out, entering details about whether they'd enjoyed their flight, if they'd gotten everything they needed, and how was the service?

If the letter complimented the service, Brian was instructed to make a copy and give it to the flight attendant. If the letter was critical—service had been too slow, the coffee was cold, the attendant had seemed brusque—it was sent to the flight attendant's supervisor. Then the flight attendant would be called in to a meeting and asked to explain, in detail, why the passenger had been unhappy. Usually months had passed and it was impossible to remember—if there had even been an incident to remember. If the supervisor decided the complaint was legitimate, the letter would go in the flight attendant's personnel file. That meant they had to file a grievance to get it removed, which could take up to six months of meetings and discussions; this is what union reps spent much of their time dealing with.

Not all the letters made it through. Management would come and check the trash cans in the office every once in a while, but if Brian saw a complaint letter that mentioned a friend of his, he'd rip it up and shove the pieces into his pocket. Later, in the bathroom, he'd throw it away.

Patt was the recipient of several of the complimentary letters

Brian had reviewed. They included statements like, "Your gals on Flight 140F/8 September from SFO-DFW were outstanding. Led by First Lady, Patt Gibbs . . . we really had an excellent in-flight dining experience . . . I know that Patt Gibbs could be a theatrical director on almost any stage the way she runs the show aboard our DC10 LuxuryLiner. Her PA announcements are the finest I have ever heard—as they say in the trade; she is a real professional." Patt *had* to do a good job; she was well aware that doing constant battle with the company over girdles, nail polish, and much more serious grievances meant that any excuse for firing her would be welcome. She took special training that qualified her to work the giant new Astroliner plane, a 747. When she had first caught sight of one, walking onto the field, her jaw had dropped. It was so big it dwarfed the terminal. She'd never seen anything like it. The Astroliner was an incredible plane, one of the best, she thought. She worked first class, a prestigious post.

Still, try as she might, she continued to incur disciplinary actions of her own. Once, she was given a C-314 for having tucked a revision to her flight manual into the front of the manual rather than slotting it in at the right page. Another time she didn't have extra batteries for her flashlight. This constant cutting away at her authority only spurred her on. Tommie sympathized. When you were an outspoken activist, she knew, if there was something that they could get you on, they would go for it. Union reps had to keep their noses clean because management would be after you in a second. Tommie's nose was always clean; Patt's not so much. But she was trying. She even conceded on one of the most horrifying job requirements: kissing the passengers.

This was a peculiarity at several airlines in the 1970s. At one point, female flight attendants at Continental were instructed to kiss every male passenger on the cheek as he exited the plane. Many of the men would swivel their faces around at the last second to catch the stewardess on the lips. At American Airlines, on flights to Hawaii the stewardesses were supposed to give departing customers leis, along with a kiss on the cheek. In one photo from that period, a man at least thirty years older than Patt, with white hair, a brightly patterned shirt, and thick-frame glasses is kissing Patt full on the mouth as he drapes a lei around her neck. Patt, dressed in the uni-

Patt being kissed by a passenger, mid-1970s.

form of neat navy minidress over a pair of slacks, is standing stiffly, her arms at her sides.

In April 1976, Patt got on a plane to Los Angeles but she didn't know why.

Dusty and Nancy had spent most of their working lives in the union. They'd been leaders, contributors, recruiters. On the line for decades, they had adeptly balanced their stewardess duties with the fight for workers' rights, and brought more women, like Patt, into union leadership positions. They'd been by all accounts successful. But something had been in the background all this time. Their slow-building anger at watching the TWU put their problems—age, marriage, pregnancy, single rooms—on the back burner year after year had finally become something that they couldn't and wouldn't hold back any longer.

Along with a couple of other similarly dissatisfied flight attendants, they'd made a decision. They asked Patt and a select few others to join them for a secret meeting in L.A. They'd carefully picked people, including two men, who held positions in the union, who had taken the organizing training the TWU offered—people they knew could lead. The group was small; it had to be. What they were planning was something radical, something that had the potential to change the career of every single American Airlines flight attendant, with ramifications for the entire airline industry. When everyone had settled in, the conspirators dropped their bombshell. They proposed that the people in the room lead a movement to take American Airlines flight attendants out of the TWU and into an entirely independent union of their own.

Patt sat back, stunned. She'd had her own complaints about the TWU, plenty of them. Her disaffection had grown with every passing year. But this was an unprecedented move. The TWU was enormous, powerful, and she had always been told—indeed, she'd told countless others—that the power of the workers lay in numbers. To leave the TWU for another formidable union, like the Teamsters, was easier to envision. But to forge their own union, by and for American flight attendants, would be to enter, she thought, into something totally unknown.

The discussion wasn't rushed. But as they debated, a thrum of excitement seemed to move through the room, affecting everyone in it one by one. The recent roadshows with management, and the pressure from the TWU to accept a contract without single rooms, had pissed off everyone in the group. Perhaps, Nancy pointed out, it was time to handle their contract negotiations themselves.

By the end of the day, they had made a decision: it was time to take their destiny out of the hands of the TWU and into their own.

Patt was under no illusions. This was going to be difficult, possibly the hardest thing she'd ever done. But she had been representing stewardesses for years and years now, and it seemed like their number always came last when the TWU made its list of workers to support. Going independent—forming their own union, just for flight attendants, and led by women—was the only way forward she could see.

The meeting broke up. Patt took a taxi back to the airport, her heart pounding. She felt fired up and energized in a way she hadn't in years. She'd had so many clashes with the TWU in the past, and she had been feeling for what seemed like forever that the way the flight attendants were dominated by men, both American's management and the TWU leadership, was stifling and infantilizing. This meeting was the natural culmination of years of pushing back against the system. It was hugely risky. She knew—no one knew better—how quick the TWU could be to exact vengeance. But the vision she couldn't get out of her head, of the flight attendants in charge of their own destiny, no longer told what to do by men, was too tantalizing to resist. She went to work.

It began with conversations with her colleagues. Autonomy was Patt's most powerful argument. She'd find women she thought might be equally fed up and launch into her sales pitch. "We're in the mechanics' union," she'd say. "They control everything, and we get the leftovers." "With our own union," she'd go on, her voice rising with passion, "we'll control our own destiny at the bargaining table." The "nickel more" theory of pattern bargaining the TWU had been espousing since the 1960s, sweetening the contracts with small improvements, wasn't good enough, Patt declared. Pattern bargaining was effective for traditional unions, such as the United Auto Workers. It wasn't effective for stewardesses, who were after the right to rest on the plane, to be able to sit down during a flight, to have a meal on board instead of picking up the scraps from uneaten passenger meals. The TWU was putting forth its best efforts for the mechanics. "Look at *their* contracts," Patt would point out. "They're paid more than us. The people who clean the plane are paid more than us. Do you want to be in a union that is spending your union dues to help all these other people? You don't work for Pan Am, Eastern, or TWA. What do you care what they do? We're going to work for *us*."

She held organizing meetings, presenting skeptical flight attendants with a slideshow she'd made that was peppered with photos of old white men chomping cigars. She wanted to hammer home the fact that the labor leadership was almost entirely male. The photos were actually of cigar makers (they had their own union), but Patt figured they illustrated her point perfectly. Men controlled the fate of women in the workplace. It was sexism, pure and simple. She'd point out to other flight attendants, "You know, if the men were in the cabin and the women in the cockpit, we'd *still* be getting paid less than them."

Not everyone was receptive. Some were; they felt that the TWU dismissed them, in Tommie's rueful framing, as the "mascots of the labor movement." Others said, "Oh, we're being paid fairly. Why do you always want to upset the applecart, Patt?"

She didn't waste time. Grassroots organizing was effective, she knew. Patt and the women she was converting to the idea made buttons and sold them for fifty cents each. The buttons, which had a white background with blue lettering, were blazoned with the acronym APFA—the name of the new union, they'd decided, would be the Association of Professional Flight Attendants. They held small fund-raisers with Patt's old trick, free cookies. They talked to colleagues one-on-one, bringing up the issues that affected everyone: the uniforms they didn't like, the advertising buttons the airline made them wear that made them feel cheap.

The organizers of the independence movement held secret meetings. Patt, Nancy, and Dusty were always there, as were Colleen Brenner and Kathy Knoop, two other union officials who were as excited as Patt about this audacious plan. The meetings moved from L.A. to Dallas, where Patt was based; it was the easiest base to reach. As time passed and the idea started catching fire, discussions turned from "Can we do this?" to "When should we do this?"

The most important decision they had to make was when to start distributing authorization-to-act cards. These same cards that Jimmy Hoffa had handed to Patt almost a decade earlier, when the flight attendants had considered becoming Teamsters, were their passports to a new union. If they could get 50 percent of American Airlines flight attendants, plus just one more, to sign the cards, the law said they could hold an election. This meant that the flight attendants would get to vote on whether or not they wanted to go independent. But cards came with a timeline. Once the first card was signed, a deadline was triggered. If they couldn't get enough flight attendants to sign cards within a year, they would lose their chance for a vote. And they'd have to start all over again collecting signatures. Each meeting would bring up the same question: How much more time did they need before they started getting people to sign the cards? For the moment, they were organizing under the radar, but as soon as the cards appeared, the TWU would start fighting back.

They decided to go for it. As their campaign became public, Patt and the others started wearing their APFA buttons on their uniforms. Buttons were as strictly regulated as every other part of the uniform, and flight attendants were permitted to wear a union button next to their wings. But the TWU raised a protest. APFA wasn't a union, they said. Take them off. Base managers did the same. Most people removed the buttons; disciplinary action was always an effective threat.

Patt found another way to spread the word about APFA. She printed stickers with the new logo and started sticking them on the planes and in the Operations offices at different airports. She made sure they were always out of sight of the passengers, but posted them where a flight attendant would certainly see them, behind the galley doors, or on the inside of the catering carts. Every time a flight attendant would open a cart, they'd be reminded of the new union. The insurrectionists came up with other ideas to get the news out. An 800 number that people could call for more information on the union would be expensive, $300 a month, but they decided it was worth it. They set up a recorded message. If a curious flight attendant called the number, she'd hear a spiel about the evil things American Airlines and the TWU were doing to the flight attendants, a laundry list of indignities that ranged from the serious (lack of pensions) to the middling (flight attendants didn't get meals on flights) to the merely irritating (having to wear a pin promoting the airline's latest offers). They started producing their own newsletter, printed on big yellow sheets. Every issue had a front-page cartoon that depicted someone from the TWU in cahoots with the company, cutting a deal that disenfranchised the flight attendants. Kathy Knoop wrote a column called Legal Eagle, about contract violations. Patt wrote a column about whatever took her fancy: the latest thing the TWU was doing, or management was doing, that had a negative impact on the flight attendants. The messaging—that the company wasn't going to open its heart and suddenly grant the flight attendants the rights they deserved as workers, and that the TWU was equally at fault—relentlessly pushed the need for a complete overhaul.

Patt had been trained by the TWU to organize in a certain style, and she replicated that style when trying to put together her rebel union. What she did was find one thing, like the single rooms issue, to build upon. "Remember how just a few months ago you didn't have single rooms?" she'd ask fellow flight attendants when they were picking up mail in Operations, or checking in at hotel reception. "They could take that away at any moment." Or she'd point out, "*You're* not getting meals on planes," as she heated trays for the pilots in the galley with a colleague. "Why do you think that is? Maybe it's because they think you're not that important." She'd highlight the things they didn't have, and assert that their working conditions and pay would never get better if they stayed with the TWU.

She kept her poker face on while she thought up new and creative ways to make the few appear like the many. The stickers APFA posted on the plane made it look to management as if there were many more people invested in the union than there were. Patt put the "tree" system she'd learned from the TWU into practice. If she told five people about the union, and each of them told five people, and so on and so forth, word would spread fast, from galley to galley, from jumpseat to jumpseat.

The pace accelerated. After each meeting, the members of the organizing team would return to their individual bases, to continue to build momentum and get the cards signed. They were taking the bureaucratic steps necessary for becoming a union: filing constitution bylaws, electing officers. The organizing committee decided Patt would be president, Kathy Knoop vice president, Linda Prosser treasurer, and Karen Chenault secretary. Soon they had reps in every base. As word of the new union circulated through the flight attendant ranks, more people came to meetings. Patt started seeing more APFA stickers on drinks carts and suitcases, ones she hadn't posted. Flight attendants began asking her about it, although always with a quick glance around first to be sure they wouldn't be overheard. On every flight she worked, she'd organize, asking her colleagues if they supported the new union or not. A "no" never deterred her. A "no" was an opportunity. She'd just try twice as hard to persuade them.

Retribution arrived without delay. On August 27, 1976, the TWU leadership removed Patt from her elected union position and revoked her membership privileges. The same dual unionism charges that had been leveled against Stewardesses for Women's Rights members just a couple of years earlier were now raised against the other founding members of APFA. The difference was that this time they were true. But Patt wrote to Tommie, president of the local, asking her to arrange travel and accommodations for a trip to New York to fight the charges.

Once members were charged under the union's constitution, a trial would be held. That was supposed to ensure due process, but the trial board was made up of TWU leaders. Elected union officials were the ones at risk—only they could be charged with dual unionism. Patt had just been removed from her position, so she wasn't charged, and the other leaders could have resigned their TWU positions. But then they'd have no control over what was happening on their bases, so they decided to fight.

Kathy Knoop was charged, as was Colleen Brenner. Colleen was high up in the TWU, the Los Angeles base chair, and presumably the leaders imagined that bringing her to trial would have a chilling effect on the independence movement. But by this point, the rebels didn't care.

Patt flew to New York for the trials. She met with Tommie while she was there. Patt had planned in advance to talk to Tommie about APFA, what they were doing, and why they were doing it. She's a feminist, Patt thought. She'll understand better than anyone why we want out of the TWU. She's active in SFWR, for Pete's sake! To Patt, that meant there was no way Tommie would want to be part of a male-dominated union when another option was available. Her hopes were high. In initial organizing meetings she had brought up the idea of trying to bring Tommie over to their side, telling the others that Tommie thought the same way they did. But, it turned out, she didn't.

Tommie, she discovered right away, was not a supporter of the indie movement. She'd been appalled when she first heard about the idea, and had only gotten more angry as she watched the campaign progress. Patt *liked* Tommie. She was personable, laid-back, friendly but not a pushover. She wasn't a traditional enemy. She certainly wasn't a favorite of management. Patt respected her, thought she was bright. But it didn't take her very long to learn that Tommie, the union president and a bastion of strength, was going to be fighting her every step of the way. It was a blow.

The trials ended. Everyone was found guilty. They were removed from office and the membership.

At this point, it hardly mattered. There were still a few APFA supporters who held union office; acting as double agents, they would pass on information to the rebels. But Patt and her fellow organizers were past the point of no return. It was either move forward and win the election, or live out the rest of their careers under the heel of vengeful TWU leaders; they'd almost certainly have to quit their jobs. It wasn't really a choice at all.

As more and more of the most active SFWR members began spending time on other things—some dedicating additional hours to union work, some going to law school, some leaving to work for NOW—SFWR slowed down. Adding conflict was the newly established Dallas chapter. Their leader (and the new national coordinator) had, Tommie had heard, been a Miss America contestant. She wore lots of makeup—voluntarily—and talked in the Texas twang that Tommie had worked so assiduously to get rid of. The New York members didn't feel much kinship with her, but Tommie, Bobbi, and Dana flew down to Dallas for the SFWR conference. As Bobbi checked in, she noticed Patt checking in on the other side of the reception desk. She was surprised; Patt had attended that one meeting in New York but she hadn't done much with SFWR since.

When they walked into the Hyatt hotel, things felt different. Tommie suddenly had the overwhelming impression she was at a meeting of a garden club. "This isn't Stewardesses for Women's Rights anymore," she thought to herself, shocked. No one had on their women's equality symbol. The women here weren't the loud, passionate feminists Tommie was used to finding at meetings. They were more decorative, tidier, more conservative. SFWR had changed, Tommie, Dana, and Bobbi felt, and not for the better.

The New York gang would always say to each other that Texas ended Stewardesses for Women's Rights. It wasn't really true. Members had moved on, finances were tight, enthusiasm had shifted to other projects. But before Tommie and her friends left the Dallas conference—early—they noticed one thing. Patt Gibbs and her crew, all promoters of the independent union, were going around collecting the signatures they needed to hold the vote on leaving the TWU. Dallas hadn't even been a part of SFWR until recently, and now it was serving as a vehicle for leaving the union. Tommie was president of Local 552, had committed herself to growing stewardess power through the TWU, and she had to watch as the Dallas stewardesses turned the SFWR conference into a means to their own end, one that would, she thought, destroy everything she was working toward.

In the end, the changes in SFWR didn't really matter. The Dallas conference was the last one it held. In New York, the final newsletter went out. Bobbi and Tommie, wrapped up in union activities, were missing from the masthead, but Dana was still on there, listed as the newsletter editor. Cindy and Kathleen were the last ones in the office. They canceled the phone line, packed up boxes, and turned in the keys. SFWR was over.

The deadline for making the independence decision was rapidly approaching, and you could cut the tension among the flight attendants with a knife. Some were convinced by APFA's arguments. The ones who had been around for many years remembered how the union had allowed no-marriage and no-aging rules to become standard practice. They hadn't forgotten how, when courts had ordered the airlines to hire back the women they had fired, the airlines had found every reason possible to prevent them from returning, and the union had done little to help. They had watched as women had fought to become pursers, with little support from the union as months stretched into years.

Cheryl Stewart, who had faced down the supervisor trying to measure her hair with a ruler, had always felt that the TWU hadn't quite known what to do with the flight attendants. And she understood what Patt was saying: that if they ran their own union, they'd control their own money, and they wouldn't have to expend energy persuading the TWU to listen. It was an argument that made sense to her, but she didn't think they should leave. The flight attendants needed, she thought, to make their voices heard under the umbrella of the TWU, not break off into their own union.

Cheryl could also see—no one could miss seeing—how the people in charge were almost always men. For the entire length of ALSSA's existence (the precursor to their current locals), a man had been either president, vice president, or both. Male pursers and stewards, despite being a tiny percentage of the membership, had always been the union leaders. And at the TWU, there was just a single woman, Claire Corbett, high up in the ranks. Dusty Roads described the stewardesses and the rest of the transport workers as living in two different worlds. "They represented a lot of subway workers and mechanics in New York and those are men whose wives basically stayed at home," she'd remember years later. "They had a hard time relating to a woman who wanted a career . . . They thought a career for a woman was taking care of them and their babies. This was not a big issue for them. The moral issue was important to us as well as the financial issue, but for them it was money. They couldn't relate to us at all. A lot of us were college-educated women; these guys were running the subways."

The divide wasn't just one of class. These bus drivers, mechanics, subway workers—many of them were white men who had grown up in conservative households and spent their lives in unions that had been staunchly anti-Communist. Their working lives had been shaped by the heyday of the American labor movement, their politics by the Cold War. Sex discrimination was to them something completely alien. The fact that a flight attendant had to share a room, or leave her job when pregnant, or wear a skirt so short that it showed her underwear when she stowed luggage in an overhead rack meant very little to them.

And then there was the money. American Airlines stewardesses paid dues to Local 552, which sent them to the TWU, which funneled money upward to the AFL-CIO. The TWU board would cut a check to the parent union and send money back to the stewardesses, after taking their cut. This was perfectly normal for a union federation, but some flight attendants (who, unlike most of the rest of the TWU membership, didn't come from union backgrounds) resented paying the salaries of the TWU leaders out of their already slim paychecks. Enough, it was starting to seem, was enough.

Brian, one of the few men with a leadership position in Local 552, was unquestionably on the side of staying with the TWU. They were making progress, he felt. The TWU leadership was beginning to realize that the flight attendants were a force to be reckoned with. True, they weren't like the subway workers, whom Brian always thought of as Archie Bunker types. But the bigger the union, the bigger your strength—though it was an old chestnut, it was, Brian believed, true. The representatives from the TWU who dealt with the stewardesses, like Ernie Mitchell, were mostly mechanics, and they knew the airlines as well as the flight attendants did. They were sympathetic, and getting more so. They'd push back when Bill Lindner tried to do things the flight attendants didn't want. It was progress; Brian could see it. Going independent would set them back years. Besides, he thought Patt was odious, a loudmouth and a bully. And Tommie, his friend and the woman who'd brought him into the union, was a TWU loyalist. He stuck with her.

It wasn't, Tommie tried to tell people, that she thought the leadership of the TWU was doing its best for the stewardesses. She was butting heads with Bill Lindner all the time. But there had been an incident that had given her hope. She was attending a training session at the AFL-CIO's learning center, and Bill was there. He had come with his wife to an evening event, and they got to chatting with Tommie. She brought up flight attendant safety certification, one of the things they had been pushing for for years and years, and for the first time she could see a change in him. He was . . . listening. Rumblings of the new union movement were getting louder, and he clearly didn't want to lose the flight attendants. Perhaps backing them in their campaign for licensing would do that. Whatever the motivation, she could see that his attitude had shifted.

If Patt's campaign had ended there—using the threat of leaving to force the TWU leadership to take action on what the flight attendants needed—Tommie could have come to terms with it. But Patt had no faith that the TWU leadership would suddenly start giving the "girls" their due. She pressed on.

Tommie was unconvinced. The more she thought about it, the crazier it seemed. We want power? she thought. We can get power *here.* Leaving the TWU would mean losing the backing of the AFL-CIO, would mean abandoning the considerable clout and influence it wielded. The women creating APFA were, in her mind, forming a sorority. *She* wanted to be connected to the labor movement. She wanted a seat at the table. And she knew they were getting there. "If we just stay in here," she'd tell people, "we'll be running the damn unions!"

Tommie had been going all out in her first year as president of Local 552. She'd gather her council of eight and hold frequent meetings, often in someone's apartment rather than at the union office. They'd review the incidents of the past weeks: supervisors who were getting out of hand, crew schedulers breaking the rules, Bob Crandall's latest misdeeds. And she knew how to get what she wanted. In May, Brian had decided to transfer to D.C. Tommie knew the council chairperson there was about to retire. "There's about to be an election in D.C.," she told Brian. "I want you to run for council rep." She even filed his paperwork for him.

"Fine," he thought. "She can put me on the ballot." He'd been on Tommie's council in New York and was willing to do the same in D.C. But Tommie knew that no one else had filed paperwork to run for chairperson. If no one else ran, the elected council rep would automatically become the chair. Brian had only been in D.C. a couple of weeks when Tommie picked up the phone and called him. "Congratulations!" she said. "You're the chairperson in D.C." He could tell she was grinning, even over the phone.

It was the kind of maneuver that had gotten Patt her first union job—elected without her knowledge after showing up at a single meeting. And, just as Patt had done, Brian went dutifully to work.

Tommie coordinated with other locals, invited newly elected officers to get involved, set up training sessions at the AFL-CIO's D.C. center. They'd do trainings on arbitration, negotiation, learning everything they could from the professional organizers at the AFL-CIO. "Bring your crew chiefs here," she'd tell everyone. "Let's get what we can out of this." Yes, Tommie thought, perhaps the TWU *had* bought into the glamour girl image of the flight attendants as much as the general public had. But that could change. She was, in fact, changing it. Some of the new TWU officers came from American and were former maintenance workers. So she built on those ties. She wasn't being called a "Commie" anymore; she was a respected colleague.

But APFA, and Patt Gibbs, were everywhere she looked. Tommie and the other anti-independence leaders decided to write an open letter to the flight attendants. They declared that they were pro-TWU, that they did not support an independent union, and they vowed that if the flight attendants voted to form APFA, they would never run for office in the new union. There would be no magical transfer of power. *They* were elected representatives. And APFA was a mess. The leaders weren't even elected. Which was true: Patt was technically the president, but there had been no vote from the membership; there was no membership yet. The elected leadership of Local 552—Tommie, Becky—and council members like Brian all wanted to stay with the TWU. It was those on the outs with the TWU who wanted to leave. Sour grapes, thought Tommie.

The letter was powerful: a flight attendant reading it would see all the names of the leadership and might think, Hmm, if we leave we won't have anyone in charge who knows anything about unions. From the signatures, it was evident that nearly every base leader was against the change.

Tommie wrote a note for the TWA newsletter (TWA was also hearing rumbles of secession) and came out swinging. Titled "I Support the TWU," her article speculated that the reason for the move toward independence was that many flight attendants did not understand the benefits of the labor movement. They didn't come from trade union families, she said, so they didn't realize that the strength of the workers came from their numbers. She delivered her own views on the independence movement: "I like the involvement and energy present, but strongly believe the direction of independent unions with no affiliations to an international organization would be an incredibly unwise move and totally adverse to the union philosophy." She referenced the number of flight attendants represented by the TWU (almost twenty thousand) and pointed to the additional numbers of their fellow airline workers and TWU members: the mechanics, technicians, flight navigators. "What do these facts and figures say?" she asked. "POWER!"

She finished by urging flight attendants to consider what leaving would mean, and what life would look like without the support of the TWU and AFL-CIO. "Unions are run by workers and workers bound together in solidarity means strength and power. Before this force is disbanded, consider the amount of time, money and effort it will take to begin again—with no support group or international affiliates fortifying your efforts."

Solidarity is what it's all about, Tommie thought. Staying in a big union with other workers meant help: if the flight attendants went out on strike, the mechanics would be on the picket line with them. Flight attendants were considered unskilled labor; they could be replaced quickly, within six weeks, the time it took them to complete their term at training school. But the airline couldn't operate without the mechanics. Safer, she thought, to have the support of other airline workers.

She wrote another letter to her own membership, directly addressing the same flight attendants Patt was trying to convince to join APFA. "Flight attendants have to learn that we can do one of two things," she wrote, her passion coming off the page. "Continue to search for the perfect and ideal union, remaining weak and vulnerable during this period, or put all of our efforts together for once and be **the** power source the Company has to face. I BELIEVE THAT WE HAVE FORGOTTEN JUST WHO OUR ADVERSARY IS IN OBTAINING OUR WORK RELATED GAINS; NOT THE INTERNATIONAL UNION, NOT EACH OTHER, **BUT THE COMPANY**."

Despite how passionate she felt about staying in the TWU, Tommie was beginning to get the uneasy feeling that she was swimming against the tide. At other airlines, flight attendants were also talking about leaving the TWU. Organized labor and the women's movement had often been at loggerheads, and this was the purest expression of that conflict.

TWA flight attendants—Local 551 in the TWU—started a bid for independence. They had begun pushing back against the TWU around the time Patt was launching the APFA campaign, during contract negotiations in which they, like the American stewardesses, felt that the union leaders were prioritizing the wrong things. TWA flight attendants in Kansas City got hundreds of signatures on a petition to "Tell Mitchell off!," referring to Ernie, who was now a TWU VP. The TWU had reacted badly, hauling the executive board of Local 551 into an emergency meeting where they were asked to swear an oath to uphold the TWU constitution. Each board member was told to utter this loyalty oath with their hand on a copy of the constitution itself, like witnesses in court swearing on a Bible. Instead of a loyalty oath, they swore that they would support TWA flight attendants and do what they wanted. The TWU leaders threatened to kick them out, and charged them, in a now familiar scenario, with dual unionism.

The TWA local was still sharing office space with American's Local 552 when they voted to leave the TWU in March 1977. TWA's new union was called the Independent Federation of Flight Attendants, but it still wasn't led by women. The new president was Art Teolis, a man. "What are you guys doing?" Tommie asked, frustrated and aggrieved by what was to her a series of grave errors that threatened to erase all the gains flight attendants had made. She and her crew reluctantly helped them pack up their boxes, Tommie telling them, "I hope you're making the right decision. But I'm staying. We're going to take this union over."

Kathleen Heenan, Tommie's SFWR compatriot, could understand better than Tommie how frustrated TWA flight attendants were. Fighting sex discrimination and helping women who had been forced out when pregnant were not issues the TWU rank and file cared about. Pregnancy was a choice, they reasoned. They ignored the fact that the EEOC had filed suit against TWA in 1976; TWA was still firing pregnant flight attendants. The case would become part of the ACLU's Women's Rights Project, and to demonstrate that pregnancy was not correlated with an inability to do your job, every lawyer the ACLU used in court was pregnant. (*Knox-Schillinger v. TWA* wouldn't be resolved until the twenty-first century.) This was fuel for Patt's APFA fire, just another display of the women's place in the TWU hierarchy.

From Kathleen's perspective, their "comrades" in the TWU, these grandfathers, as she thought of them, were just biding their time. Once Kathleen had been representing a fellow stewardess in a dispute, and a manager at JFK, Dick Ferris, was repeatedly nasty to her in the hearings. She complained about it. But the response from the TWU leadership was, "Well, we'll just find somebody else to do your work." She quit the airline entirely in 1977.

More change started coming. Northwest flight attendants joined the Teamsters. One large group, made up of flight attendants from Braniff, Continental, United, and other airlines, formed the Association of Flight Attendants. Before this, these airlines had been part of the pilots' union, which had controlled their contract negotiations in much the same way the TWU did for American. AFA, their new union, wasn't fully independent—it was still affiliated with the pilots' union—but the flight attendants at these airlines held a series of elections between 1975 and 1979, at the end of which they could bargain for themselves. And AFA was led almost entirely by women.

Then the TWU lost another group of flight attendants, from Pan Am. They had been with the TWU for decades, in a unique umbrella local with other Pan Am workers including cleaners, commissary workers, and mechanics. But the president of the Pan Am local was a mechanic, the vice president was a mechanic, and although there were almost as many flight attendants as mechanics in the local, they had only one representative on the board, out of nine. The flight attendants voted with their feet and formed the Independent Union of Flight Attendants. They soon secured themselves a much better contract.

Tommie was depressed, but not defeated. They still had Eastern, Southern, and a handful of smaller airlines. They would stick with the TWU and take power, even if the men didn't want to give it. She had faith; she knew they could do it.

The players had chosen their sides. Tommie couldn't understand why Patt was giving up a chance to play with the big boys, to be part of a major union. She even suspected that some of Patt's motivation for going independent was personal. Patt had wanted to be a negotiator and the TWU had shot her down; Tommie had seen her stomping down the hallway in a huff after a meeting. Patt had, Tommie imagined, in a fit of pique, thought, "Okay, fine. I'll go another route." The two had plenty in common, she knew. The women's movement, for one—they were both strong, radical feminists. But they didn't see eye-to-eye on this one essential thing.

For Patt's part, she had had high hopes that Tommie would see the light when it came to independence. As she got to know Tommie better, she could see that their approaches were totally different. They fought battles for the same things, and Patt admired her, but their passion presented itself in very different ways. Shock and awe was Patt's method. Communication and deal-making was Tommie's.

But Patt was sick of fighting on two fronts: the old conservative white men in management, and the old conservative white men in the TWU. She had been discouraged. As a unionist, she didn't think the flight attendants were making the progress they should be. Now she was thriving, full of the energy that the prospect of a truly independent union was giving her.

Tommie had a network of supporters. Brian was one, Becky another. She and Tommie developed a plan to make change from within the TWU. They would ramp up training and increase resources. But Tommie felt like she was trying to hold back a tidal wave. Swept up in a maelstrom of passion, angst, and ideals, the flight attendants pushing for an independent union were flush with empowerment. It was hard to fight that, to advise caution. Nevertheless, she kept trying.

The battle over whether to stay or to go was reaching its peak. Conflicts were starting to erupt over everything, down to the bulletin board in Operations. The TWU supporters posted their opinion on the board. Then APFA complained about not being permitted to post theirs. Lawyers became involved. Patt and her team were canvassing heavily, asking people to sign authorization-to-act cards every chance they got. Patt even staked out the employee parking lot. That way the crew had to pass her on their way from their cars to the AirTran station, where employees boarded the little train that circulated around the Dallas airport. Everyone came through there, they were a captive audience.

Patt had her table, with cards for people to sign, propaganda about why the flight attendants should be independent, her yellow sheets, her APFA buttons. Becky, Tommie's VP, set up a competing table stocked with information about why it was better to stay in the TWU. Tensions rose fast and tempers exploded. There were screaming matches over the tables, shouts of "Get off our fucking turf!" in the parking lot, Patt quick to get in another person's face. At this point anywhere was fair game, thought Patt; their deadline was rapidly approaching. You had to stand your ground, couldn't let the other side see you as weak. She started handing out cards on flights, but she couldn't know in advance if her target was a TWU supporter, which led to heated confrontations.

Then someone called the police on her, saying that she was in the employee parking lot with a tire chain and crowbar, threatening people and intimidating them into signing cards. She'd been in the parking lot, yes, but certainly not with weapons. She was arrested. But she had a witness, and was quickly released. She suspected it wasn't the TWU that had called the cops, but management. Management might not have liked the TWU but at least it was a known quantity; negotiating with a rogue union headed by a militant like Patt was something to be avoided at all costs.

It was ironic, in a way. That approach, tire chains and crowbars, was the one she'd always associated with Jimmy Hoffa. Hoffa himself had disappeared in 1975. He had been in prison from 1967 to 1971, when Richard Nixon commuted his sentence, though with the stipulation that he could not be involved in union activity until 1980. He had been replaced as Teamsters president by Frank Fitzsimmons but had been searching for ways to regain his leadership position when he was reported missing. In the days and weeks that followed, conspiracy theories as to what had happened abounded. Had the Mafia executed him? Had a friend turned on him? Was he dead, or kidnapped? Patt had her own theory: that the Teamsters leadership, under the direction of Fitzsimmons, had persuaded the mob to kill Hoffa. She didn't like Fitzsimmons, and knew he didn't want Hoffa back in charge. She was saddened by the news of his disappearance. Though she knew Hoffa's history wasn't, as she put it, lily-white, he'd been an ally. And she respected what he'd done for his workers. It felt like the end of an era.

She had achieved, she realized, an entirely new understanding of why the Teamsters had become so militant. Now, she thought angrily, she'd have been willing to sell her soul to the devil if he could start making progress and changes in the way women were treated, both in the airline industry and in general. She had thought Hoffa a thug. Now she understood why he did the things he did, and she almost wished she could adopt some of those same methods.

CHAPTER TWENTY

Election Day

THE YEAR WAS almost up. The last few weeks of the campaign were frenetic. Patt handed out cards like a Vegas dealer, persuading members of her crew on each flight to take cards and get them signed, instructing them to bring them back on the next trip, extending the network all over the country. The TWU didn't sit back and take it. As Patt and her co-conspirators worked to get the cards signed, the TWU started a campaign to persuade flight attendants not to sign. They tried scare tactics, trumpeting the negative effects of going independent: think of the power you'll lose, the prestige, the resources! The independence movement taking hold at other airlines was worrying. Losing the American Airlines flight attendants (and their dues) would leave a big hole in the budget. At every opportunity, the TWU trumpeted the benefits of staying put. But time was running out.

Organizing APFA had taken over Patt's life to the extent that it took her much longer than it should have to realize her smoking had gotten out of control. Cigarettes were still permitted on every flight, although the flight attendants had to smoke theirs in the galley, or before everyone boarded. (Passengers weren't supposed to see them smoking.) Patt's fellow organizers would come to town, staying overnight at her house, which doubled as APFA headquarters; they were all smokers. Shana, her partner, was a smoker. It never occurred to anyone to go outside for their cigarette. One day Patt realized that she was smoking all the time. She was up to four packs a day, sometimes more, unthinkingly lighting up as her frantic pace of work continued.

She decided to tackle the problem with her usual single-minded dedication. I sleep eight hours a night and I'm not smoking then, she told herself. So I'll try to go for eight hours at a time awake. She still carried cigarettes and a lighter around with her, and she kept a carton of cigarettes in the house. But for every pack she didn't smoke, she put the money it would have cost her in a jar. Every time she wanted a cigarette, she'd chew a vitamin C tablet instead. She'd always associated cigarettes with coffee, which she drank black with lots of sugar. So she switched to coffee with cream, which didn't trigger the same craving. She stopped smoking and never looked back.

Though Patt was consumed by the campaign for independence, she continued to fly planes in the little spare time she had. And she became health-obsessed; she and Shana still had the vitamin store. Shana and Patt kept their relationship at least partly under wraps. Their house had two bedrooms; they used only one but could point to the other as "Shana's room" if anyone asked. Patt had other Texan friends, Margo and Carolyn, who were stewardesses a bit older than she was. They had become lovers at the charm farm and had been together for decades. But every week before the house cleaner came over, Patt knew, they'd go into the second bedroom and mess it up, making it look like someone had been sleeping there. Patt had plenty of other lesbian friends who were stewardesses, many of whom, like her, never came out to their parents because they were too afraid of rejection. She'd even discovered that two of her instructors at the charm farm had been a couple. They'd just had to keep it hidden from almost everyone.

Patt was traveling all the time now, drumming up support for APFA at bases around the country. All of a sudden, she noticed, she was more popular than before. Women were inviting her to stay over; she'd enter a bathroom and someone would try to kiss her. She was flattered. She had a couple of one-night stands, enjoying the attention. Part of it was people trying to lay traps for her, she figured. But she didn't care. She did it anyway.

As May 1977 neared, it was time to deliver the cards. The process worked like this: first, the cards were handed over to the National Mediation Board. The board would look through them, check the signatures against the signatures the company supplied from its files, investigate for any signs of fraud, and then count them. If

APFA had the 50 percent plus one that they needed, they'd have a majority and could call for an election. The election would be conducted by ballot. Each flight attendant who wanted to could cast her vote to stay put or to leave for the new union. If APFA had the votes, the American Airlines flight attendants would leave the TWU and embark on their new path.

Patt and her fellow organizers packed up all their cards in shoeboxes and flew with them to Washington, D.C. Mailing them in seemed too risky. And they couldn't risk stowing them in their checked luggage either, knowing that the baggage handlers were TWU members. Instead, Patt, Kathy, and the others carried the shoeboxes onto the plane under their arms, then tucked them carefully under their seats. Patt kept bending down to check on them during the flight, just in case.

The cards were counted. They had the votes. They had known they did—they had counted the cards themselves before packing them into the shoeboxes—but somehow it hadn't felt real until it was confirmed by the board. It was the first step, and they'd succeeded. They went back to normal life. Patt worked her flights, performing each task automatically: welcoming passengers aboard, picking up glasses, depositing trays. But her mind was on this huge thing they'd launched. There was no turning back now.

From there, things moved fast. Ballots were sent to every flight attendant at American. The ballot listed only two options: stay in the TWU or make APFA their new union. First in alphabetical order, APFA was top on the ballot. The date of the count was announced: May 10, 1977.

Patt and the rest of the organizing committee—Kathy Knoop, Linda Prosser, Nancy Collins, Dusty Roads, and the others, numbering almost twenty—flew back to D.C. for the count. There was one danger. If less than a majority of the flight attendants voted, they'd have no representation at all, leaving them without a union. Voting was essential, no matter which way it went. Even Tommie had put out a newsletter urging people to vote, even if they didn't vote to remain. To be without a union was to both groups unthinkable. But the risk existed.

The day arrived. The APFA organizers were tense as they filed into the room where the count would take place, a cavernous space at

the National Mediation Board offices. The TWU had an equal number of representatives there, but Tommie was not among them—she
was back in the local's office in New York. She sent Brian as her
primary representative. She had a bad feeling about the vote and
thought she should stick close to the office in case things didn't go
their way. She had an idea that the TWU wouldn't react well if the
flight attendants decided to leave.

The process was a slow one. Ballots were counted in groups. First
they had to be sorted and authenticated. The ballots were secreted
inside envelopes that had then been inserted into bigger envelopes.
Once the outer envelopes had been verified, the mediators started
opening the heap of ballot envelopes. They were counted manually,
and each vote was read out loud. Brian would run out at intervals and
call Tommie from a pay phone to let her know what was happening.

Their fears of a no-union result were allayed early; a large majority of the more than five thousand American flight attendants had
cast their ballots and there were over four thousand votes to be
counted. Patt's heart was racing as she heard each vote called. After
a while, the result began to become clear. Vote after vote was read
out loud: "APFA." "APFA." "APFA." Eventually the TWU reps left
the room and didn't come back. Brian went to the pay phone. "Tommie," he said, "it's not looking good."

It was late at night by the time the count was finished. The
excitement among the APFA founders had been rising through the
afternoon and into the evening. Patt was beside herself. Their year of
planning, working, persuading—it had worked. They—themselves,
the women—were going to be in charge of their own destiny. The
board, all ballots finally tallied, declared APFA the winner. Patt
closed her eyes. It was a moment to savor.

The leaders of the new flight attendants' union went back to their
hotel and celebrated. They had rented a suite, everyone chipping in
to pay for it, and they crowded in, squashing onto the bed and bal-
ancing on the arms of the chairs, chattering and exclaiming. They
toasted with champagne, made ecstatic phone calls. They changed
the outgoing message on their hotline, the 800 number they'd set up
to one that declared victory. It had been a long day, an exhausting
year, but they were no longer tired.

They went back the next day to receive their official certification. A photo taken at that moment showed sixteen women and one man, the founders of APFA, with joyous faces. They're each making the "V for victory" sign with their fingers, except for Dusty Roads, who's sitting at the front like a queen. Patt is holding up the certification. She's grinning from ear to ear.

Professionals at Last

BRIAN CALLED TOMMIE and told her the news. She was crushed. The union—*her* union—was gone. The flight attendants had made a huge mistake, she knew that much. But, she told herself, she'd known there was a chance this would happen. And now that they'd lost, there was something urgent she had to do. She was heartsick. But grieving for her loss would have to wait until morning. She picked up the phone.

She called three women on her union council, flight attendants she was close to, and whom she knew had access to cars. "Get to the office," she told them, although it was already after dark. "I'll explain there." She put on her jacket and headed out. When her colleagues arrived, she told them what she had in mind. They were no longer part of the TWU, she announced. Now they were APFA. And they had to move fast. The TWU would be coming for every scrap of paperwork they possessed. "Every grievance, every list of addresses, every complaint against the company," she said. The TWU would be outraged that the flight attendants had left, and they'd feel entitled to everything the union had. "You all know I didn't want to go with APFA," she told them. "But that's our union now. And we need those papers. Our union can't function without them."

They got to work, packing up everything they could carry, loading box after box with the union's most important documents. They packed until almost midnight, then loaded it all into three cars and drove it up to Tommie and Al's apartment in Bronxville.

The next morning, Tommie went back to the union office. When she opened the door the first thing she noticed was Ernie Mitchell, the one-armed bandit. She'd always gotten along well with Ernie, but when she saw him waiting for her, flanked by two other TWU officers, there was an icy silence. She looked around. The office was empty. The rest of the paperwork, everything they hadn't been able to fit in their cars, leftover files and folders and boxes—it was all gone. And her desk had been turned upside down. Ernie had heard the results of the election and had arrived at 7 a.m., determined to grab the local's documents, lists, every bit of paper of any importance. The TWU had taken everything they could find. The office was cleared out. But they knew they hadn't got it all.

"What the fuck have you done, Tommie?" Ernie asked her. He was in a rage, all three of them were. They'd been outflanked on two fronts. First they'd lost the flight attendants, and now they'd been beaten to the punch when it came to their records.

"Those documents belong to APFA now," Tommie replied. "They're part of the union's history. And I'm turning them over to the folks that are working hard to create something. Because they worked for a whole year without even being elected."

"Where's your loyalty?" Ernie asked, practically spitting.

"My loyalty," she said, tired and upset, but holding firm, "is to the flight attendants."

He snorted at that. "Those documents are TWU property."

Tommie sighed. "You'd have done the same thing in my shoes." She looked around the bare room. "You didn't have to do this, Ernie," she said reproachfully. "You know how hard we worked to stay." He ignored her.

Tommie felt she had lost the union, and she had. But she certainly wasn't going to complain about the flight attendants' decision to the TWU. And overturning her desk had, she thought, been the act of a petulant child.

A day later, Kathy Knoop and Colleen Brenner, the victors in the independence fight, drove up to Bronxville and knocked on her door. They thanked her profusely, animosity and gloating both set aside for the moment. There wasn't enough space in their car for everything Tommie had taken; they had to go rent a van and then come back. Then they had to drive all the papers back to Dallas, which was APFA headquarters. But they were grateful. Without these records, APFA would have been starting from nothing. Now they had all the active disputes, grievances, all the cases in the system. It was a beginning.

For years afterward Tommie would ask the TWU for the remainder of the local's paperwork. She knew exactly where it was, in the basement of the TWU headquarters in New York. "Guys, come on," she'd cajole. "It's our property." But it didn't work. The TWU knew how to hold a grudge.

Tommie, who had gone from being president of a union of fifty-five hundred flight attendants to being an ordinary member of a rookie union still finding its feet, took a vacation. Then she went back to flying.

Nineteen seventy-seven was the year women got to be in charge, or at least they got to try. Bella Abzug threw herself into the Democratic primary race for mayor of New York City; Bobbi worked on her campaign. Bella hadn't given up her trademark oversized hat (she wore it, she said, so people would recognize that she was a professional, not a secretary). Her nickname, "Bellicose," was in Bobbi's opinion completely appropriate. Still, Bella got things done. Bobbi knew she was a great leader, and she worked hard on the campaign to help distract herself from the battle over the future of the union. Bella lost to Ed Koch.

A few months later, Bella attended the National Women's Conference in Houston. She had been appointed the head of the National Commission on the Observance of International Women's Year by Jimmy Carter, who in the same year chose Carin Clauss as the first woman solicitor of labor. (Carin would become Patt's mentor, eventually encouraging her to go to law school.) The national conference was a landmark event for the second-wave feminist movement, drawing thousands of women from around the country. Tommie, still in the liminal space of the post-election daze, decided to go, taking Dana with her. SFWR necklace layered over her overalls, her mass of curly hair freed from the parted-in-the-middle, pulled-back style she wore on board, Tommie fit right in amid the sea of ERA tote bags and T-shirts emblazoned with the *Ms.* logo. It was unbelievable, she thought, in the best way, a true celebration of women who wanted to propel the women's movement forward. (Phyllis

Schlafly held her own conference down the street at the same time.) Three First Ladies attended; so did Maya Angelou, and the leaders of NOW. The electricity in the air thrilled Tommie to her core, and even the proximity of Schlafly couldn't kill it. They listened to earthshaking speeches by the big names, but the memory that stuck with Tommie was of a small circle discussion. A Mormon woman, representing Utah at the conference, told the story of how she'd left her husband and the church had taken her children from her. By the end of the story, she, Tommie, and all the other women in the circle were crying. It should have been a moment of pain, and it was, but it was also a moment of power.

Management at the airline didn't react well to the American flight attendants' decision. Now the women had no powerful union behind them, so placing obstacles in their path was easy. The moment they were certified, Patt got on the phone and called Charlie Pasciuto. She was the leader now, and she needed to set a meeting with the

In Houston at the National Women's Conference, 1977. Left to right: Diane McEwen, Tommie, Dana.

company. She had to introduce the new officers, find out which griev-ances were in progress. "We won the election, Charlie," she told him, trying—but not that hard—to keep the triumph out of her voice.

His reaction was disappointing. "So?"

She requested a meeting, but he was having none of it. Manage-ment had decided to be as uncooperative as possible, doing only what was required by law. He told her right off the bat that American wasn't going to recognize APFA's dues check-off cards. This meant that American would no longer automatically collect union dues from the flight attendants' paychecks, the way they had done for Local 552. Patt was shocked. She had assumed the company would honor the cards; they always had for the TWU. It was a slap in the face. But it was also a wake-up call. Her fight wasn't over.

She moved on. "We need to figure out an extension for the griev-ances in progress," she told him. The TWU had absconded with the paperwork Tommie and her helpers hadn't managed to grab, and APFA would need time to catch up.

"No extensions will be granted," was Charlie's curt answer. Patt started to panic. If no extensions were granted and APFA couldn't catch up in time, flight attendant grievances could be dismissed, and the members would, rightfully, be furious that the union they'd voted for was leaving them in the lurch.

"Fine," she said, angry now. "Our lawyers will set up a meeting and we'll get all of this worked out. We're the union now, and you're going to have to deal with us whether you like us or not."

"Fine, Gibbs," Charlie replied. "But remember, I don't have to make your life easier." He hung up the phone.

Patt had disliked Charlie ever since she'd seen him drinking in the hotel bar with Colleen Boland all those years ago. In the time since, she'd watched him, on the other side of the bargaining table, denying the flight attendants' demands at every opportunity. And when she'd seen him out on the roadshow trying to sell the flight attendants on a contract without single rooms, she'd hated him even more. Now he'd made it clear he was going to oppose her every chance he got. Let's do it, she thought. She knew she was a match for him.

Patt realized almost instantly how ill-prepared APFA was. For a year they'd poured all their energy into organizing, without time or energy to spare for figuring out how to operate if they won. They needed a dues structure in place, had to scramble to do basic things such as set up a bank account. Charlie knew they were in disarray, and, like any good company man, he took advantage of it.

They also had to elect officers. Patt had been chosen as temporary president of APFA by the founding members, but now they had to hold a real election, in which the brand-new flight attendant membership would get to decide who ran the union. Patt expected that she would be voted in as president again; everyone knew she had put her heart and soul into this.

Then something unexpected happened. The former leaders of Local 552, the ones who had signed the letter saying that they would never run for office if the flight attendants left the TWU, ran for office. Tommie was one of them. She'd been infuriated and saddened in equal parts by the decision to go independent, but she'd grieved enough. She wasn't one to dwell on the past; she looked forward. The conference in Houston had reenergized her. The flight attendants, she realized, had chosen what they wanted, and she wasn't going to pout in a corner. So APFA was now her union, whether she liked it or not, and contracts and negotiations were coming up. They had to get back in the game. She announced her candidacy.

Brian, though he'd been just as anti-APFA as Tommie, thought of it as the only practical move. He talked to other former officers: "You have to remember what's on the other side of the wall," he'd say. "What's on the other side of the wall is the company. And if we're going to be together, we've got to *be together.* It doesn't mean we can't argue and debate when we're in meetings, but once we come to a vote, everybody has to go down the same path." Part of his motivation was less virtuous, though. "It's our union, too," he thought. "We're not going to let it go just because we didn't vote for it. And we've got more experience than a lot of these idiots in Dallas." Those "idiots in Dallas" included Patt. But Brian was all in.

Becky, too, picked herself up. As early as September 1977 she requested to serve as Dallas–Fort Worth base chairperson until elections could be held. In a letter she sent to all DFW flight attendants, she outlined her reasons: "Together we have been through cruel months of dissension and inner turmoil. The defeat of Local 552 in the representation election was a heartbreak for many of us, and there are things about our new union with which many of us are uncomfortable. But, this IS our union—yours and mine. I know that it's up to me as a member to do what I can to build a strong union—a union of which I can be proud."

Patt had thought everything would fall into place after they'd won the independence vote. But it was harder than she'd thought to create a union out of nothing. As the election approached, internal conflict was frequent; differences of opinion as to how APFA should be run became more and more common. Patt and Kathy Knoop—whom she always referred to by her last name (kah-NOOP)—were butting heads constantly. A board meeting was held and it became clear to Patt that Knoop had more support and that she, Patt, was about to be yanked out of office. Thwarted, she decided to step down. She resigned her temporary presidency. Kathy Knoop took over until the election could be held.

Kathy ran for president. Becky Kroll, backed by the TWU group, ran too. And Patt ran, backed by her own group of loyal supporters. Tommie ran for vice president. American Airlines was moving its headquarters from New York to Dallas. Tommie had left Texas a long time before and swore she'd never go back. Al's job at the Bank of New York was in New York; her home was in New York. And the vice president job would stay in New York, where Employee Relations (and Charlie Pasciuto) would also remain.

The election was held in Dallas. There were four mediators counting the ballots, at long tables set up expressly for that purpose. Patt and her crew and Tommie and hers were allowed to observe the count from chairs cordoned off at one side of the room; they weren't permitted near the tables. The room was tense, but quiet. Conversation was discouraged. Tommie and Patt, who had been enemies for a full year, started talking in hushed voices. They wondered aloud how it was going to go, asked each other how the last year had been. The rest of Tommie's and Patt's teams watched them closely. Tommie realized, almost surprised, that she liked Patt. She was a character—that Tommie had already known—but Patt was obviously passionate about making things better for the workers, and that was, after all, Tommie's goal too. Tommie had a flight and needed to leave before all the votes had been tabulated. She knew what time the results would come in, though, and when she got off the plane she ran over the tarmac to a pay phone. She called the union hotline with her heart pounding. The message at the other end of the 800 number read out the winners. Kathy Knoop had won the presidency. Tommie was elected vice president. And the division reps were a mix of all the parties. Tommie was horrified. By this time it was clear that there were three camps in the new union: the Gibbs supporters, the Knoop supporters, and the former officers of Local 552. She'd just been elected with Patt's worst enemy. "What have we done?" she asked herself.

She couldn't imagine how they would ever manage to work together—her, the TWU stalwart, with Knoop, one of the leaders of the independence movement. But she pulled herself together. Kathy Knoop was known to be difficult, but she was, Tommie thought wryly to herself, no more difficult than Patt. One of her team, who had been elected as a division rep, went into a panic when she heard the results, and said to Tommie, "I'm not going to do this!" "Yes, you are," Tommie told her. "Because the membership elected us. Think about it. They're tired of all this division. And so they're going to make us work together." Just after the election, she and Knoop had to fly to New Orleans to attend the National Academy of Arbitrators convention and, since the new union had so little money, they had to share a room. Tommie smiled through it. She'd had plenty of practice.

Post-election, Patt retreated again. She couldn't work under Knoop, no matter what. Even though APFA had been her baby, her passion, almost her obsession, that was a bridge too far. She got her commercial pilot's license, taking lessons from Edna Gardner Whyte, who had been a pioneering woman pilot and a contemporary of Amelia Earhart. Sometimes when Edna raced, Patt flew with her. Edna was a vicious competitor and a tough teacher. If Patt did something wrong, Edna would reach over to the other side of the cockpit and yank her earlobe, yelling the whole time. Patt bought a plane, a Luscombe 8E. She learned to fly acrobatics, and opened her own flight school. She broke up with Shana and started dating someone new.

The newly elected APFA officers went into bargaining almost immediately after taking office. The negotiating team, led by Kathy and Tommie, would be up against Charlie and the rest of management. The first meeting was held in a big conference room in New

York. About to enter, Tommie was struck by an idea. She stopped and pulled Kathy aside. "Let's be late to this party," she said. "Let's let them sweat a little bit and wonder where we are." Pasciuto knew as well as anyone that the conflicts at the brand-new union had resulted in a bizarre slate of officers, officers who had been at each other's throats just a few months earlier. Tommie suggested that she and Kathy arrive late, just by a few minutes, and then walk in side by side. "Just trust me," she said. When she and Kathy entered the room together and took their seats, everyone's heads turned. Tommie had the pleasure of watching, in real time, Charlie realize that the new union officers were going to be able to work together. He'd been assuming, not without reason, that the infighting would continue and that the company would be able to take full advantage of their fragmentation. She could see him thinking, "I'm in trouble." It was a brilliant start.

As the first two-year term came to a close, those who wanted to run for union office for the upcoming term had to announce their candidacy. Patt decided she would try for president one last time. She began working with another woman, Sarah, who was also running for office. They needed a president, vice president, secretary, treasurer, and five division reps, a total of nine positions to form a slate that would, they hoped, dislodge Kathy Knoop. Patt and Sarah flew to Chicago to try to recruit Susan French, a flight attendant who was running as a division rep there. A lanky young woman with exuberant curly hair, dressed in overalls, a T-shirt, and white sneakers, met them in a Pizzeria Uno. Patt and Sarah asked if she would run with them. "Oh, there's no way I'm going to run with you," Susan replied. "I want to win." She'd run as an independent, she told them; she wasn't supporting Kathy either. Then she asked Patt a direct question: "Are you a lesbian? Everybody says you're a lesbian."

"Yeah," Patt said, "I am. What difference does it make? Do you go around asking Knoop and everyone else what their sexual preferences are?"

"Well," Susan said, "I see your point."

To Patt, Susan seemed way out there, weirdly hostile. All she'd wanted to know was whether Susan would be campaigning against her. But she said, "It doesn't make any difference whether I'm a lesbian or not. I'm the better candidate for this union."

Her sexual orientation was known to most people by now, but Kathy Knoop tried to make it a campaign issue anyway. Patt had to officially come out of the closet. "Fine," she said. "I'm gay. What of it?" And then she won, beating Kathy Knoop by overwhelming numbers.

Patt was, finally, the elected president of APFA, the union she'd worked so hard for. And Susan had won too; she was a division rep. She had a husband, it turned out, but she never talked about him. When Patt found out, she asked Susan, "Why didn't you tell us you were married?"

Susan replied, "What difference does it make?"

Well, thought Patt, that was fair.

Patt had been president for a year when contract bargaining time came around again. Tensions were running high. Pasciuto and his cronies had convinced themselves that Patt would take the flight attendants out on strike if they didn't get what they wanted. In the middle of the bargaining period, management sent out a letter to everyone in the company. "We are interviewing for flight attendants," it announced. "If you have a sister, a mother, a daughter, a friend, anybody, including a pet gorilla, have them contact us."

A gorilla could do their job? The flight attendants were not amused. When Patt got her hands on the memo, she immediately decided there was no way Pasciuto was getting away with this. Time to teach him a lesson. At the next bargaining session, there was no sign of her. Pasciuto and the rest of management were sitting on one side of the table, the union reps on the other, ready to begin, but Patt was nowhere in sight. "Where's Gibbs?" Pasciuto was asking, when the door flew open. Patt raced into the room wearing a gorilla suit. She made a flying leap onto the table and ran around it, making monkey noises. She stomped over to Pasciuto and started raking through his hair with her fingers. Having silenced the room, she took her gorilla head off, threw the memo on the table in front of him, and said, "Even a gorilla can replace us, Charlie? That's how valuable we are to American Airlines?" The union reps around the table loved it. The executives were speechless. Charlie was livid.

He slammed his fist down on the table, snatched up his papers, and left.

From being told she walked like a gorilla back in 1962 to donning a gorilla suit to piss off management twenty years later, Patt had come far. She was, at last, in charge of the union she'd given an entire year of her life to creating, and she continued to lead in her iconoclastic, loudmouthed, no-holds-barred way. Her approach still caused friction. One letter from a member, written on Sheraton stationery, practically begged her not to make waves. "Try to work <u>with</u> the company," the flight attendant pleaded. "Try not to antagonize and/or irritate Crandall." But that wasn't Patt's style.

Patt and Susan continued working together, not bringing up Susan's husband or Patt's sexuality again. They were getting along, though. Patt no longer thought Susan was "out there." Susan was a hard worker and clearly passionate about the same things Patt was; she'd stand in the back at meetings and shout to make herself heard. They became, as the weeks went by, friends.

Not long after the election, they both flew with Linda Prosser to the Caribbean to organize new flight attendants. The union was trying to save money, so Susan and Linda bunked together. Patt, as president, got the single room to herself. Linda had to fly home early, and to avoid paying for a second room she moved Susan's things into Patt's room before she left. And that was that. Susan and Patt are still together.

Bit by bit, APFA found its footing. The union grew over the years; it now represents twenty-eight thousand flight attendants, and it's still independent, answering to no one but its members.

The key to *staying* strong and independent, the flight attendants learned, was serving their common interests. Patt and Tommie ended up working together in a surprisingly effective way. When major arbitrations arose that demanded two union representatives, the members often sent them together, despite their wildly different styles, utilizing the strengths of each and forcing them to become teammates.

And they admired each other, their mutual respect growing as the years passed. When one was in a leadership position, they'd hire the other to work on arbitrations. When they were advocates together, they learned, they were strong advocates. And they knew their power against the company only grew when they stood shoulder to shoulder.

There was a moment in the thick of the weight battles of the early 1990s that Tommie would always look back on with a smile. Sherri Cappello, at the time APFA's vice president, had been fired for being over her maximum permitted weight. She'd worked for American Airlines for twenty-five years. When her case came to arbitration, Sherri was represented by Susan French, Patt's partner, and Patt and Tommie were both sitting on the board for the union. Despite warnings from people who thought Patt was too difficult to deal with, Tommie flew out to Los Angeles and worked with Patt and Susan for two days straight, strategizing and planning Sherri's defense. They had dinner together each night, reminiscing about the old days with surprising fondness. And they won Sherri's case for her. Tommie even reprised her trick from the first meeting APFA had attended in 1977: when the arbitration opened, they all walked into the room together, united, and watched management start to sweat.

Epilogue

FOR THE TWU, the mass movement of flight attendants into independent unions was a bloodbath. It had taken less than three years for almost every flight attendant in the country to shift her allegiance. It was a seismic change in an industry that had relied for so long on the passivity of its workers. Around fourteen thousand of them left, 10 percent of the total membership: a huge blow to the TWU's prestige and finances. The number of women represented by the TWU also, unsurprisingly, dropped dramatically. By decade's end, the male-dominated organizations that had lorded it over the flight attendants had been decisively thrust aside. The flight attendants didn't dismiss organized labor as a path to power; they simply wanted to march down that path themselves rather than be led.

The flight attendants were, by many measures, unique in their position in the labor actions of their time. In the 1970s, other women were organizing to seize more control over their working lives. An organization of women clerical workers called 9to5 was created in 1975; they joined SEIU (the Service Employees International Union) in 1981. CLUW, the Coalition of Labor Union Women, had its first major convention in 1974. Thirty-two hundred women, all trade union members, turned up with the aim of winning more power in their unions and putting more women in leadership positions at the largest union organizations. At the meeting, one speaker, Myra Goldberg, famously called out George Meany (president of the AFL-CIO), Leonard Woodcock (president of the United Auto Workers), and Frank Fitzsimmons (president of the Teamsters) by name, saying, "You can tell them we didn't come here to swap recipes!" But these organizations, CLUW from the beginning and 9to5 a few years after its founding, sought to build power *within* traditional labor structures. They were pushing to make change from the inside, but Patt and her colleagues saw no way forward for women in a male-dominated organization (there wouldn't be a woman on the Executive Council of the AFL-CIO until 1980). They were forging a different path.

Today, APFA, which Patt worked so hard to build, is the only independent flight attendants' union to survive. Another union, the Association of Flight Attendants, is also flourishing. In 2004, in what was termed a "pink collar" merger, the AFA joined the Communications Workers of America, which had roots in organizing telephone operators. It currently represents almost fifty thousand flight attendants.

Still, the years after APFA's formation were turbulent ones for the airlines. On October 24, 1978, something happened that irreversibly changed the lives of everyone in the industry: the government deregulated the airlines, removing entry restrictions and price controls. For once, Robert Crandall and the flight attendants were in agreement—deregulation would be a disaster. Crandall and the flight attendants could see bankruptcy and job losses, respectively, in their futures once airlines were no longer required by law to serve smaller airports.

Tommie and Charlie Pasciuto joined forces and went to Washington together to try to talk lawmakers out of deregulation. Management and the union were united in believing this would decimate their industry. But it had no effect. Even Ted Kennedy, someone Tommie had always thought of as an advocate for labor, was in favor of it. The other politician throwing his support behind deregulation? Unexpectedly, it was Ralph Nader, who had been a part of SFWR's fight to remove hazardous cargo from passenger planes. He believed, erroneously, that the change would lower ticket costs for consumers.

Deregulation devastated the airlines, leading to heavy losses, company-union conflicts, and the bankrupting of eight major carriers and more than a hundred smaller ones. After two decades of progress in securing better employment conditions, flight attendants lost their jobs by the thousands, employee protections disappeared overnight, and revenue shortfalls were subsidized out of airline workers' wages. And it didn't benefit consumers, either. Airlines started cutting routes to save money, which in turn created the "hub and spoke" system the United States has now. (That's why, if you want to fly from Eugene, Oregon, to Marquette, Michigan, you have to spend all day flying and have two layovers.) It was the end of an era, and the beginning of the penny-pinching airline oligarchy of today.

The labor movement grew increasingly fractured at the same time, perhaps epitomized by Reagan's breaking of the 1981 air traffic controllers' strike. Fifty percent fewer workers voted in union elections in 1982 than in 1979. As the labor movement lost members and momentum throughout the '80s, conditions deteriorated at the airlines in tandem. Brian used to hold a desirable flight from San Francisco, where he had moved, to Honolulu; there was just an hour's layover before the return flight, and the trip always went to the most senior flight attendants. In 1985, the airline, squeezed for money, changed the route, adding a Maui leg, and sticking the crew in Honolulu hotels for hours before they flew back on an all-nighter. Brian flew this line so often that one night in Honolulu, killing time on the layover, he was in a 7-Eleven buying juice when he heard one of the women working there say to the other, "He's a little crazy. He thinks he lives in San Francisco but he's in here every night."

It was a wake-up call. He thought, "You know what, I *am* in here every night. I'm here more than I'm in my apartment." The flying had gone to hell, and the AIDS crisis was ravaging San Francisco. He put in for a transfer to Dallas.

Some things improved with time. In 1987 a federal smoking ban came down. It applied only to domestic flights under two hours, but it was something. SFWR had tried to raise public awareness of the health hazards; the flight attendants were breathing in secondhand smoke through their entire workday. On more than one flight, Bobbi watched as a drunk passenger dropped a lit cigarette between the seats; she'd have to climb around trying to find it. It took another thirteen years for smoking to be prohibited on all flights. Much of the credit was due to flight attendants, who had been pressing the government for years to enact this measure. It was another first for them—the first federal legislation regulating smoking in the workplace.

Nineteen ninety-three was a memorable year for American

Airlines flight attendants, one that would leave deep scars. Twenty thousand flight attendants went on strike just before the busy travel period around Thanksgiving. They'd been unable to come to a resolution with management on work rules, scheduling, and benefits, and were in desperate straits. The strike was in the news everywhere. *Time* and *U.S. News & World Report* called the flight attendants "the new face of labor." President Clinton managed to pull together an agreement just before Thanksgiving, but the five-day strike pitted Crandall (who had hastily trained other employees to replace the strikers) and the flight attendants against each other in a bitter face-off, and the anger is still fresh in the minds of those who worked there at the time.

After September 11, 2001, the industry changed again. In the following two years, nearly 20 percent of the flight attendants in the United States lost their jobs, and several airlines, including United and U.S. Airways, filed for bankruptcy. At American, everyone was working frantically to keep the airline in business, both labor and management. The flight attendants' contracts were gutted in an attempt to save money.

There was one bright spot, though. In 2003, in response to 9/11, Congress finally agreed that flight attendants should be safety certified. Flight attendants would now be licensed by the Federal Aviation Administration, the way pilots and mechanics were. A battle they'd been fighting for decades was finally, victoriously, over.

Weight remained one issue that was never fully resolved to everyone's satisfaction. Court cases against the airlines were brought; some plaintiffs won, some lost. And it was tough for the union to negotiate because it didn't affect all the members. Women who prided themselves on their svelte figures often didn't want to sacrifice any other advantage they might win in collective bargaining in order to get a loosening of the weight restriction. When Patt's second term as union president was over, she went back on the line only to be put on mandatory leave. She was 154 pounds, nearly 30 pounds over her maximum allowed weight. American was enforcing a new policy that, in Patt's opinion, was designed to get rid of more senior (and highly paid) flight attendants. They weighed everyone returning from unpaid leave and suspended them immediately if they were over the limit, rather than allow them to fly while losing weight, which had become the standard procedure. She found a doctor who would give her injections of human growth hormone (HGH), normally given to children of below average height. But it also reduced weight. It was expensive, around $100 a shot, and she had to get the injections at least once a week, but it worked. She also ran twice a day, three miles each time. She was drinking so much water that she passed out on the street.

The constant chipping away at women's self-esteem through the weigh-ins went on and on, albeit on a somewhat reduced scale. After a lawsuit, in 1991 American Airlines relaxed its standards and reinstated some of the flight attendants who had been fired for weight. Other airlines replaced their weight charts with "proficiency tests," which could include being able to move swiftly down an aisle, and fit through the emergency exit. But every small win had to be fought for tooth and nail.

The stewardess rebellion changed the entire airline industry, one of the largest businesses in the United States. From eliminating strictures on eyeglasses and nail polish to opening the job to men to securing the right to be married and to get older, their efforts made the inside of the airplane cabin look very different. Their work changed the demographics of the ranks permanently. In the late 1960s, the average flight attendant held her job for eighteen months. By 1978, the average tenure was seven years. By 1980, more than 50 percent of working female flight attendants were married. The effects of getting rid of the no-marriage rule and age ceiling had ramifications that stretched over decades. In 1980, the median age of a flight attendant was thirty; in 2007, it was forty-four.

In 2014, the EEOC cosponsored an event titled "The Civil Rights Act @ 50: The Pioneering Role of Flight Attendants in Fighting Sex Discrimination." A panel of women discussed their perspectives and experiences. Sonia was on the panel, as was Mary Pat Laffey. The EEOC chair, Jenny Yang, spoke about the long-ranging effects of the flight attendant rebellion: "Flight attendants' civil rights strides also extended beyond Title VII and the airline industry, as they prevailed in striking down arbitrary age restrictions for women in the workplace and began to change views about women's roles at home and in our society." Their slew of court cases and EEOC complaints laid a solid groundwork for women in other industries to bring their own claims challenging sex discrimination.

One example can be seen in a 1977 case, when a decision came down from the Supreme Court. Dianne Rawlinson had applied for a job as a prison guard in Alabama, but her height and weight were under the requirements: prison guards needed to be at least five foot two and 120 pounds. Rawlinson was 110 pounds. She filed a sex discrimination complaint with the EEOC, which filed a lawsuit alleging that the height and weight standards discriminated against women and were not essential requirements for the job. In other words, they were not bona fide occupational qualifications. You could draw a direct line from the stewardesses' BFOQ hearings held at the EEOC in the late 1960s to the decision in *Dothard v. Rawlinson.* The case went all the way to the Supreme Court, and was its first case in which the bona fide occupational qualification defense was used. The justices decided that the height and weight requirements were not BFOQs and that they did indeed discriminate against women. The decision meant that an entire swath of law enforcement jobs were now open to women.

Before flight attendants had begun to bring their claims to the EEOC, no one know how the BFOQ exception was going to be interpreted. If it had been interpreted broadly, allowing companies to create sex based exceptions for whatever jobs they wanted, Title VII would have been rendered more or less useless for women. When the EEOC, in reviewing the stewardesses' situation, decided on a narrow interpretation of the BFOQ, this led to the courts restricting employers from using the BFOQ to justify sex discrimination. This in turn led to the elimination of state protective laws and the opening up of many more job opportunities for women. Thanks to the efforts of flight attendants, it became established that when the basic duties of a job can be performed by members of any sex, an employer cannot legally restrict the job to members of one. In jobs where just men, or just women, had traditionally been hired, as in the *Dothard* case, this would change everything.

And the legal challenges to sex discrimination led by the flight attendants are still benefiting the disenfranchised. *Sprogis* in particular—Mary Burke Sprogis's case about being fired for marriage—is still being cited in cases where gender identity and sexual orientation have been challenged as sex discrimination. And Mary Pat Laffey's lawsuit, which helped to demolish the distinction between "women's work" and "men's work," was a landmark that opened doors for women in all kinds of professions.

Charlie Pasciuto retired in 1988. Patt had often said to him, "Charlie, you should kiss my hand for making sure you always have a job." But they ended up with a relationship of mutual respect. Pasciuto had been an old-school negotiator: he did his job for the company, but his word was his bond, something Tommie, Patt, Becky, and every other union leader appreciated. If he said you had a deal, you had a deal. He'd even mellowed a bit as the years went on; the flight attendants took to calling him "Uncle Charlie," sometimes even to his face. Crandall invited Patt to make a speech at Pasciuto's retirement dinner. (When it was her turn to speak, Crandall played the theme music from *Jaws.*) Patt told the audience how Pasciuto often asked her when she was going to give him an honorary union membership. She'd always reply, "Your seniority number would have to be one million and one before you'd ever become a member of APFA." She went on to give him, in front of the crowd, an honorary membership in APFA. Seniority number: 1,000,001.

Pasciuto died in 2008. Patt was working in Hawaii and couldn't get back for the wake, but Susan went in her place. She introduced herself to Pasciuto's wife, Mary, and his kids. "I'm Susan French," she said. "You probably don't remember me, but maybe you'll remember Patt Gibbs." "Patt Gibbs!" Mary exclaimed. She and her children started reminiscing about Pasciuto coming home every night and complaining, "That goddamn Patt Gibbs is ruining my life again!" "If it makes you feel any better," Susan replied with a smile, "Patt always used to come home and say, 'That goddamn Charlie Pasciuto is ruining my life!'" It cheered everybody up.

Robert Crandall retired from American Airlines in 1998 and went on to work as a director for other corporations; he also served on the board at Halliburton.

Cindy Hounsell became an attorney and, later, president of a nonprofit organization helping women plan for retirement.

Dusty Roads came out as a lesbian and she and her wife, Jean, live in California.

Brian has retired and lives in New York City.

Becky retired in 2013 and lives in Texas.

Bobbi took a buyout after forty-four years as a flight attendant, angry about how airline workers were fighting for a few extra dollars while CEOs were profiting by millions.

Dana is now a musician and yoga teacher.

Kathleen Heenan had three children and started a new career. She taught birding in NYC public schools for fifteen years.

Cheryl Stewart, now Cheryl Stewart-Gaymon, is still flying. Her goal is to get to seniority number 1. She's currently number 14.

Sonia eventually returned to D.C. and got a job at the U.S. Department of Housing and Urban Development before retiring to Sarasota, Florida. She published her memoir in 1999 and, at the age of ninety-three, is still frequently interviewed about and honored for her contributions to the fight for equal rights for women.

Tommie timed her maternity leave carefully. In 1978, Congress had passed the Pregnancy Discrimination Act, which forced employers to treat pregnancy like any other temporary disability. This meant that women were to be neither fired nor prevented from returning to work on account of pregnancy and childbirth. Flight attendants could now keep their jobs when they got pregnant, using sick leave and vacation days to cobble together some semblance of parental leave. Tommie hoarded her leave until she'd accumulated a decent amount of time off. She'd been working for ten years. She left office in June 1980 to have her first child, a daughter named Sawyer; her second daughter, Allison, was born five years later.

Tommie became union president again in 2004 and remained president until she retired from the airline in 2008. She'd been a flight attendant for thirty-eight years. Gloria Steinem mentioned her by name in her book *My Life on the Road*, in a section dedicated to the achievements of flight attendants. Tommie and Al live in the Berkshires, where she dedicates her time to social justice activism and her three grandchildren.

Patt was reelected president of the union and ran it from 1985 to 1988 in her unorthodox style, once leading picketing outside Crandall's own home. She worked on and off as a flight attendant until 2004, though she graduated from law school in 1988 (Charlie Pasciuto wrote her a letter of recommendation; he'd recovered from the gorilla incident) and began to practice as a lawyer. Carin Clauss, who became Patt's mentor, was the commencement speaker at her graduation ceremony, and the audience was full of Patt's flight attendant friends and colleagues, including Dusty and Nancy, all in uniform. She got married. To a man: her brother's lover, who had AIDS. Her spouse was entitled to travel passes from American Airlines; it helped his family visit him when he got really sick. Her supervisor, well-intentioned but stunningly obtuse, sent her a congratulations card.

She lives with Susan in Texas and still flies frequently for her job as a senior international union rep. And her reputation lives on. Flight attendants often approach her to ask, "Are you the real Patt Gibbs?"

The story of flight attendants in labor is far from over, although this era of achievement shines particularly bright. Deregulation of the airlines was the end of a period that stands out for its hard-won victories in both the labor movement and the women's movement. The women in this book asked themselves how they could make change when there was an institution actively denying them their rights and the organization that was supposed to represent them wasn't doing its job. By standing up to an industry that preferred its women docile, pretty, and young, they demonstrated to the world that power was available—you just had to reach out and grab it. They defied the assumption that marriage was every woman's crowning ambition, that a company-regulated appearance was a necessary qualification for a worker, and that women were created to serve and not to lead. It became clear to them that the labor movement can't win without women. And strong unions can't be built unless every member has representation and power.

Flight attendants are still at the forefront of the labor movement. In 2019, during the government shutdown, many airport employees were furloughed or forced to work without pay. In the chaos of the shutdown, a new voice emerged. Sara Nelson, a flight attendant since 1996 and president of the Association of Flight Attendants since 2014 (and a front-runner for president of the AFL-CIO in 2022), was suddenly everywhere. She was talking to workers and urging unity, seen with Bernie Sanders and Tim Kaine, being interviewed on CNN and PBS—nearly always dressed in her United Airlines uniform, wings pinned to her lapel, striped scarf tied jauntily around her neck.

Nelson had become the new face of labor. As militant as Patt and Tommie, she never backed down from a fight, never stopped advocating for radical action, always asked incisive questions of her fellow labor leaders. "Almost a million workers are locked out or being forced to work without pay. Others are going to work when our workspace is increasingly unsafe," she said. "What is the Labor Movement waiting for?"

Her most audacious move? Calling for a general strike—a strategy many Americans thought was consigned to the dustbin of labor history. It was, said the *New York Times,* "an idea so radical that it has scarcely been invoked in public by the head of a national union in generations." Afterward, she was asked by a labor historian whether such a thing was too inflammatory to talk about publicly. "Strike, strike, strike, strike, strike, strike, strike," Nelson responded, urging him to "say it—it feels good."

Acknowledgments

FIRST AND FOREMOST, thanks to the women who entrusted me with their stories, and told them with such grace, humor, and astounding memory for detail. Patt, Tommie, and Sonia, I will be forever grateful. I feel extraordinarily lucky that you let me share this piece of your history, and appreciate your endless patience with my visits, calls, emails, texts, and questions.

Also thanks to the many other women (and a few men) who took the time to speak with me, dig up photos, connect me with other flight attendants, and generally let me pester them for several years, especially Dana, Bobbie, Becky, Cindy, Kathleen, Cheryl, and Brian. And big thanks to Patricia Ireland, Joan Dorsey, Carin Clauss, and Bonnie Tiburzi Caputo—your stories were enlightening and our interviews such a pleasure, even if not every detail could make it into the book.

This story built on the work of many writers and researchers; first among them is Kathleen Barry. Help with my own research came from too many places to name, but Jennifer Brissette at APFA, Linda Hutchinson at the EEOC, and the librarians at the University of Texas at Arlington archives went above and beyond; thank you so much.

Big thanks to Adam Conover, who gave me the idea for this book during an interview. Ewa Beaujon and Daniella Byck, superlative fact-checkers—thank you! All remaining errors are, of course, my own. Martha Curren-Preis, thanks both for reading and for saving me many, many hours of hunting for documents. Julia Cooke and Maggie Doherty shared excellent advice and much-needed encouragement. Sarah Ellis, Jennifer Shahade, and Karen O'Reilly, for reviewing the dreadful early drafts and being kind about them—I am grateful! John Rosenberg, I'm eternally thankful to you for showing me how this was a story, and for your wise, thoughtful comments.

My agent, the smart, encouraging, patient, and extremely fun Lauren Sharp—I very obviously couldn't have done this without you. I am so grateful. And enormous thanks to the editor I was so privileged to have, Kris Puopolo, whose brilliance and sense of humor made this book so much better (and make her such a pleasure to hang out with). Carolyn Williams, thank you for your help with literally everything and also your sunny attitude!

At Doubleday, a huge "thank-you!" to Elena Hershey, Anne Jaconette, Roland Ottewell, Nicole Pedersen, Maria Carella, Emily Mahon, Beth Meister, and Chris Dufault. What a gift to have your help.

A big arm raise to my Pomobuddies for their support, humor, and the structure of virtual coworking, without which this writing process would have been infinitely more painful. To my parents, for a lifetime of love, encouragement, and reading—I know how lucky I am. The biggest of hugs to Yael and Annabel, my unflagging cheerleaders. And to Alan, thank you—for everything.

Notes

INTRODUCTION

vii   "This morning, sight-seeing": Michele Martin, "Winged Women: Steward-esses, Sexism, and American Society" (master's thesis, Dominican University of California, 2017), 6.

vii   Stewardesses were required: Kathleen M. Barry, *Femininity in Flight: A History of Flight Attendants* (Durham, NC: Duke University Press, 2007), 112.

vii   well after nearly every other industry: Barry, *Femininity in Flight*, 97.

viii   But their work turned Title VII: Patricia K. Willis, "The Stewardesses for Women's Rights: Opening Closed Doors for Radical Change" (dissertation, State University of New York, 2004), 347.

viii   for decades to come: Barry, *Femininity in Flight*, 144.

CHAPTER ONE: HONEYBUNS ON THE CHARM FARM

4   "Okay, I'll interview": Author interview with Patt Gibbs.

5   "the first fundamental is appearance": Victoria Vantoch, *The Jet Sex: Stewardesses and the Making of an American Icon* (Philadelphia: University of Pennsylvania Press, 2013), 112.

5   American Airlines Barbie: Jazz Hands, "American Airlines Stewardess #984, Vintage Barbie Fashion," YouTube video, July 18, 2019.

5   "I love it": Drew Whitelegg, "From Smiles to Miles: Delta Air Lines Flight Attendants and Southern Hospitality," *Southern Cultures* 11, no. 4 (2005): 7–27.

5   United, wanting to appeal: Arlie Russell Hochschild, *The Managed Heart: Commercialization of Human Feeling* (Berkeley: University of California Press, 1983), 97–98.

5   TWA, like Pan Am: Bruce Handy, "Glamour with Altitude," *Vanity Fair*, May 28, 2014.

5   Pacific Southwest was known: Paula Kane, with Christopher Chandler, *Sex Objects in the Sky: A Personal Account of the Stewardess Rebellion* (Chicago: Follett, 1974), 44.

5   with an hourglass figure: Kane, *Sex Objects in the Sky*, 13.

5   "high moral character": Hochschild, *The Managed Heart*, 97.

6   "superior background": ClickAmericana, "Pretty, Thin, Young and Single? Check Out These Sexist Stewardess Job Requirements of the '50s & '60s," n.d., accessed August 13, 2021, https://clickamericana.com/topics/money-work/fly-girls-stewardess-job-requirements-of-the-50s-60s.

6   "all American" girl: Kane, *Sex Objects in the Sky*, 30.

6   "a high school graduate": Michelle Higgins, "63 Years Flying, from Glamour to Days of Gray," *New York Times*, March 17, 2012.

7   Patt was under twenty-one: Author interview with Patt Gibbs.

7   The contract also specified: From personal records of Patt Gibbs.

7   It had been less than a decade: Barry, *Femininity in Flight*, 112.

7   "basic among the qualifications": Barry, *Femininity in Flight*, 112.

8   The stewardesses' union had: Barry, *Femininity in Flight*, 112.

8   Other airlines soon added: Barry, *Femininity in Flight*, 112.

8   By the middle of the 1960s: Barry, *Femininity in Flight*, 113.

8   Her parents signed: Author interview with Patt Gibbs.

8   The only difference: From personal records of Patt Gibbs.

8   And this campus: Handy, "Glamour with Altitude."

9   Eastern Airlines had the Silverliners: Silverliners, "Become a Part of an Organization with a Common Bond," n.d., accessed August 13, 2021, www.thesilverliners.org/.

9   United the Clipped Wings: Clipped Wings, "History of Clipped Wings," n.d., accessed August 13, 2021, https://unitedclippedwingsinc.org/history/.

9   Continental the Golden Penguins: "Mary Lenore Holloway [obituary]," *The Oregonian*, April 11–13, 2016.

9   bars were affixed: Handy, "Glamour with Altitude."

9   an alarm system: Dooley, "Battle in the Sky," 103.

9   United launched a stewardess school: Dooley, "Battle in the Sky," 105.

9   In addition to safety training: Handy, "Glamour with Altitude."

10   Continental sent its trainees: Barry, *Femininity in Flight*, 47.

10   "C.R.'s honeybuns": Email from Patt Gibbs, April 2021.

10   the Greensboro lunch counter sit-ins: "Woolworth's Lunch Counter," Civil Rights Movement, History.com, October 27, 2009 (updated May 17, 2021), www.history.com.

10   Supervisors kept a close eye: Kane, *Sex Objects in the Sky*, 37.

10   An entire class was dedicated: Author interview with Patt Gibbs.

10   Before that, airlines argued: Richard Witkin, "Aviation: Stewardess; First Negro Girl to Obtain a Position as Air Hostess Hired by Mohawk," *New York Times*, December 29, 1957.

11   around fifty Black stewardesses: Barry, *Femininity in Flight*, 117.

11   about fifteen thousand: Barry, *Femininity in Flight*, 117.

11   Stewardesses might have entered: Kane, *Sex Objects in the Sky*, 35.

11   There was a saying: Kane, *Sex Objects in the Sky*, 73.

11   Patt and her fellow trainees: Suzanne Lee Kolm, "Women's Labor Aloft: A Cultural History of Airline Flight Attendants in the United States 1930–1978" (PhD dissertation, Brown University, 1995), 147.

11   "You walk like a gorilla": Vantoch, *The Jet Sex*, 53.

11   In the beauty salon: From personal records of Patt Gibbs.

14   "We choose just": Item found via search on eBay (July 10, 2021) for "Vintage 1960 American Airlines 'Stewardess College' Reproduction Print Advert."

15   The women sang the graduation song: Kane, *Sex Objects in the Sky*, 40.

15   After the month and a half: Author interview with Patt Gibbs.

CHAPTER TWO: GLOVES TO GRIEVANCES

16    $650 ($5,648 in 2021 dollars): "Value of 1962 US Dollars Today," Inflation Tool, accessed August 13, 2021, www.inflationtool.com.

16   Stewardesses who left off the girdle: Author interview with Patt Gibbs.

17   Afros were specifically forbidden: " 'Natural' Hair Style Grounds Steward-ess," *New York Times*, September 23, 1969.

17   to straighten their hair: Barry, *Femininity in Flight*, 119.

17   Each stewardess would fill out: Barry, *Femininity in Flight*, 120.

20   By November, the chair: Author interview with Patt Gibbs.

20   Nancy was a slim: Author interview with Patt Gibbs.

21   Under their leadership were: Barry, *Femininity in Flight*, 87.

22   She agreed: Author interview with Patt Gibbs.

23   A stewardess never addressed a captain: Author interview with Patt Gibbs.

23   "I did call him Bob": Author interview with Patt Gibbs.

CHAPTER THREE: THE AIR STRIP

26   He wanted to add airline workers: "Hoffa Offers Air Stewardesses Special Division in Teamsters," *New York Times*, February 21, 1961.

26   The Teamsters were a formidable union: Barry, *Femininity in Flight*, 85.

27   She'd been scared: Email from Patt Gibbs, May 2021.

27   "stew zoos": Kane, *Sex Objects in the Sky*, 43.

28   Frederic Simpson: Barry, *Femininity in Flight*, 91.

28   Barbara Roads: Flora Davis, *Moving the Mountain: The Women's Movement in American Since 1960* (New York: Simon & Schuster, 1991), 20.

29   The *Daily News* described: Barry, *Femininity in Flight*, 131.

29   Dusty, a charming, strong-willed stewardess: Barry, *Femininity in Flight*, 122.

29   A group of seventeen stewardesses: Vantoch, *The Jet Sex*, 204.

29   "Would you be good enough": *Employment Problems of the Older Worker (The Airline Stewardesses Case): Hearings on H.R. 10634 and Similar Bills, Day 1, Before the Select Subcommittee on Labor of the Committee on Education and Labor,* 89th Cong. 397 (1965) (statement of James H. Scheuer, U.S. Represen-tative, New York).

30   When Colleen finished her testimony: *Employment Problems: Hearings on H.R. 10634,* 409 (statement of James G. O'Hara, U.S. Representative, Michigan).

30   They had, though, made the news: Kathleen M. Barry, " 'Too Glamorous to Be Considered Workers': Flight Attendants and Pink-Collar Activism in Mid-Twentieth-Century America," *Labor* 3, no. 3 (2006): 119–38.

30   Many stewardesses who aged out: Author interview with Patt Gibbs.

31   It said that she felt: Author interview with Patt Gibbs.

31   She was one of six individuals: Email from Patt Gibbs, April 2021.

32   The industry started launching: Barry, *Femininity in Flight*, 179.

32   The new look included: Gillian A. Frank and Lauren Gutterman, "How Flight Attendants Organized Against Their Bosses to End 'Swinging Stewardesses' Stereotyping," *Jezebel*, November 29, 2018.

32   "When a Braniff International hostess": Braniff Airways Foundation, "Air Strip I Advertisement—Braniff International," YouTube video, March 14, 2021.

33   There was also a Braniff Barbie: Belief Media, "braniff-barbi-04.jpg [image]," n.d., accessed August 13, 2021, www.beliefmedia.com.au.

33   Ken, in his pilot uniform: Something About The Boy, "1967 The Braniff International Pilot Ken," n.d., accessed August 13, 2021, https://something abouttheboy.com.

33   Unashamedly performative: Vantoch, *The Jet Sex*, 168.

33   This campaign: Martin Khoury, "Branding Braniff International," Belief Media, n.d., accessed August 13, 2021, www.beliefmedia.com.au /branding-braniff-international.

33   Wells issued a blunt rebuttal: Vantoch, *The Jet Sex*, 169.

33   A year later, Braniff reported: Walter Carlson, "Advertising: Braniff, Pucci and 'Air Strips,'" *New York Times*, June 28, 1966.

CHAPTER FOUR: SONIA IN FANTASYLAND

34   His first ask was that she write a speech: Author interview with Sonia Pressman Fuentes.

34   It was now officially illegal: Barry, *Femininity in Flight*, 127.

35   "reasonably necessary": Title VII of the Civil Rights Act of 1964, 42 U.S.C. sec. 2000e, Pub L. 88-352, www.eeoc.gov/statutes/title-vii-civil-rights-act-1964.

36   The EEOC staff, shocked: "Interview with Barbara 'Dusty' Roads," *People's Century: Half the People*, PBS, n.d., accessed August 13, 2021, www.pbs.org /wgbh/peoplescentury.

36   Although the EEOC had no power: Dennis A. Deslippe, "Organized Labor, National Politics, and Second-Wave Feminism in the United States, 1965–1975," *International Labor and Working-Class History* 49 (1996): 143–65.

36   The march from Selma to Montgomery: CNN Editorial Research, "1965 Selma to Montgomery March Fast Facts," CNN, updated February 25, 2021, https://edition.cnn.com.

36   By the end of the first year: Barry, *Femininity in Flight*, 152.

36   Around 27 percent: Deslippe, "Organized Labor, National Politics."

36   And stewardesses were coming to the EEOC: Barry, *Femininity in Flight*, 152.

37   In 2019, he'd also be publicly named: Gabriel Sherman, "'She Was Shaking Uncontrollably': Powerful Men, Disturbing New Details in Unsealed Jeffrey Epstein Documents," *Vanity Fair*, August 9, 2019.

38   But then the reference arrived: Author interview with Sonia Pressman Fuentes.

38   She knew the EEOC had limited funds: Author interview with Sonia Pressman Fuentes.

38   Franklin Delano Roosevelt Jr. was one: Author interview with Sonia Press-
      man Fuentes.

38   "Mr. Jackson and Mrs. Hernandez are Negroes": Cabell Phillips, "Frank-
      lin Roosevelt Jr. to Head Equal Job Opportunity Agency; Panel, Created in
      Rights Act, Will Begin Work in July," *New York Times*, May 11, 1965.

39   He knew, Sonia quickly realized: Author interview with Sonia Pressman
      Fuentes.

39   At his first EEOC press conference: Phil Tiemeyer, *Plane Queer: Labor, Sexu-
      ality, and AIDS in the History of Male Flight Attendants* (Berkeley: University
      of California Press, 2013), 88.

39   The Reverend Dr. Pauli Murray: Dooley, "Battle in the Sky," 143.

40   Berg, Sonia soon saw: Sonia Pressman Fuentes, *Eat First—You Don't Know
      What They'll Give You: The Adventures of an Immigrant Family and Their
      Feminist Daughter*, Kindle ed. (Philadelphia: Xlibris, 1999), chap. 23.

40   He did, however, nickname her: Author interview with Sonia Pressman
      Fuentes.

40   "How," she asked herself: Author interview with Sonia Pressman Fuentes.

41   The idea was so absurd: Author interview with Sonia Pressman Fuentes.

41   "You're asking me to speak": Author interview with Sonia Pressman
      Fuentes.

41   "At the White House Conference": Tiemeyer, *Plane Queer*, 88.

42   Griffiths pointed out that the airlines: Tiemeyer, *Plane Queer*, 90.

43   *The Feminine Mystique:* Mitra Toossi and Teresa L. Morisi, "Women in the
      Workforce Before, During, and After the Great Recession," U.S. Bureau of
      Labor Statistics, July 2017. https://www.bls.gov.

43   the 38.3 percent: Mitra Toossi and Teresa L. Morisi, "Women in the Work-
      force Before, During, and After the Great Recession," U.S. Bureau of Labor
      Statistics, July 2017, www.bls.gov.

43   by 1966 her book had sold: "FMC Program Segments 1960–2000: Betty
      Freidan and *The Feminine Mystique*," PBS, n.d., accessed August 13, 2021.
      http://www.pbs.org/fmc/segments/progseg11.htm.

44   The location was the basement: Author interview with Sonia Pressman
      Fuentes.

44   Sonia had plenty of suggestions: Email from Sister Joel Reed (NOW
      cofounder) to Sonia Pressman Fuentes, December 6, 2002.

44   They worked in government: Betty Friedan, *The Feminine Mystique*,
      Kindle ed. (New York: W. W. Norton, 2001 [originally published 1963]),
      Epilogue.

44   Betty jotted down: National Organization for Women (NOW), "Honoring
      Our Founders & Pioneers," n.d., accessed August 13, 2021, https://now.org
      /about/history/honoring-our-founders-pioneers/.

44   That meeting also established: National Organization for Women (NOW),
      "Founding: Setting the Stage," n.d., accessed August 13, 2021, https://now
      .org/about/history/founding-2/.

45   Caruthers Berger: Barbara J. Love, ed., *Feminists Who Changed America,
      1963–1975* (Urbana: University of Illinois Press, 2006), 38.

46   A lawyer, feminist, and civil rights activist: Author interview with Sonia
        Pressman Fuentes.

46   This was a win for both groups: Vantoch, *The Jet Sex,* 202.

46   It petitioned the EEOC: Fuentes, *Eat First,* Kindle ed., chap. 23.

47   She continued with her secret work: Author interview with Sonia Pressman
        Fuentes.

47   One picket sign read: Deslippe, "Organized Labor, National Politics."

47   The *Post* wasn't the only paper: Author interview with Sonia Pressman
        Fuentes.

47   Her bombing plan wasn't taken up: NOW, "Honoring Our Founders &
        Pioneers."

47   Jobs, at least most jobs: Fuentes, *Eat First,* Kindle ed., chap. 23.

48   They'd stay late: Leila J. Rupp and Verta Taylor, *Survival in the Doldrums:
        The American Women's Rights Movement, 1945 to the 1960s* (New York: Oxford
        University Press, 1987), 180.

48   Griffiths's speech helped inspire: Barry, *Femininity in Flight,* 153.

CHAPTER FIVE: WHAT THE BFOQ?

49   She was reinstated: Author interview with Patt Gibbs.

50   homosexuality was classified: Mark L. Ruffalo, "Setting the Record
        Straight: Homosexuality and DSM," *Psychology Today,* June 22, 2019.

52   The accompanying television ad: Flight, "The Easter[n] Air Lines Losers
        (1967)," YouTube video, March 26, 2017.

52   New ones were opening up: Flight, "The Easter[n] Air Lines Losers (1967)."

52   And in 1967: Katherine Lagrave, "From Stewardess to Flight Attendant: 80
        Years of Sophistication and Sexism," *Condé Nast Traveler,* March 8, 2017.

52   He asked more questions: Author interview with Patt Gibbs.

52   It was suddenly obvious: Author interview with Patt Gibbs.

53   Finally, Bateman was reinstated: Barry, *Femininity in Flight,* 149.

54   maintaining a secret marriage: Chicago-Kent College of Law at Illinois
        Institute of Technology, "The Civil Rights Act @ 50: The Pioneering Role
        of Flight Attendants in Fighting Sex Discrimination," YouTube video,
        October 31, 2014.

54   Maiden names, not married names: Tamar Lewin, "Ex-Stewardesses vs.
        United," *New York Times,* February 24, 1984.

54   Some supervisors would scan: Gail Collins, *When Everything Changed: The
        Amazing Journey of American Women from 1960 to the Present* (New York:
        Little, Brown, 2009), 20.

54   trying to catch stewardesses: Chicago-Kent College of Law at Illinois, "The
        Civil Rights Act @ 50."

54   Continental Airlines removed: Cathleen M. Dooley Loucks, "Battle in the
        Skies: Sex Discrimination in the United States Airline Industry, 1930 to
        1978" (thesis, University of Nevada, Las Vegas, 1995), https://digitalscholar
        ship.unlv.edu.

54   In the early 1960s: Davis, *Moving the Mountain,* 17.

54   The average length of service: Dooley, "Battle in the Sky," 161.

54   One American Airlines ad: Flashbak, "People Keep Stealing Our Steward-
      esses [advertisement]," n.d., accessed August 13, 2021, https://flashbak.com.

54   "If that figure ever": Kane, *Sex Objects in the Sky*, 103; Fredric C. Appel,
      "Airlines Vie with Cupid for Stewardesses: Girls Hold Job for 2½ Years on
      Average," *New York Times*, April 26, 1965.

55   Finally, the union and the company: Danis Binder, "Sex Discrimination in
      the Airline Industry: Title VII Flying High," *California Law Review* 59, no.
      5 (1971): 1106.

56   And there was no letting up: Barry, *Femininity in Flight*, 147.

56   Just twelve days later: Tiemeyer, *Plane Queer*, 89.

56   qualified this decision: Phil Tiemeyer, "Male Stewardesses: Male Flight
      Attendants as a Queer Miscarriage of Justice," *Genders* (June 1, 2007), 4.

57   The inclusion of "sex" in Title VII: Author interview with Mary Pat Laffey
      Inman.

58   The firm would continue: Tiemeyer, *Plane Queer*, 91.

58   What men couldn't do: Tiemeyer, *Plane Queer*, 90.

58   And, Freidin argued: Dooley, "Battle in the Sky," 163.

59   They provided testimonials: Barry, *Femininity in Flight*, 158.

59   The schedules were too irregular: Dooley, "Battle in the Sky," 219.

59   "As an acceptable and useful job": Barry, *Femininity in Flight*, 156.

59   One United ad: *The Media Guy* (blog), "Nicki Minaj Took My Seat in Busi-
      ness Class, Plus a Visit with Flight Girl Daniela!," September 2, 2015,
      https://mediamindsetter.blogspot.com.

59   A close-up of a smiling: *The Media Guy*, "Nicki Minaj Took My Seat."

59   The copy read: Dooley, "Battle in the Sky," 209.

61   As the hearing progressed: Dooley, "Battle in the Sky," 228.

61   Colleen, in a gesture: Dooley, "Battle in the Sky," 225.

61   She was thrilled with the idea: Author interview with Mary Pat Laffey
      Inman.

62   She'd officially resigned: Barry, *Femininity in Flight*, 160.

62   An entire new set of hearings: David Dismore, "September 12, 1967: Femi-
      nists and Labor Unions Take On Sexist Airline Industry," Feminist Major-
      ity Foundation, September 12, 2014, https://feminist.org/.

62   She had brought an EEOC complaint: U.S. Equal Employment Opportunity
      Commission, "Filing a Lawsuit," n.d., accessed August 13, 2021, www.eeoc
      .gov/filing-lawsuit.

62   Stewardesses needed to be single: Barry, *Femininity in Flight*, 162.

62   Her letter to Mason: Harold Jackson, "Martha Griffiths [obituary]," *Guard-
      ian*, April 28, 2003.

63   Though her case set: Stroud v. Delta Air Lines, 544 F.2d 892 (5th Cir. 1977),
      https://openjurist.org/544/f2d/892.

CHAPTER SIX: BLACK MOLLIES

65   Patt, nervous, wanted a lawyer: Author interview with Patt Gibbs.

65   But he was, she quickly learned: Author interview with Patt Gibbs.

67   It was a message that only: Author interview with Patt Gibbs.

67   By the late 1960s: Barry, *Femininity in Flight*, 99.

67   A 1967 ad gave credit: *The Media Guy,* "Nicki Minaj Took My Seat."

67   Another boasted about the increased size: ClickAmericana, "Pretty, Thin, Young and Single?"

67   American took another tack: *The Media Guy,* "Nicki Minaj Took My Seat."

69   Patt flew with one woman: Email from Patt Gibbs, May 2021.

69   The weight limits were derived: Bob Baker, "Airline Sued for Weight Discrimination," *Los Angeles Times,* September 10, 1990.

70   At American Airlines: Baker, "Airline Sued for Weight Discrimination."

71   Geritol was an alcohol-based liquid: Wikipedia, "Geritol," last modified July 28, 2021, https://en.wikipedia.org.

71   Patt had moved from her trailer: Email from Patt Gibbs, May 2021.

72   If they got pregnant: Carrie N. Baker, "The History of Abortion Law in the United States," Our Bodies, Our Selves, September 14, 2020, www.our bodiesourselves.org.

72   In most states in the 1960s: Collins, *When Everything Changed,* 161.

73   Usually, once a stewardess became pregnant: "Kathleen Heenan [interview]," NYU Libraries: Oral Histories, November 21, 1985, https://digital tamiment.hosting.nyu.edu.

73   around $5,000 a year (around $44,000 in 2021 dollars): "Value of 1964 US Dollars Today," Inflation Tool, accessed August 13, 2021, www.inflation tool.com.

74   That meant she had a regular schedule: "Heenan [interview]," NYU Libraries.

74   This wasn't the age of shuttle buses: Author interview with Patt Gibbs.

74   Even when she'd flown all night: "Heenan [interview]," NYU Libraries.

74   She and her friends occasionally dated: "Heenan [interview]," NYU Libraries.

75   She met her husband: "Heenan [interview]," NYU Libraries.

75   In 1968, TWA decided: *The Media Guy,* "Nicki Minaj Took My Seat."

75   The airline issued stewardesses: ClickAmericana, "Pretty, Thin, Young and Single?"

75   The print ads featured: ClickAmericana, "Pretty, Thin, Young and Single?"

75   "Fly 'Foreign Accent' with us": ClickAmericana, "Pretty, Thin, Young and Single?"

75   Kathleen, along with her fellow stewardesses: Barry, *Femininity in Flight,* 181.

75   "pictured us wearing": Kathleen Heenan, "Fighting the 'Fly-Me' Airlines," *The Civil Liberties Review* (December 1976/January 1977): 58.

77   A friend had a passenger die: Author interview with Kathleen Heenan.

77   There was a spate of hijackings: Thom Patterson, "How the Era of 'Skyjackings' Changed the Way We Fly," CNN, October 2, 2017.

77   A union rep has credibility: Author interview with Kathleen Heenan.

CHAPTER SEVEN: THINK OF HER AS YOUR MOTHER

78   While the age rules: Barry, *Femininity in Flight,* 122.

78   Throwing fuel on the fire: Carney Maley, "Flying the 'Unfriendly Skies':

Flight Attendant Activism, 1964–1982," (PhD dissertation, Boston University, 2011), 130.

78   Pan Am was an exception: Barry, *Femininity in Flight*, 248.

78   It was an entire industry: Barry, *Femininity in Flight*, 114.

78   And that industry was booming: Barry, *Femininity in Flight*, 111.

79   This was far from the first: Kane, *Sex Objects in the Sky*, 77.

79   She talked about how: U.S. Senate, *Hearings, Volume 1* (Washington, DC: U.S. Government Printing Office, 1967), 200–201.

79   "To us a few more months": U.S. Senate, *Hearings*, 203.

81   She was sitting on a chair: *The Media Guy* (blog), "Daniela:::Deux," April 24, 2014, https://mediamindsetter.blogspot.com.

82   The headline, black and bold: Barry, *Femininity in Flight*, 179.

84   Patt sat at the table: Photo emailed from Patt Gibbs, July 17, 2021.

84   less than $5,000 a year (around $44,000 in 2021 dollars): "Value of 1968 US Dollars Today," Inflation Tool, accessed August 13, 2021, www.inflation tool.com.

84   And then she leaked it: Author interview with Patt Gibbs.

86   Charlie had lost a lot of people their jobs: Author interview with Tommie Hutto-Blake.

88   Both Fred and Colleen had: From personal records of Patt Gibbs.

CHAPTER EIGHT: DO WOMEN AGE FASTER ON AIRPLANES?

90   The second hearing took place: Tiemeyer, *Plane Queer*, 244.

90   The psychologists submitted statements: Author interview with Sonia Pressman Fuentes.

90   United Airlines argued that: Dooley, "Battle in the Sky," 200.

90   The stewardess was the face: Equal Employment Opportunity Commission, "Termination or Reassignment of Airline Stewardess After Reaching 32 Years of Age Held Unlawful Sex Discrimination," in *CCH EEOC Decisions* (New York: Commerce Clearing House, 1973), 20.

90   women between the ages of thirty-eight and fifty: Maley, "Flying the 'Unfriendly Skies,' " 112.

90   The airline executives worried: Dooley, "Battle in the Sky," 224.

90   The point was to prove: Author interview with Patt Gibbs.

91   And these airlines continued: Personal communication from Sonia Pressman Fuentes.

91   The slate of people: Personal records of Sonia Pressman Fuentes.

91   The decision was not unanimous: Maley, "Flying the 'Unfriendly Skies,' " 131.

92   Three individual decisions: Barry, *Femininity in Flight*, 160.

92   The airline had attempted to argue: Dooley, "Battle in the Sky," 251.

92   Obviously, therefore, the requirement: Equal Employment Opportunity Commission, "Termination or Reassignment of Airline Stewardess."

92   The second case, *Colvin v. Piedmont Aviation:* Equal Employment Opportunity Commission, "No-Marriage Ban and Age Limitation on Employment of Airline Stewardesses Violate Title VII," in *CCH EEOC Decisions* (New York: Commerce Clearing House, 1973), 30.

92   Another violation of Title VII: Georgia Panter Nielsen, *From Sky Girl to Flight Attendant: Women and the Making of a Union* (Ithaca: New York State School of Industrial and Labor Relations, Cornell University, 1982), 86.

92   *Neal v. American Airlines:* Equal Employment Opportunity Commission, "Termination of Airline Stewardess After Marriage Viewed as Unlawful Sex Discrimination," in *CCH EEOC Decisions* (New York: Commerce Clearing House, 1973), 25.

92   American, still firing stewardesses: Nielsen, *From Sky Girl to Flight Attendant*, 86.

92   The EEOC rejected: Equal Employment Opportunity Commission, "Termination of Airline Stewardess After Marriage."

92   that applied to a class of employees: Nielsen, *From Sky Girl to Flight Attendant*, 86.

92   There didn't have to be differences: Barry, *Femininity in Flight*, 161.

93   When Charlie asked exactly: Author interview with Sonia Pressman Fuentes.

93   She was shocked and saddened: Author interview with Sonia Pressman Fuentes.

93   they would strike: "Hostesses Agree to an Airline Pact," *New York Times*, August 11, 1968.

93   They could see the way: "Job Limits Lifted for Stewardesses," *AFL-CIO News*, August 17, 1968, https://archive.org/.

94   The new contract wording: Personal communication from Sonia Pressman Fuentes.

94   The pregnancy restriction: Personal communication from Sonia Pressman Fuentes.

94   but the biggest obstacle: "Job Limits Lifted for Stewardesses," *AFL-CIO News*.

94   And American agreed: From personal records of Patt Gibbs (1971 American Airlines contract).

94   when they refused reassignment: From personal records of Patt Gibbs (1971 American Airlines contract).

94   humorous headlines: Press clippings, document collection of Sonia Pressman Fuentes, Arthur and Elizabeth Schlesinger Library on the History of Women in America, Harvard Radcliffe Institute, Cambridge, MA.

94   But the courts would not always see: Barry, *Femininity in Flight*, 161.

95   Everyone else went back to flying: Email from Patt Gibbs.

95   First of all, while American would no longer: Author interview with Sonia Pressman Fuentes.

95   As well, the agreement: From personal records of Patt Gibbs (1971 American Airlines contract).

95   It was a not-so-subtle way: Notes, document collection of Sonia Pressman Fuentes, Schlesinger Library.

95   "She told me": Willis, "The Stewardesses for Women's Rights," 146.

96   And TWA had come to an agreement: Barry, *Femininity in Flight*, 147.

96   This concession: Willis, "The Stewardesses for Women's Rights," 246.

96   Its failure to protect: Willis, "The Stewardesses for Women's Rights," 246.

96   The essential ruling: Vantoch, *The Jet Sex*, 205.

96   Mary Burke Sprogis: Sprogis v. United Air Lines, 517 F.2d 387 (7th Cir. 1971).

96   In 1968, the EEOC authorized: Dooley, "Battle in the Sky," 176.

96   and she took United to court: Dooley, "Battle in the Sky," 232.

96   The court followed the EEOC's lead: Barry, *Femininity in Flight*. 164.

96   It was the beginning of a shift: Barry, *Femininity in Flight*, 164.

97   By the time the legal judgment: Dooley, "Battle in the Sky," 229.

97   United had gotten rid of: Vantoch, *The Jet Sex*, 205.

97   although it had held on to: Barry, *Femininity in Flight*, 148.

97   But the *Sprogis* decision: Barry, *Femininity in Flight*, 169.

97   United had to give Sprogis her job back: Dooley, "Battle in the Sky," 176.

97   and United had to pay: Barry, *Femininity in Flight*, 164.

97   And it wasn't the longest-lasting case: "Sex Discrimination Case Suit Settled for $37 Million," *New York Times*, October 8, 1986.

97   United had to pay: James Warren, "Airline Ends Sex-Bias Suit For $33 Million," *Chicago Tribune*, July 10, 1986.

CHAPTER NINE: IN AND OUT OF UNIFORM

98   So in their continuing efforts: Barry, *Femininity in Flight*, 99.

98   "status gloves with a touch of fishnet": Marylin Bender, "Airlines Are Going Sky High for Fashionable Stewardesses," *New York Times*, August 23, 1967.

98   Patt immediately started wearing: Author interview with Patt Gibbs.

98   In early 1969, American introduced: Barry, *Femininity in Flight*, 181.

98   The "Field Flowers" serving garment: *The Today Show*, "Style in the Skies: Flight Attendant Fashion over the Years, from Hot Pants and Go-Go Boots to More Sophisticated and Glamorous Looks," NBC, April, 19, 2011, www.today.com.

98   The shift from the highly tailored: Author interview with Patt Gibbs.

99   On another layover: Email from Patt Gibbs, May 2021.

99   Every stewardess knew about: Author interview with Kathleen Heenan.

99   At Pan Am, management had upgraded: "Stewardesses Get New Look at Pan Am," *New York Times*, February 17, 1969.

99   And Canadian Pacific Air Lines: Joan Sangster and Julia Smith, "Thigh in the Sky: Canadian Pacific Dresses Its Female Flight Attendants," *Labor* 14, no. 1 (2017): 39–63.

100   They grieved the suspension: Joan Sangster and Julia Smith, "Beards and Bloomers: Flight Attendants, Grievances and Embodied Labour in the Canadian Airline Industry, 1960s–1980s," *Gender, Work & Organization* 23, no. 2 (2016): 183–99.

100   After feminist picketing: Joan Sangster and Julia Smith, "#MeToo: Fighting Sexism Through Labour Activism," *Canadian Dimension* 52, no. 2 (October 2018).

100   Three years later Southern gave in: Barry, *Femininity in Flight*, 183.

101   "save the satisfaction that comes from": "Which Stewardess Is the Girl on Your Flight?" *New York Times*, June 8, 1969.

101   While bra-burning existed: Roxane Gay, "Fifty Years Ago, Protesters Took

on the Miss America Pageant and Electrified the Feminist Movement," *Smithsonian*, January/February 2018.

101   high heels, and girdles: Lee Thornton, "Florynce Kennedy Says Miss America Pageant Is 'Superfluous' and 'Unnecessary,'" NPR, September 17, 1983.

101   triumphantly crowned a sheep: Gail Collins, *America's Women: Four Hundred Years of Dolls, Drudges, Helpmates, and Heroines* (New York: William Morrow, 2003), 440.

101   Florynce Kennedy: Gay, "Fifty Years Ago."

101   Miss America would have its first Black contestant: Gay, "Fifty Years Ago."

101   The Miss America protest: Gay, "Fifty Years Ago."

101   a women's liberation group: *The Woodstock Whisperer/Jim Shelley* (blog), "New York Radical Women 1968," September 7, 2016, https://woodstock whisperer.info.

101   Other women's groups were gaining: Marion Lockwood Carden, *The New Feminist Movement* (New York: Russell Sage Foundation, 1974), 190.

101   Members performed a sort of subversive theater: https://digpodcast.org /2020/09/27/w-i-t-c-h/.

101   and leafleting bridal fairs: JoFreeman.com, "W.I.T.C.H.: The Womens International Terrorist Conspiracy from Hell," n.d., accessed August 13, 2021, www.jofreeman.com.

102   And court cases that invoked: Barbara Allen Babcock, *Sex Discrimination and the Law: History, Practice, and Theory* (Boston: Little, Brown, 1996), 489.

102   The next decade would see: Dorothy Sue Cobble, "'A Spontaneous Loss of Enthusiasm': Workplace Feminism and the Transformation of Women's Service Jobs in the 1970s," *International Labor and Working-Class History* 56 (1999): 23–44.

102   In 1970, the United Auto Workers: Rupp and Taylor, *Survival in the Doldrums*, 153.

102   Even the new president: Vantoch, *The Jet Sex*, 2.

103   And Patt said, "I would": Author interview with Patt Gibbs.

103   She and Anna continued to date: Author interview with Patt Gibbs.

104   Her year of self-doubt was over: Author interview with Patt Gibbs.

CHAPTER TEN: FLYING PIANOS

109   Tommie had been so excited: Author interview with Tommie Hutto-Blake.

109   The center provided job training: Sullivan Progress Plaza, "Our Founder," n.d., accessed August 13, 2021, https://progressplaza.com/about-us/our -founder/.

113   When Tommie graduated: Author interview with Tommie Hutto-Blake.

115   Bobbi (her real name was Barbara): Author interview with Tommie Hutto-Blake.

116   "I propose that the women": Collins, *When Everything Changed*, 205.

117   The rallying slogan?: Katie Reilly, "'Don't Iron While the Strike Is Hot': These Are the Precursors to 'A Day Without a Woman,'" *Time*, March 7, 2017.

117 Women held teach-ins: Linda Napikoski, "Women's Strike for Equality," ThoughtCo., updated February 25, 2019, www.thoughtco.com.

117 free, accessible abortion: Maggie Doherty, "Feminist Factions United and Filled the Streets for This Historic March," *New York Times,* August 26, 2020 (updated September 3, 2020).

117 Four union leaders: Barry, *Femininity in Flight,* 188.

118 And the more commercials she saw: Author interview with Tommie Hutto-Blake.

118 She felt more like punching them: Notes from Tommie Hutto-Blake provided to author in an email, July 9, 2021.

118 Still, it was hard to blame the men entirely: *The Media Guy,* "Nicki Minaj Took My Seat."

118 "you work hard so you deserve this": Barry, *Femininity in Flight,* 100.

118 Another United ad: Item found via search on eBay (July 10, 2021) for "1967 United Airlines stewardess businesman photo vintage print ad."

120 Every once in a while: Author interview with Brian Hagerty.

120 Even the mechanics made: Office of Occupational Statistics and Employment Projections, *Occupational Outlook Handbook, 1974–75 Edition: Part 2; Bulletin of the United States Bureau of Labor Statistics, No. 1785* (Washington, DC: U.S. Bureau of Labor, 1975).

120 "But they'll think I'm a flight attendant": "Kathleen Heenan [interview]," NYU Libraries.

121 Walking into the cockpit to see: Author interview with Tommie Hutto-Blake.

121 They'd open a mini bottle of vodka: Author interview with Brian Hagerty.

121 The huge new 747 had been introduced: Author interview with Patt Gibbs.

122 Eventually, passengers were just told: Author interview with Patt Gibbs.

122 The lounge had its own piano: Part of the collection of the American Airlines CR Smith Museum.

122 Other passengers could join in: Author interview with Bobbi Lennie.

122 "Put a piano in a room full": FM1156, "American Airlines 747 the Coach Lounge 1970's TV Commercial HD," YouTube video, January 7, 2018.

122 But the 747 was there: United Jet Mainliner, "1971 American Airlines '747 Coach Lounge' Commercial," YouTube video, December 19, 2016.

124 They wrote their own vows: Author interview with Tommie Hutto-Blake.

CHAPTER ELEVEN: PREGNANCY AND PURSERS

125 She moved to her own apartment: Author interview with Sonia Pressman Fuentes.

126 Zia was born: Fuentes, *Eat First,* Kindle ed., chap. 29.

126 The life of a housewife: Fuentes, *Eat First,* Kindle ed., chap. 29.

126 She looked at the woman: Author interview with Sonia Pressman Fuentes.

126 She'd hoped he'd take her with him: Author interview with Sonia Pressman Fuentes.

127 "We don't need any further studies": Sonia Pressman Fuentes, "The Law Against Sex Discrimination in Employment and Its Relationship to Statistics," *The American Statistician* 26, no. 2 (1972).

127   "it would be anomalous for you": Fuentes, "The Law Against Sex Discrimination."

128   When the man who'd hired her: Author interview with Sonia Pressman Fuentes.

128   "Listen, guys": Author interview with Sonia Pressman Fuentes.

129   When the Supreme Court finally upheld: Fuentes, *Eat First*, Kindle ed., chap. 24.

129   The negotiating team had scraped: Author interview with Patt Gibbs.

129   In 1970, there were 169 million: Drew Whitelegg, *Working the Skies: The Fast-Paced, Disorienting World of the Flight Attendant*, Kindle ed. (New York: New York University Press, 2007), chap. 1.

129   Patt knew that the average baggage handler: Ryan Patrick Murphy, *Deregulating Desire: Flight Attendant Activism, Family Politics, and Workplace Justice* (Philadelphia: Temple University Press, 2016), 24.

130   In July 1971, Bella Abzug: Feminist Majority Foundation, "Part II—1971," n.d., accessed August 13, 2021, https://feminist.org.

130   She pointed out that in 1970 in Virginia: Feminist Majority Foundation, "Part II—1971."

130   The same year, the Professional Women's Caucus: Feminist Majority Foundation, "Part II—1971."

130   Title IX, which made discrimination: Editors of Encyclopaedia Britannica, "Title IX," Encyclopaedia Britannica, n.d., accessed August 13, 2021, www.britannica.com.

130   Patt did additional training: From personal records of Patt Gibbs.

CHAPTER TWELVE: THE CASE OF MARY PAT

132   At least that's what the new contract said: Author interview with Mary Pat Laffey Inman.

133   He posted the bids: Author interview with Mary Pat Laffey Inman.

133   She had been a stewardess for a decade: Author interview with Mary Pat Laffey Inman.

134   He loved the Northwest: Email from Michael Gottesman.

134   "We did a study": Author interview with Michael Gottesman.

134   The VP wasn't the only one: Barry, *Femininity in Flight*, 199.

134   They'd ignore her completely: Author interview with Mary Pat Laffey Inman.

135   "we know that women": Author interview and follow-up email with Michael Gottesman.

135   The EEOC filed an amicus brief: Dooley, "Battle in the Sky," 41.

135   It was revealed that in many cases: Author interview with Michael Gottesman.

135   When Mike asked why: Dooley, "Battle in the Sky," 43.

135   Northwest protested that Asian: Dooley, "Battle in the Sky," 44.

136   Northwest, like its fellow airlines: Dooley, "Battle in the Sky," 45.

136   She had rallied the other women: Author interview with Michael Gottesman.

136   The total amount of money: Dooley, "Battle in the Sky," 46.

136 The *Laffey* case was: Barry, *Femininity in Flight*, 170.

136 General Electric: Rogers v. General Electric Company, 781 F. 2d 452 (5th Cir. 1986).

137 Northwest got rid of the purser role: Author interview with Mary Pat Laffey Inman.

137 The final appeal was held: Author interview with Michael Gottesman.

137 They won everything: Author interview with Michael Gottesman.

137 Thanks to compound interest: Email from Michael Gottesman.

137 It was the largest monetary judgment: Author interview with Michael Gottesman.

137 Mary Pat continued to fly: Author interview with Mary Pat Laffey Inman.

CHAPTER THIRTEEN: MEN ON BOARD

138 He took Pan Am to court: Barry, *Femininity in Flight*, 167.

138 The court's decision hammered home: Weeks v. Southern Bell Telephone Co., 408 F.2d 228, 235 (5th Cir. 1969).

138 Employers taken to court: Barry, *Femininity in Flight*, 169.

139 Pan Am's cutoff: Diaz v. Pan American World Airways, Inc., 311 F. Supp. 559 (S.D. Fla. 1970).

139 was twenty-six: Tiemeyer, *Plane Queer*, 106.

139 The *Diaz* case was the end: Tiemeyer, *Plane Queer*, 106.

139 Before *Diaz,* just a few: Barry, *Femininity in Flight*, 159.

139 Now men leapt at the opportunity: Tiemeyer, *Plane Queer*, 106.

139 Alternative names he'd debated: Vantoch, *The Jet Sex*, 20.

139 From now on: Author interview with Patricia Ireland.

140 "Half of these guys are queens": Author interview with Brian Hagerty.

140 They absorbed all the little things: Author interview with Brian Hagerty.

140 He had just signed a lease: Author interview with Brian Hagerty.

141 It went on all winter: Kamelia Angelova, "Amazing Pictures of the Oil Crisis of 1973," *Business Insider*, August 30, 2011, www.businessinsider.com.

141 By September 10 he was: Author interview with Brian Hagerty.

142 "But don't worry about Tommie": Author interview with Brian Hagerty.

142 "Hi, I'm Tommie": Author interview with Tommie Hutto-Blake.

142 Quick to sense an opportunity: Author interview with Brian Hagerty.

142 If she asked him for paperwork: Author interview with Tommie Hutto-Blake.

142 "Tired businessmen flying home": Robert Lindsey, "U.S. Airlines Seek Stewards to Work Aloft," *New York Times*, April 7, 1972.

143 "It wasn't until I saw my first steward": Anna Quindlen, "Flight Attendants: An Old Stereotype Is Given the Air," *New York Times*, April 23, 1978.

143 Quindlen would continue: Anna Quindlen, "Public & Private; in Thin Air," *New York Times*, May 16, 1993.

143 The men's uniform: Part of the collection of the American Airlines CR Smith Museum.

144 It is absurd: Author interview with Patt Gibbs.

144 She wrangled a meeting: Author interview with Patt Gibbs.

144   And the regulation applied: Author interview with Patt Gibbs.

144   Occasionally the union could: Author interview with Tommie Hutto-Blake.

145   Men also came in handy: Author interview with Patricia Ireland.

145   Women had long been subjected: "SFWR Organizational Meeting (Washington DC) [recording]," NYU Libraries: Oral Histories, n.d., accessed August 13, 2021, http://digitaltamiment.hosting.nyu.edu.

145   Dana had a friend who: Author interview with Dana Olson.

145   She wasn't the only one: Author interview with Patt Gibbs.

145   Robert Crandall: Author interview with Brian Hagerty.

146   Everyone knew some women: Author interview with Patt Gibbs.

146   In later years: Author interview with Tommie Hutto-Blake.

147   No sooner would she explain: Author interview with Joan Dorsey.

147   While there might have been: Tiemeyer, *Plane Queer,* 121.

147   In a 1969 New York State suit: Tiemeyer, *Plane Queer,* 91.

147   Delta's CEO, Tom Beebe: Tiemeyer, *Plane Queer,* 121.

148   They kept saving and bought: Author interview with Patt Gibbs.

148   And the world was catching up: Tiemeyer, *Plane Queer,* 1–3.

CHAPTER FOURTEEN: GO FLY YOURSELF

150   Along with increasing numbers: Barry, *Femininity in Flight,* 119.

150   with Latinx and Asian Americans: Barry, *Femininity in Flight,* 120.

150   A few days after Martin Luther King Jr.: History.com, "Fair Housing Act," January 27, 2010 (updated January 28, 2021), www.history.com.

150   The Black Panther Party: History.com, "Black Panthers," November 3, 2017 (updated January 26, 2021), www.history.com.

150   Discrimination was rife: Casey Grant, *Stars in the Sky: Stories of the First African American Flight Attendants,* Kindle ed. (Shelbyville, KY: Wasteland, 2014), chap. 4.

150   Pilots would occasionally: Grant, *Stars in the Sky,* chap. 2.

151   That was her first experience: Author interview with Cheryl Stewart-Gaymon.

152   Her supervisor wrote down three inches: Author interview with Cheryl Stewart-Gaymon.

152   "Really?" asked Cheryl: Author interview with Cheryl Stewart-Gaymon.

153   She wore her clown makeup: Author interview with Kathleen Clements.

153   In the mid-1960s: Barry, *Femininity in Flight,* 120.

153   If she were lighter-skinned: Author interview with Sharon Dunn.

153   Kathleen watched with pleasure: "Heenan [interview]," NYU Libraries.

154   "Stewardess Lancy Lee": *The Media Guy,* "Nicki Minaj Took My Seat."

154   "Can't pronounce her full name?": *The Media Guy,* "Nicki Minaj Took My Seat."

154   Sociologist Arlie Russell Hochschild: Amy S. Wharton, "The Sociology of Emotional Labor," *Annual Review of Sociology* 35 (2009): 147–65.

154   when she did she was referring to stewardesses: Hochschild, *The Managed Heart,* 127.

154   And the key element: noluckBoston13, "1968 American Airlines Commercial," YouTube video, March 2, 2017.

154 "Enjoy yourself": Vantoch, *The Jet Sex*, 172.

157 Pacific Southwest Airlines ran: PSA, "Commercials," n.d., accessed August 13, 2021, www.psa-history.org.

157 Carol, the ad specified: ClickAmericana, "Pretty, Thin, Young and Single?"

157 National Airlines had the dubious honor: Barry, *Femininity in Flight*, 177.

158 The campaign infuriated the stewardesses: Letter, Stewardesses for Women's Rights Collection, Tamiment Library and Robert F. Wagner Labor Archives, New York University Libraries.

158 The stewardesses joined the almost: Gillian Frank and Lauren Gutterman, "Sexism Takes Flight [transcript]," *Sexing History* (podcast), n.d., accessed August 13, 2021, https://gill-frank.squarespace.com.

158 The agency owner, Bill Free: Stuart Lavietes, "F. William Free, 74, Ad Man Behind 'Fly Me' [obituary]," *New York Times*, January 8, 2003.

158 NOW also picketed: Barry, *Femininity in Flight*, 194.

158 to write letters to the airline: Dooley, "Battle in the Sky," 123.

158 National had a 19 percent increase: "F. William Free, 74 [obituary]."

158 The agency created a follow-up ad: Leonard Sloane, "Advertising: New 'Fly Me' Spots," *New York Times*, August 30, 1972.

158 Getting the message across: Carden, *The New Feminist Movement*, 161.

159 But wearing a "Fly Me" T-shirt: Author interview with Carin Clauss.

CHAPTER FIFTEEN: STEWARDESSES FOR WOMEN'S RIGHTS

160 On September 20, 1973: Billie Jean King Enterprises, "Battle of the Sexes," n.d., accessed August 13, 2021, www.billiejeanking.com.

160 And Billie Jean was scoring: Author interview with Patt Gibbs.

160 But she could see that Billie Jean: Author interview with Tommie Hutto-Blake.

160 Earlier that year she'd threatened: Adam Augustyn, "Battle of the Sexes," Encyclopaedia Britannica, September 13, 2020, www.britannica.com.

160 Her advocacy got results: Billie Jean King Enterprises, "Equality," n.d., accessed August 13, 2021, www.billiejeanking.com.

160 Billie Jean couldn't get a credit card: Collins, *When Everything Changed*, 250.

161 On average, a woman needed: Collins, *America's Women*, 438.

161 Young women in Texas: Author interview with Tommie Hutto-Blake.

161 He and Tommie took trips: Author interview with Tommie Hutto-Blake.

161 They went back and bought two more: Author interview with Tommie Hutto-Blake.

161 They weren't the only ones mesmerized: "About Us," *Ms.*, n.d., accessed August 13, 2021, https://msmagazine.com/about/.

162 Tommie read every word: Linda Napikoski, "Articles in the First Issue of Ms. Magazine: The Debut of Feminism's Famous Magazine," ThoughtCo., updated July 3, 2019, www.thoughtco.com.

162 Sandra Jarrell was the first speaker: "Why They Don't Want to Be Sex Symbols," *Washington Post*, August 22, 1973, Stewardesses for Women's Rights Collection.

162 It had been her idea: Undated *Washington Post* article, Stewardesses for Women's Rights Collection.

163 It was true that flight attendants had unique access: "Interview with Barbara 'Dusty' Roads," *People's Century.*

163 When it came time, toward the end: Interview with Dana Olson.

164 Tommie, Dana, and Bobbi walked: Author interview with Tommie Hutto-Blake.

164 Stewardesses for Women's Rights: Flyer, Stewardesses for Women's Rights Collection.

164 Tommie, Bobbi, and Dana were already: Collins, *When Everything Changed,* 401.

164 Then, in January 1973, *Ms.* ran: *Ms.,* January 1973.

165 In these letters: Letters, Stewardesses for Women's Rights Collection.

165 copied out the addresses: Letter, Stewardesses for Women's Rights Collection.

165 They made general comments: Letter, Stewardesses for Women's Rights Collection.

165 "because of his own personal preferences": Letter, Stewardesses for Women's Rights Collection.

165 "I saw the new uniform": Letter, Stewardesses for Women's Rights Collection.

165 One woman had received four anonymous letters: Letters, Stewardesses for Women's Rights Collection.

165 Letters referenced instances: Letters, Stewardesses for Women's Rights Collection.

165 When stewardesses turned up at union meetings: "SFWR Organizational Meeting (Washington DC) [recording]," NYU Libraries.

165 "If we could get Stewardesses for Women's Rights active": "SFWR Organizational Meeting (Washington DC) [recording]," NYU Libraries.

166 One new member proposed: Letter, Stewardesses for Women's Rights Collection.

166 How to convince the young stewardesses: "SFWR Organizational Meeting (Washington DC) [recording]," NYU Libraries.

167 Florynce Kennedy: Margaret Busby, "Florynce Kennedy [obituary]," *Guardian,* January 9, 2001.

167 Margaret Sloan-Hunter turned up: Kayomi Wada, "National Black Feminist Organization (1973–1976)," BlackPast, December 29, 2008, www.blackpast.org.

167 National conferences, they decided: Author interview with Tommie Hutto-Blake.

167 The entrance fee was just $5: Willis, "The Stewardesses for Women's Rights," 197.

167 Around a hundred stewardesses: Letter, Stewardesses for Women's Rights Collection.

167 Gloria Steinem, Margaret Sloan-Hunter: Willis, "The Stewardesses for Women's Rights," 165.

167 an activist in the Redstockings: Willis, "The Stewardesses for Women's Rights," 110.

168 Union leaders, though: Willis, "The Stewardesses for Women's Rights," 108.

168 The two-day conference neatly balanced: "Women's Rights Reach New High with Wings," *New York Times*, March 12, 1973.

168 Tommie loved it: Author interview with Tommie Hutto-Blake.

169 $25,000 (around $153,200 in 2021 dollars): "Value of 1973 US Dollars Today," Inflation Tool, accessed October 2, 2021, www.inflationtool.com.

169 grant from the Stern Family Fund: Barry, *Femininity in Flight*, 193.

169 They designated $9,000: Parsons et al., "Organizational Logic and Feminist Organizing."

169 That decision didn't sit well: Parsons et al., "Organizational Logic and Feminist Organizing."

169 They got it cheap: Willis, "The Stewardesses for Women's Rights," 317.

169 They filled a library with materials: Survey, Stewardesses for Women's Rights, Stewardesses for Women's Rights Collection.

169 In January 1974: News clipping, January 24, 1974, Stewardesses for Women's Rights Collection.

169 Al, Tommie's husband: Author interview with Tommie Hutto-Blake.

169 And they decided to invite: Author interview with Tommie Hutto-Blake.

169 The address was impressive: Willis, "The Stewardesses for Women's Rights," 336.

170 If she had to, Dana told her: News clipping, n.d., Stewardesses for Women's Rights Collection.

170 The reporter, Anna Quindlen: Author interview with Dana Olson.

170 This conference had two themes: Letter to David R. Hunter from Stewardesses for Women's Rights, February 25, 1974, Stewardesses for Women's Rights Collection.

170 Discussions were held: Chandler, *Sex Objects in the Sky*, 85.

170 "Delta is an air line run by professionals": Item found via search on eBay (July 10, 2021) for "1973 Delta Airlines Ad Rose Wynne Stewardess."

171 "4,000 Christas": Item found via search on eBay (July 10, 2021) for "1974 Delta Airlines Ad Christa Beck Stewardess."

171 "2,200 Anitas": Item found via search on eBay (July 10, 2021) for "1971 Delta Airlines Vintage Look Metal Sign—Stewardess Anita Johnson & 747 Jet."

171 Captains and other male: Item found via search on eBay (July 10, 2021) for "973 Delta Airlines Paul Hunt Vintage Print Ad."

171 not one of thousands: Item found via search on eBay (July 10, 2021) for "Vintage Ad Print Delta Airlines, 1972 6.5 x 10."

171 matching set: Item found via search on eBay (July 10, 2021) for "1978 Delta Airlines: Dot Turnipseed Vintage Print Ad."

171 They created task forces: Willis, "The Stewardesses for Women's Rights," 171.

171 Tommie came home exhilarated: Author interview with Tommie Hutto-Blake.

171 She went alone: "Oral Histories," NYU Libraries, n.d., accessed August 13, 2021, https://digitaltamiment.hosting.nyu.edu.

171   One woman approached her: "Oral Histories," NYU Libraries.

171   Cindy listened to a woman: "Oral Histories," NYU Libraries.

172   And the panels, which gave: Willis, "The Stewardesses for Women's Rights," 176.

172   Cindy, well-spoken: Author interview with Tommie Hutto-Blake.

172   Even the work itself had an air: Author interview with Cindy Hounsell.

172   She joined more committees: "Oral Histories," NYU Libraries.

172   She scaled up at SFWR: "Stewardesses for Women's Rights Policy and Procedure Manual," n.d., Stewardesses for Women's Rights Collection.

172   the head of the New York chapter: "Stewardesses for Women's Rights Policy and Procedure Manual," n.d., Stewardesses for Women's Rights Collection.

172   As she became more active in the union: "Oral Histories," NYU Libraries.

173   SFWR could at times feel dominated: "Oral Histories," NYU Libraries.

173   At Pan Am, when she'd: "Oral Histories," NYU Libraries.

173   "If I had to organize these people": "Oral Histories," NYU Libraries.

173   She'd enthuse about how wonderful: Author interview with Cindy Hounsell.

173   She'd try identifying: Author interview with Tommie Hutto-Blake.

174   Afterward, when Tommie ran into her: Author interview with Tommie Hutto-Blake.

174   She handed over a newsletter: Author interview with Tommie Hutto-Blake.

174   And Patt went: Author interview with Patt Gibbs.

174   The membership of SFWR: Willis, "The Stewardesses for Women's Rights," 127.

174   In October 1974: Stewardesses for Women's Rights, "Face from Membership Survey—October 5, 1974," Stewardesses for Women's Rights Collection.

174   It was a numerically insignificant amount: Barry, *Femininity in Flight*, 190.

174   She'd schedule a meeting but people: Author interview with Bobbi Lennie.

174   Thirteen local chapters: Kathy Sanderson, Donna Boone Parsons, J. Helms Mills, and Albert Mills, "Riding the Second Wave: Organizing Feminism and Organizational Discourse—Stewardesses for Women's Rights," *Management & Organizational History* 5, nos. 3–4 (2010): 360–77.

174   Tommie, Dana, and Bobbi became editors: Author interview with Dana Olson.

174   It went out each month: Author interview with Tommie Hutto-Blake.

175   Bobbi took some of the photos: Author interview with Bobbi Lennie.

175   The newsletter suggested: Willis, "The Stewardesses for Women's Rights," 197.

175   When SFWR members started: Author interview with Tommie Hutto-Blake.

176   The San Francisco chapter sold: Letter, Stewardesses for Women's Rights Collection.

176   Stewardesses who might have been: Author interview with Patt Gibbs.

176   "just wonderful": "Oral Histories," NYU Libraries.

176   Tommie learned (and would never forget): Author interview with Tommie Hutto-Blake.

176   One flight attendant confided: Gloria Steinem, "Gloria Steinem on How

Female Flight Attendants Fought Sexism in the Skies," *Condé Nast Traveler,* March 25, 2016.

176 More financial help came in: Douglas Martin, "Stewart R. Mott, 70, Off-beat Philanthropist, Dies," *New York Times,* June 14, 2008.

176 was famous for donating money: "Loan Agreement," November 5, 1974, Stewardesses for Women's Rights Collection.

176 Then SFWR was offered: Parsons et al., "Organizational Logic and Feminist Organizing."

176 They briefly considered it: Memo, May 2, 1974, Stewardesses for Women's Rights Collection.

177 They hashed the question out: Author interview with Tommie Hutto-Blake.

177 SFWR also helped stewardesses: Heenan, "Fighting the 'Fly-Me' Airlines," 52.

177 Betty Southard Murphy: Letter, Stewardesses for Women's Rights Collection.

177 a lawyer in the Department of Labor: Penn State University Libraries, "Betty Southard Murphy," n.d., accessed August 13, 2021, https://libraries.psu.edu.

177 gave them free legal advice: Memo, June 4, 1974, Stewardesses for Women's Rights Collection.

177 as did Kathleen Peratis: Women's Rights Project; American Civil Liberties Union, "Memorandum," n.d., Stewardesses for Women's Rights Collection.

177 When new legislation passed: "Oral Histories," NYU Libraries.

177 Pioneered by Kathie Sarachild: Barry, *Femininity in Flight,* 192.

177 the prominent feminist who'd spoken: Linda Napikoski, "Feminist Consciousness-Raising Groups," ThoughtCo., updated October 14, 2019, www.thoughtco.com.

177 A much-used text by Verne Moberg: Photo, Association of Professional Flight Attendants Records, University of Texas at Arlington Library, https://legacy.lib.utexas.edu.

177 Tommie found these sessions: Author interview with Tommie Hutto-Blake.

177 SFWR's third conference: Willis, "The Stewardesses for Women's Rights," 184.

178 With panels staffed: Willis, "The Stewardesses for Women's Rights," 180.

178 Pregnant flight attendants had: News clipping, "Stewardesses Challenge Airlines," n.d., Stewardesses for Women's Rights Collection.

178 At the San Francisco conference: Willis, "The Stewardesses for Women's Rights," 180.

178 In 1973, one out of every ten planes: News clipping, "Stewardesses Challenge Airlines," n.d., Stewardesses for Women's Rights Collection.

178 thus exposing crew and passengers: Barry, *Femininity in Flight,* 194.

178 Ozark Airlines carried more radioactive cargo: Letter, Stewardesses for Women's Rights Collection.

178 The transport of radioactive cargo: Letter, Stewardesses for Women's Rights Collection.

178   SFWR partnered with Nader's organization: Willis, "The Stewardesses for Women's Rights," 262.

179   The FAA was neglecting: Willis, "The Stewardesses for Women's Rights," 262.

179   So Tommie, Dana, and Bobbi swapped: Author interview with Tommie Hutto-Blake.

179   Employee Relations staff from American: Author interview with Tommie Hutto-Blake.

179   The same outgoing personalities: Author interview with Tommie Hutto-Blake.

179   It worked: Barry, *Femininity in Flight*, 194.

CHAPTER SIXTEEN: WE REALLY MOVE OUR TAILS FOR YOU

180   SFWR's safety campaign: Liz Ritch, "Public Relations Up-date," n.d., Stewardesses for Women's Rights Collection.

180   SFWR's campaign against: Letter, Stewardesses for Women's Rights Collection.

180   "pinched, fondled, leered at": "Stewardesses Battle Sex-Object Image," *Los Angeles Times*, April 5, 1972.

180   Joan Rivers made stewardesses: "Flight Attendants Publically Slandered [Local 552 press release]," Stewardesses for Women's Rights Collection.

180   She drove both Bobbi and Cindy: "Oral Histories," NYU Libraries.

180   constantly promoting the very image: Author interview with Bobbi Lennie.

180   They joined a massive letter-writing campaign: Undated union newsletter, Stewardesses for Women's Rights Collection.

180   Harry Reasoner: Letter to Reasoner from Dana Olson, Stewardesses for Women's Rights Collection.

181   "should remain patches": Letter, Stewardesses for Women's Rights Collection.

181   SFWR went wild: Willis, "The Stewardesses for Women's Rights," 326.

181   Dana, by this time: Maley, "Flying the 'Unfriendly Skies,'" 198.

181   It worked—Reasoner went on the air: Letter, Stewardesses for Women's Rights Collection.

181   mentioning Dana's letter specifically: Personal communication from Tommie Hutto-Blake.

181   It noted, farther down: Vantoch, *The Jet Sex*, 183.

181   The commercial showed: Classic Airliners & Vintage Pop Culture, "PSA: Pacific Southwest Stewardess Commercial—1972," YouTube video, March 19, 2012.

182   Domestic airlines didn't have a monopoly: Print advertisement, Stewardesses for Women's Rights Collection.

182   Air France asked with a wink: Barry, *Femininity in Flight*, 178.

182   Finnair created print ads: *The Media Guy*, "Nicki Minaj Took My Seat."

183   One turned just slightly toward the camera: Creations by Adam, "Southwest Airlines Hostesses Hotpants Ad 1972," YouTube video, September 10, 2007.

183   The airline operated from Love Field: Wikipedia, "Dallas Love Field," last modified August 20, 2021, https://en.wikipedia.org.

183   It was a new airline: "New Texas Airline 'Loves' Its Passengers," *New York Times*, August 8, 1971.

183   Southwest milked this campaign: Kolm, "Women's Labor Aloft," 231.

183   Southwest dug its heels in: Tiemeyer, *Plane Queer*, 242.

183   Now it was doubling down: Print advertisement, Stewardesses for Women's Rights Collection.

183   At SFWR headquarters, Tommie: Willis, "The Stewardesses for Women's Rights," 331.

184   and producing bumper stickers: Undated news clipping, Stewardesses for Women's Rights Collection.

184   The NAB agreed: Barry, *Femininity in Flight*, 194.

184   Bobbi was always butting heads: Willis, "The Stewardesses for Women's Rights," 339.

184   She went to the cockpit for help: Author interview with Cindy Hounsell.

184   More than ten ambulances: Email from Cindy Hounsell, June 6, 2021.

185   But the campaign had in reality: News clipping, *Time* (February 11, 1974), Stewardesses for Women's Rights Collection.

185   When Continental's stewardesses protested: News clipping, *Time* (February 11, 1974), Stewardesses for Women's Rights Collection.

185   One story that circulated widely: Willis, "The Stewardesses for Women's Rights," 210.

185   The group had already tried raising this issue: Barry, *Femininity in Flight*, 195.

186   If someone called in to say: Author interview with Cindy Hounsell.

186   Around a hundred SFWR members: Maley, "Flying the 'Unfriendly Skies,' " 184.

186   The ending was solemn: Barry, *Femininity in Flight*, 196.

186   one was on a feminist show: Barry, *Femininity in Flight*, 264.

187   The next newsletter featured: Newsletter, Stewardesses for Women's Rights Collection.

187   the commercial displayed prominently: Maley, "Flying the 'Unfriendly Skies,' " 184.

187   The companies always responded defensively: Willis, "The Stewardesses for Women's Rights," 212.

187   Firestone: Maley, "Flying the 'Unfriendly Skies,' " 190.

187   which produced an ad: Willis, "The Stewardesses for Women's Rights," 210.

187   Bobbi's husband was a social worker: Author interview with Bobbi Lennie.

187   She grew tired of defending: Author interview with Cindy Hounsell.

187   They'd dutifully signed it: "Oral Histories," NYU Libraries.

188   For many flight attendants: Author interview with Tommie Hutto-Blake.

188   And the stewardesses were fighting: Author interview with Tommie Hutto-Blake.

188   SFWR, Tommie thought: Author interview with Tommie Hutto-Blake.

189   "I know you can do it": Author interview with Tommie Hutto-Blake.

189   Dusty was a unionist: Author interview with Tommie Hutto-Blake.

189   SFWR did serve as: Frieda Shoenberg Rozen, "Turbulence in the Air: The
       Autonomy Movement in the Flight Attendant Unions" (PhD dissertation,
       Pennsylvania State University, 1988), 210.

189   Cindy Hounsell, at Pan Am: Author interview with Tommie Hutto-Blake.

189   Cindy was working as a shop steward: Author interview with Cindy
       Hounsell.

189   Through a combination of happenstance: Author interview with Tommie
       Hutto-Blake.

189   Patt Gibbs had also wanted: Author interview with Tommie Hutto-Blake.

190   That was yet another reason Tommie: Author interview with Tommie
       Hutto-Blake.

190   There was, one wrote: Letter, Stewardesses for Women's Rights Collection.

190   The unions were too concerned with: Letter, Stewardesses for Women's
       Rights Collection.

190   SFWR member Liz Rich gave an interview: News clipping (March 14,
       1974), Stewardesses for Women's Rights Collection.

190   On occasion, they'd stop SFWR: Letter, Stewardesses for Women's Rights
       Collection.

190   There was a general feeling of uneasiness: Letter, Stewardesses for Wom-
       en's Rights Collection.

CHAPTER SEVENTEEN: FIRST THE COMMIES, THEN THE FEMINISTS

191   As base chair, Tommie now worked: Author interview with Tommie Hutto-
       Blake.

191   In early 1974, the Air Line Stewards: Barry, Femininity in Flight, 200.

191   TWA became Local 551: Author interview with Tommie Hutto-Blake.

191   Moving into airline-specific locals: Barry, Femininity in Flight, 200.

191   Tommie's passion for union work: Author interview with Tommie Hutto-
       Blake.

191   These men had much in common: Author interview with Tommie Hutto-
       Blake.

192   She towered over Charlie Pasciuto: Author interview with Patt Gibbs.

192   "It's because I know the rules": Author interview with Tommie Hutto-Blake.

192   On occasion Tommie would really: Author interview with Tommie
       Hutto-Blake.

192   She could be pulled off the flight: Author interview with Tommie Hutto-
       Blake.

193   At Pan Am in 1968: Vantoch, The Jet Sex, 189.

193   In 1970, United: Dooley, "Battle in the Sky," 326.

193   A year later the company: Dooley, "Battle in the Sky," 328.

193   At Braniff, a program: Dooley, "Battle in the Sky," 323.

193   had given the women some leeway: Dooley, "Battle in the Sky," 323.

193   Then in 1972 : Dooley, "Battle in the Sky," 317.

193   A male flight attendant had: Loucks, "Battle in the Skies."

194   In fact, she pointed out: Author interview with Tommie Hutto-Blake.

194   The arbitrators, though, would often: Author interview with Brian Hagerty.

194   It didn't matter for men: Author interview with Brian Hagerty.

194   One incident brought Tommie: Author interview with Tommie Hutto-Blake.

195   Memo after memo came from Eastern: Memo, Stewardesses for Women's Rights Collection.

195   Eastern was always changing the rules: Letter, Stewardesses for Women's Rights Collection.

195   Stewardesses continued to file: Letter, Stewardesses for Women's Rights Collection.

195   Some women took the airlines to court: "Stewardess Is Reinstated but Weight Policy Stands," *New York Times*, August 7, 1974.

195   But even when these individuals: Robert Lindsey, "Air Stewardesses Fight Weight Rule," *New York Times*, March 4, 1972.

195   The leash grew tighter: Dooley, "Battle in the Sky," 342.

196   After all this, her lack of progress: Dooley, "Battle in the Sky," 341.

196   SFWR collected application forms: Photo, Stewardesses for Women's Rights Collection.

196   TWA's application asked: TWA job application, Stewardesses for Women's Rights Collection.

196   A recruiting pamphlet for TWA: Print advertisement, Stewardesses for Women's Rights Collection.

196   It only fanned the flames: Author interview with Cindy Hounsell.

197   Raiding meant stealing members: Barry, *Femininity in Flight*, 85.

197   He pointed to mailings: Letter from Transport Workers Union of America, Stewardesses for Women's Rights Collection.

197   Lindner's letter had ordered: Letter from Transport Workers Union of America, Stewardesses for Women's Rights Collection.

197   Kathleen helped Cindy compose: "Oral Histories," NYU Libraries.

198   Finally, he stuck his finger: Author interview with Tommie Hutto-Blake.

198   She took advantage of the situation: Author interview with Tommie Hutto-Blake.

199   Tommie used the center: Author interview with Tommie Hutto-Blake.

199   Becky was a union rep: Interview with Becky Kroll.

199   She joined SFWR: Email from Tommie Hutto-Blake, July 9, 2021.

199   Becky would tell SFWR members: Author interview with Becky Kroll.

199   She still paid her dues: Author interview with Tommie Hutto-Blake.

199   It wasn't just the general movement: Parsons et al., "Organizational Logic and Feminist Organizing."

200   The San Francisco chapter sent: Letter, Stewardesses for Women's Rights Collection.

201   They argued that excluding: Letter, Stewardesses for Women's Rights Collection.

201   They dealt with the issue: Letter, Stewardesses for Women's Rights Collection.

201   Even though they were getting: Parsons et al., "Organizational Logic and Feminist Organizing."

201   Cindy and Kathleen, die-hard members: "Oral Histories," NYU Libraries.

201   The differences of opinion: Parsons et al., "Organizational Logic and Feminist Organizing."

CHAPTER EIGHTEEN: THE SINGLE ROOM CONTRACT

202   And the average seniority was now: Tiemeyer, *Plane Queer,* 110.
202   Everyone had different sleep schedules: Willis, "The Stewardesses for Women's Rights," 135.
202   Either everyone gets single rooms: Author interview with Tommie Hutto-Blake.
202   Contract negotiations were about to begin: Author interview with Tommie Hutto-Blake.
203   He had come to an agreement: Barry, *Femininity in Flight,* 201.
203   And management required the TWU: Becky Kroll, "A Brief History of the APFA" (unpublished manuscript, 1992), Association of Professional Flight Attendants Records, 12.
203   The United States was going through: Murphy, *Deregulating Desire,* 35.
203   But the problem was this: Author interview with Tommie Hutto-Blake.
203   Patt, part of the local Dallas committee: Author interview with Patt Gibbs.
203   Donna passed that on to Lindner: Email from Tommie Hutto-Blake.
203   "Just you sit back and watch": Author interview with Tommie Hutto-Blake.
204   Charlie was incensed: Author interview with Tommie Hutto-Blake.
204   American, he declared: Photo, Association of Professional Flight Attendants Records, IMG 4287.
204   The TWU went out on the road again: Author interview with Tommie Hutto-Blake.
205   New York was the first stop: Photo, Association of Professional Flight Attendants Records, IMG 4285.
205   The two men Charlie had brought: Author interview with Tommie Hutto-Blake.
206   The votes were tallied: Author interview with Tommie Hutto-Blake.
207   he loved using the word: Author interview with Tommie Hutto-Blake.
207   The captain had turned around: Author interview with Tommie Hutto-Blake.
207   "back there is my wife": Author interviews with Tommie Hutto-Blake and Brian Hagerty.
207   When the results of the third vote: Murphy, *Deregulating Desire,* 35.
207   by an overwhelming margin: Author interview with Tommie Hutto-Blake.
207   Later that year, Tommie ran: Photo, Association of Professional Flight Attendants Records, IMG 4336.
208   When they'd counted the votes: Author interview with Tommie Hutto-Blake.
208   She was the leader of a local: Cindy Hounsell, "Stewardesses Moving Towards Independent Unions [news clipping, n.d.]," Stewardesses for Women's Rights Collection.

CHAPTER NINETEEN: STAY OR GO?

211   When Brian Hagerty needed: Author interview with Brian Hagerty.
211   That meant they had to file: Author interview with Brian Hagerty.

211   Not all the letters made it through: Author interview with Brian Hagerty.

212   They included statements like: From personal records of Patt Gibbs.

212   She took special training: From personal records of Patt Gibbs.

212   Still, try as she might: Author interview with Patt Gibbs.

212   Tommie sympathized: Author interview with Tommie Hutto-Blake.

212   Many of the men would swivel: Willis, "The Stewardesses for Women's Rights," 99.

212   In one photo from that period: From personal records of Patt Gibbs.

215   It wasn't effective for stewardesses: Author interview with Patt Gibbs.

215   "Look at *their* contracts": Author interview with Patt Gibbs.

216   The photos were actually of cigar makers: Author interview with Patt Gibbs.

217   An 800 number: Photo, Association of Professional Flight Attendants Records, IMG 4385.

217   They set up a recorded message: Author interview with Patt Gibbs.

218   Patt put the "tree" system: Author interview with Patt Gibbs.

218   The pace accelerated: Author interview with Patt Gibbs.

219   Retribution arrived without delay: Murphy, *Deregulating Desire*, 52.

219   The same dual unionism charges: Photo, Association of Professional Flight Attendants Records, IMG 4859.

219   The difference was that this time: Photo, Association of Professional Flight Attendants Records.

219   Once members were charged: Author interview with Patt Gibbs.

219   Patt flew to New York: Photo, Association of Professional Flight Attendants Records, IMG 4333.

219   Tommie, she discovered right away: Author interview with Patt Gibbs.

220   At this point, it hardly mattered: Author interview with Patt Gibbs.

220   As more and more of the most active: Author interview with Dana Olson.

220   Adding conflict was the newly established: Author interview with Tommie Hutto-Blake.

220   The New York members didn't feel: Email from Tommie Hutto-Blake.

221   Tommie was president of Local 552: Author interview with Tommie Hutto-Blake.

221   In the end, the changes in SFWR: Author interview with Tommie Hutto-Blake.

221   Cindy and Kathleen were the last ones: Author interview with Cindy Hounsell.

221   The deadline for making the independence decision: Letter, Stewardesses for Women's Rights Collection.

222   Cheryl Stewart, who had faced down: Author interview with Cheryl Stewart-Gaymon.

222   Cheryl could also see: Willis, "The Stewardesses for Women's Rights," 342.

222   There was just a single woman: Author interview with Patt Gibbs.

222   For the entire length: Barry, *Femininity in Flight*, 83.

222   Male pursers and stewards: Barry, *Femininity in Flight*, 199.

222   Dusty Roads described the stewardesses: "Interview with Barbara 'Dusty' Roads," *People's Century.*

222   The divide wasn't just one of class: Murphy, *Deregulating Desire*, 48.

222   And then there was the money: Author interview with Tommie Hutto-Blake.

223   Brian, one of the few men: Author interview with Brian Hagerty.

223   It wasn't, Tommie tried to tell people: Author interview with Brian Hagerty.

223   Rumblings of the new union movement: Author interview with Tommie Hutto-Blake.

225   But APFA, and Patt Gibbs: Author interview with Tommie Hutto-Blake.

225   Tommie wrote a note: Newsletter, n.d., Stewardesses for Women's Rights Collection.

226   She finished by urging flight attendants: Newsletter, n.d., Stewardesses for Women's Rights Collection.

226   Solidarity is what it's all about: Author interview with Brian Hagerty.

226   She wrote another letter: Newsletter, n.d., Stewardesses for Women's Rights Collection.

226   Despite how passionate she felt: Barry, *Femininity in Flight*, 198.

227   TWA flight attendants—Local 551: Murphy, *Deregulating Desire*, 42.

227   "Tell Mitchell off!": Murphy, *Deregulating Desire*, 55.

227   TWA's new union was called: Rozen, "Turbulence in the Air," 256.

227   a man: News clipping, n.d., Stewardesses for Women's Rights Collection.

227   "What are you guys doing?": Author interview with Tommie Hutto-Blake.

227   From Kathleen's perspective: Author interview with Kathleen Heenan.

228   Northwest flight attendants joined: Nielsen, *From Sky Girl to Flight Attendant*, 127.

228   Before this, these airlines had been: Barry, *Femininity in Flight*, 198.

228   Then the TWU lost another group: "Stewardesses Moving Towards Independent Unions [news clipping, n.d.]," Stewardesses for Women's Rights Collection.

228   But the president of the Pan Am local: "Oral Histories," NYU Libraries.

228   The flight attendants voted with their feet: Barry, *Femininity in Flight*, 203.

228   Tommie was depressed: Author interview with Tommie Hutto-Blake.

228   The players had chosen their sides: Author interview with Tommie Hutto-Blake.

228   Patt had, Tommie imagined: Author interview with Tommie Hutto-Blake.

228   The two had plenty: Author interview with Tommie Hutto-Blake.

229   For Patt's part, she had had high hopes: Author interview with Patt Gibbs.

229   But Patt was sick of fighting: Author interview with Patt Gibbs.

229   Tommie had a network of supporters: Author interview with Becky Kroll.

229   The battle over whether to stay: Author interview with Patt Gibbs.

229   Patt and her cohorts were canvassing: Author interview with Patt Gibbs.

229   Patt had her table, with cards: Author interview with Patt Gibbs.

230   She started handing out cards: Author interview with Patt Gibbs.

230   She had achieved, she realized: Author interview with Patt Gibbs.

CHAPTER TWENTY: ELECTION DAY

232   Though Patt was consumed by the campaign: Author interview with Patt Gibbs.

232   Patt was traveling all the time now: Author interview with Patt Gibbs.

233   Patt and her fellow organizers packed up: Author interview with Patt Gibbs.

233   Patt and the rest of the organizing committee: "Representation Election [union mailing]," Stewardesses for Women's Rights Collection.

234   The leaders of the new flight attendants' union: Author interview with Patt Gibbs.

235   A photo taken at that moment: From personal records of Patt Gibbs.

CHAPTER TWENTY-ONE: PROFESSIONALS AT LAST

238   For years afterward Tommie would ask: Author interview with Tommie Hutto-Blake.

238   Tommie, who had gone from being president: Photo, Association of Professional Flight Attendants Records.

238   Then she went back to flying: Photo, Association of Professional Flight Attendants Records.

238   Bella hadn't given up her trademark: Laura Mansnerus, "Bella Abzug, 77, Congresswoman and a Founding Feminist, Is Dead," *New York Times,* April 1, 1998.

238   Her nickname, "Bellicose": Author interview with Bobbi Lennie.

238   A few months later, Bella attended: Author interview with Patt Gibbs.

238   Tommie fit right in: Author interview with Tommie Hutto-Blake.

239   A Mormon woman: Author interview with Tommie Hutto-Blake.

240   "Fine, Gibbs": Author interview with Patt Gibbs.

241   contracts and negotiations were coming up: Author interview with Tommie Hutto-Blake.

241   Brian, though he'd been just as anti-APFA: Author interview with Brian Hagerty.

241   Becky, too, picked herself up: Photo, Association of Professional Flight Attendants Records.

242   Kathy Knoop took over: Email from Patt Gibbs.

242   She was a character: Author interview with Tommie Hutto-Blake.

243   "What have we done?": Author interview with Tommie Hutto-Blake.

243   She couldn't imagine how they: Author interview with Tommie Hutto-Blake.

243   The newly elected APFA officers: Author interview with Tommie Hutto-Blake.

245   Her sexual orientation was known: Photo, Association of Professional Flight Attendants Records.

246   He slammed his fist down: Author interview with Patt Gibbs.

246   One letter from a member: Photo, Association of Professional Flight Attendants Records.

246   Patt and Susan continued working together: Author interview with Tommie Hutto-Blake.

246   Bit by bit, APFA found its footing: Association of Professional Flight Attendants Records, "About APFA," n.d., accessed August 13, 2021, www.apfa.org/about-apfa/.

246   The key to *staying* strong and independent: Author interview with Tommie Hutto-Blake.

246   And they admired each other: Author interview with Tommie Hutto-Blake.

247   There was a moment: Author interview with Tommie Hutto-Blake.

EPILOGUE

249   For the TWU, the mass movement: Rozen, "Turbulence in the Air," 3.

249   Around fourteen thousand of them left: Barry, *Femininity in Flight*, 203.

249   The number of women represented by the TWU: Barry, *Femininity in Flight*, 203.

249   The flight attendants were, by many measures: United Auto Workers, "Coalition for Labor Union Women (CLUW) Founded Today in 1974," March 24, 2016, https://uaw.org/.

249   putting more women in leadership positions: Ruth Milkman, "Women Workers, Feminism and the Labor Movement Since the 1960s," in *Women, Work, and Protest: A Century of US Women's Labor History* (New York: Routledge, 2013).

249   At the meeting, one speaker: Hornbake Library, " 'CLUW: The First Decade,' 1985 (Full Length)," YouTube video, September 23, 2018.

250   there wouldn't be a woman on the Executive Council: Elaine Woo, "Joyce Miller Dies at 84; Voice for Women in Labor's Top Ranks [obituary]," *Chicago Tribune*, July 18, 2012.

250   Today, APFA: Email from Tommie Hutto-Blake.

250   In 2004, in what was termed: Barry, *Femininity in Flight*, 221.

250   which had roots in organizing: Barry, *Femininity in Flight*, 221.

250   It currently represents: Association of Flight Attendants-CWA (AFA-CWA), "About AFA," n.d., accessed August 13, 2021, www.afacwa.org/about_afa.

250   Still, the years after APFA's formation: Author interview with Tommie Hutto-Blake.

250   Tommie and Charlie Pasciuto joined forces: Author interview with Tommie Hutto-Blake.

251   The labor movement grew increasingly fractured: Lane Windham, *Knocking on Labor's Door: Organizing in the 1970s and the Roots of a New Economic Divide*, Kindle ed. (Chapel Hill: University of North Carolina Press, 2017), 356.

251   It was a wake-up call: Author interview with Brian Hagerty.

251   In 1987 a federal smoking ban: Joe Sharkey, "What Flying Was Like Before the Smoke Cleared," *New York Times*, February 23, 2015.

251   On more than one flight: Author interview with Bobbi Lennie.

251   It took another thirteen years: Jocelyn Pan et al., "Smoke-Free Airlines and the Role of Organized Labor: A Case Study," *American Journal of Public Health* 95, no. 3 (2005): 398–404.

251   Much of the credit was due: Pan et al., "Smoke-Free Airlines."

251   It was another first for them: Vantoch, *The Jet Sex*, 213.

251   Nineteen ninety-three was a memorable year: Adam Bryant, "A Strike at American Airlines Disrupts Travel of Thousands," *New York Times*, November 19, 1993.

252   The strike was in the news: "The New Face of Labor Fights an Old Struggle," *U.S. News & World Report*, December 6, 1993.

252   President Clinton managed to pull together: Ted Street, "What Really Happened in the 1993 American Flight Attendants Strike," TheStreet, November 27, 2013, www.thestreet.com.

252   There was one bright spot: Barry, *Femininity in Flight*, 220.

252   A battle they'd been fighting: Whitelegg, *Working the Skies,* chap. 3.

252   Weight remained one issue: Bob Egelko, "United Flight Attendants Win Weight-Bias Appeal," SFGate, June 21, 2000.

252   some lost: Somini Sengupta, "Airline Wins Suit on Weight Limits of Attendants," *New York Times,* December 18, 1997.

252   And it was tough for the union: Author interview with Tommie Hutto-Blake.

252   She was 154 pounds: Bob Baker, "Airline Sued for Weight Discrimination," *Los Angeles Times,* April 10, 1990.

253   It was expensive: Author interview with Patt Gibbs.

253   After a lawsuit: Baker, "Airline Sued for Weight Discrimination."

253   in 1991 American Airlines: Barry, *Femininity in Flight,* 218.

253   and reinstated some of the flight attendants: Vantoch, *The Jet Sex,* 213.

253   "proficiency tests": Barry, *Femininity in Flight,* 218.

253   which could include being able to move: Tamar Lewin, "USAir Agrees to Lift Rules on the Weight of Attendants," *New York Times,* April 8, 1994.

253   In the late 1960s: Whitelegg, *Working the Skies,* chap. 1.

253   By 1978, the average tenure: M. Smolensky, E. Lee, D. Mott, and M. Colligan, "A Health Profile of American Flight Attendants," *Journal of Human Ergology* 11, Suppl. (1982): 104.

253   By 1980, more than 50 percent: Barry, *Femininity in Flight,* 172.

253   In 1980, the median age: Population Reference Bureau, "The Changing Demography of U.S. Flight Attendants," PRB, June 3, 2009, www.prb.org /usflightattendants/.

253   In 2014, the EEOC cosponsored: U.S. Equal Employment Opportunity Commission, "Waiting with Their Wings to Fight Workplace Sex Discrimination [press release]," October 24, 2014, www.eeoc.gov.

254   One example can be seen in a 1977 case: Dothard v. Rawlinson, 433 U.S. 321, 97 S. Ct. 2720 (1977).

255   Charlie Pasciuto retired in 1988: Author interview with Tommie Hutto-Blake.

255   Crandall invited Patt: Author interview with Patt Gibbs.

255   Charlie died in 2008: Author interview with Patt Gibbs.

256   Tommie timed her maternity leave carefully: Dawn Rosenberg McKay, "The Pregnancy Discrimination Act of 1978," The Balance Careers, updated June 22, 2020, www.the balancecareers.com.

256   Flight attendants could now keep: Dooley, "Battle in the Sky," 193.

256   Tommie hoarded her leave: Author interview with Tommie Hutto-Blake.

256   She left office in June 1980: Author interview with Brian Hagerty.

256   Patt was reelected president: Author interview with Patt Gibbs.

257   She worked on and off: From personal records of Patt Gibbs.

257   though she graduated: Photo, Association of Professional Flight Attendants Records, IMG 3836.

257   Carin Clauss, who became: From personal records of Patt Gibbs.

257   Flight attendants are still at the forefront: Erik Loomis, "Is a General Strike What's Needed to End the Shutdown," *Atlantic,* January 25, 2019.

258   In the chaos of the shutdown: Natasha Hakimi Zapata, "Sara Nelson Is the

Face of America's Resurgent Labor Movement," Truthdig, October 4, 2019, www.truthdig.com.

258   As militant as Patt and Tommie: Zapata, "Sara Nelson Is the Face."

258   "Almost a million workers": Zapata, "Sara Nelson Is the Face."

258   It was, said the *New York Times:* Kitroeff, "The Shutdown Made Sara Nelson."

258   Afterward, she was asked: Kitroeff, "The Shutdown Made Sara Nelson."

Index

Page numbers in *italics* refer to illustrations.